Hanging
From a Tree
By My Knees

THE JERRY MASTERS STORY
"Let It All Hang Out"

Hanging
From a Tree
By My Knees

THE JERRY MASTERS STORY
"Let It All Hang Out"

JERRY MASTERS

Hanging From a Tree By My Knees
The Jerry Masters Story
"Let It All Hang Out"
By: Jerry Masters

Published by Crossover Publications LLC, 870 N. Bierdeman Road, Pearl, Mississippi 39208, www.crossoverpublications.com
(601) 664-6717, Fax: (601) 664-6818

Library of Congress Control Number: 2009944152

ISBN 978-0-9819657-4-1

Printed in the USA

Cover concept and direction by Randall M. Mooney
Cover design and graphic arts by R. Matthew Mooney
Cover photos by Tommy Wright, Dick Cooper, and Sam Melhorn

Introduction

What do Charlie Rich, Willie Nelson, Bob Dylan, Joe Cocker, Rod Stewart, Paul Simon, Burt Reynolds, Bob Seger, Liza Minelli, Donny Osmond, Jerry Lee Lewis, Steve Winwood, Paul Anka, Wayne Newton, Kris Kristofferson, Johnny Rivers, Cat Stevens, Boz Scaggs, Ronny and the Daytonas, The Hombres, Clarence Carter, The Osmonds, Wilson Pickett, J.J. Cale, Bobby Womack, Leon Russell, Luther Ingram, Jim Capaldi, Canned Heat, Percy Sledge, Candi Staton, Simon & Garfunkle, Blackfoot, Mary MacGregor, Kim Carnes, Dr. Hook, Foxy, Mac Davis, Rita Coolidge, Andy Williams, Peter Yarrow, Traffic, and Will McFarlane all have in common?

The answer is Jerry Masters! Jerry started his music career playing bass for the great Charlie Rich and before the first decade was over he had moved on touring with Ronny and the Daytonas supporting the hit song, Little GTO. From the musicians of that group he went on to form The Hombres who had the hit song, Let It All Hang Out, a song that has experienced a revival on You Tube and on the hit TV show, Cold Case.

With over 50 years in rock music, Jerry Masters went from sixties rock star to recording engineer, working with many of the most recognized performers in the world. He mixed and engineered some of the greatest songs and recordings of our time.

Jerry then moved on to make Rock and Roll history with the remarkably creative folks at Muscle Shoals Sound. Were it not for the incredible work at that North Alabama recording studio Rock Music would have a huge hole in its history. Jerry reinvented himself in the seventies and went from playing music to creating music with the greatest entertainers and musicians in the business. He quickly became one of the best recording engineers to sit at a console.

Jerry's new book is a fabulous and fun read. While the news and the music magazines may have told you what the publicists and the handlers of the stars wanted you to know, Jerry shares wonderful behind the scenes stories of working with the world's greatest stars. This is not a "dirt" book or "tell all." It is clear in every chapter that Jerry had great respect and became dear friends with most all of the people he worked with in music. In fact he rat's himself out more than anything and shares honestly how he made his way through the alley's of the rock scene and survived. *RANDALL M. MOONEY*

Foreword

Ah...how to begin. When I first heard Jerry was writing his story, I thought immediately, "I'll read that one". What a life—from Arkansas, to engineering some of the best records ever made, to serving as an elder in Mississippi, he has a story to tell.

I first met Jerry in 1981. I'd moved to Muscle Shoals the year before, and had heard some of the old war stories about the early days there—his name came up frequently. Who would've thought he'd move back to the scene of the (dare I say) crimes, and then go through a personal metamorphosis that would become evident to all—especially the ones who knew him before. We ended up working and traveling together a lot during that time, and they are some of the most important and special days of our lives.

I'll cut through a little here, and say that Jerry never pulls any punches or minces any words. He's a very straight shooter, and you will find out what he's thinking. To be honest, we both had to work through some knotholes in our relationship, and at times, it seemed, it could have gone either way. But he just doesn't walk away in the middle of something, and through all the late night sessions, drives and conversations, a grace emerged, and he's remained one of my most faithful friends; a friendship truly forged in the messy circumstances of life.

It would be my desire that his story would inspire all who read it to simply be who you are, and that's the best of who you are. Catch the wind, go through the doors that open, and don't let disappointment keep you down long. Keep pressing on and stand for what you believe. That should be all of our stories.

WILL MCFARLANE

Acknowledgements

When I first started writing, I had no idea it was going to be a book. I was only writing my memoirs in order for my children and grandchildren to know what I had spent my life doing and why I wasn't around very much. When my good friend Randall Mooney said he wanted to publish my book, I buckled down and started writing like I had never written before.

Not having any professional writing experience, I had no idea what I was doing. I wasn't even writing in chapters or anything. I was just writing. So I must first thank Kathy Dixon for taking what seemed liked five thousand paragraphs and making them into a book. Thank you so much, Kathy, for going above and beyond the call of duty.

Of course the person that paid the biggest price was my wife, Edie. All the many hours I spent upstairs on that %$$#@ computer. And the worst part was that I wouldn't let her read a single word of it until the book came out. I wanted her to read it at its very best, and that's what she and you are getting ready to read. Thanks for dinner, Edie, and thanks for all the hours you spent by yourself downstairs, never complaining one single time, even when I said, "I'll be down in just a second." Also, thank you so much for the last twenty-nine years of happiness and joy you have brought me since God put us together in Miami in 1980. I love you, Edith Ann.

I also want to thank my good friend and 1957 Little Rock Central High classmate, mentor, and practically co-author, Joyce Whittecar Brewer, in Miami. Thanks for the article in Tiger Rag, which really inspired me, and for the first edit of this book. Thanks for continuously encouraging me, making such great suggestions, and not holding back when it took courage to get in my face and tell it like it is. You're a complete and total joy, Joy, and I simply could not have made it without you and your continuous love and support on a daily basis. Also, thank you Joanie and Beni.

Randall Mooney, my friend above all friends, and brother, you are priceless. Thank you, Lord Jesus, for bringing him into my life.

JERRY MASTERS

Dedication

I would like to dedicate this book to my Mother, Marjorie Dyer Masters, who made the Heavenly Transition on December 17th, 1998. After being abandoned with four boys, she dedicated the remainder of her life to making sure we all had food, shelter, clothing and unconditional love, until she finally had to cut the apron strings one by one.

First me, born in 1939, then Terry Lyn, born in 1943, Dennis Ray, born in 1945, and James Harry "Jimbo" Masters, born in 1948 and made the Heavenly Transition in 1975.

She literally went above and beyond the call of duty as a Mother until her passing. I will be forever grateful to her and consider her a role model for Mothers everywhere who devote their entire lives to their children. All she asked of us was that we graduate from high school, which we did. Thanks Mom. I still pick up the phone to call you now and then, especially when the Razorbacks are playing. I'll see you in the morning.

Chapter

I

I was 5 years old; I remember it like it was yesterday. There were seven of us living in a two bedroom house of about 850 square feet. My grandparents, my parents, and two younger brothers, Terry and Dennis, all lived in this quaint little house located on 2016 S. Cedar Street in Little Rock, Arkansas. My youngest brother, Jimbo, wasn't to come along till three years later.

I was sleeping on a small cot up against the wall to the living room. On the other side of the wall was an upright piano that I'm sure had never been tuned. But my mother could play the keys off of it. She often played piano and organ in church (only if it was Baptist, of course), and she was called on quite often. My grandfather was a deacon and charter member of South Highland Baptist Church in Little Rock. Every so often they would get together, along with a couple of bottles of bourbon, with friends they had known all their lives, Curtis and Elsie Stover. What a crew they were. Elsie was one of those ladies that never knew when to hush. Curtis was quiet with a gentle spirit— and very tolerant. He was also a guitar player who played the best rhythm guitar I had ever heard at that time. I remember it so well. They were playing a song called "Goofus."

I never was that crazy about my mother's piano technique, because she used her left hand like a bass player and a drummer. I called it "boom-chic-a-boom" playing. But that night, she and Curtis playing rhythm guitar sounded like music from heaven. That night, laying there in the bed, listening to that music, I knew that I was supposed to be involved in music for my entire life, no matter what. It was like a *spirit of music* crept into my soul, never to leave. It's still there today. Any chance I get to be involved with music, whether it be on guitar, bass, recording it in a studio, recording it live, mixing it, or just listening to it, it doesn't matter. Music became my life that night on 2016 S. Cedar Street in Little Rock, Arkansas, my hometown.

Skipping ahead a few years, my baby brother, James Harry "Jimbo," was born. It was 1948, and my dad left us, high and dry. At the time, we were living with another couple out on Fourche Dam Pike, about 200 feet from where the small Fourche River enters the Arkansas River. The other couple we were living with was a wonderful lady and my mom's best friend, Dot Coates, and her husband, a man we called Chief. He was mostly Native American, and was a very interesting man. They had two wonderful daughters, Bobbie and Lou.

The adults used to have a wild party at times. There was a lot of hanky-panky going on, and that might have had something to do with my dad eventually leaving, but mother never said a single word about him. She never tried to convince us that he was a bad man. She was determined for us to simply remember him as our father, and that was it.

One of the most traumatic times in my life came while we were living there. I was going to an elementary school, and I was in the third or fourth grade. I do know that I skipped the second grade there, because I was so far ahead of the other students. I already knew what they were trying to teach, so they moved me on up to the third grade. I finally had my very first girl friend. I don't remember too much about her except that I was incredibly smitten by her and just knew I was in love. About two days into our romance, she finally decided she liked another boy more than she liked me. It caused a feeling of rejection to come on me that I still live with to this day.

I remember it so well—she blew me off on a Friday, and I spent the entire weekend in my robe. I never even got dressed. I walked around the house like I had lost my best friend, because I was so emotionally devastated by her rejection of me. It was more than I could handle, but there was no one else there to help me or even talk to me about it. All I needed was for someone to put their arm around me and say, "It's going to be alright Jerry. You're young and things like this are going to happen all through your life." But not one single person in that house noticed what a deep depression it had put me in.

That was my last memory of living out by the river. It was about then that my dad split, and we were pretty much orphans for about two years, as I remember. My mother wasn't allowed custody of us until she could prove she could support us. We got spread out all over town. Terry and Dennis were in an orphanage, and Jimbo was living with some couple that lived out in the country. I was released to my grandfather and pretty much spent my life at the Little Rock Boys Club at 8th and Scott Street. That became my second home until I was a senior in high school.

Once mother got custody of us, we moved into the Highland Courts on 12th Street, only a block or two before you go to the entrance roads to Fair Park and the City Zoo. I went to Woodruff Elementary School, right across the street from Lamar Porter Field. By then mother had gotten a job at the Safeway Grocery Store as a meat wrapper. If she worked enough overtime, along with her regular salary, she had enough to support us and bring us all back together. What a great feeling it was when we were all finally back together and a family again. The hard part was her working twelve to fourteen hours a day, which left little time for her to be at home with us preparing meals and such. Therefore, guess who became the man of the house … yep, little old Jerry. I wanted a life of my own, but I had three brothers who depended on me to just be there and make sure they had the bare minimum of a family relationship. Needless to say, we ate a lot of spam and bologna sandwiches and cereal.

Being as immature as I was, I took my authority a bit too seriously, and it was rough going there for quite a few years. But we still had tons of fun with each other. It seemed like it was always them versus me. When they wouldn't clean their room or if they were making too much noise, I'd go in there and start throwing kids all over the bedroom. I was very gentle, but I was also quite stern at certain times, because mother would always blame me if the bedrooms were too much of a mess or the kitchen was a mess when she got home.

For some reason, I took a lot of pride in having my own room, so I kept it very neat. I still have that virtue—I guess that's what you would call it today. I like for things to be neat and in order. I can't stand messes. Even if I'm visiting somewhere else, I'll clean up a messy countertop if need be. It was also very funny how my little brothers would find ways to get back at me. I had a small shelf on the wall right above my bed that had all kinds of what I called *whatnots* on it—little trinkets and animals and stuff like that. Just a little decoration that I thought was cool.

Small apartments weren't very well built back then, so the walls were quite thin. My brothers would wait until I was about half-asleep at night, then they would start beating on that very wall, and all those little trinkets and whatnots would fall all over me in bed. They would just laugh their little butts off, but it made me furious at the time. Now that I think about it, it was pretty ingenious on their part and quite funny, too. We would make darts out of needles and match sticks with little pieces of paper for wings. They were so cool. I threw one once and hit Dennis right in the tip of his nose, and it just stuck there. We were on the floor laughing so hard we were crying, and he was just standing there crying with that dart in the end of his nose. It was a very memorable time for all of us.

We were a family, in spite of where we lived or what kind of income we had. The housing project we lived in was called Highland Courts. It was basically government subsidized housing for people that could not afford homes. It was located at 12th and Highland in West Little Rock. And it was our home. Your rent was based on your income. It was what you would call the *white ghetto* back in those days. To most people we were just white trash.

We used to get around by standing down on 12th Street hitchhiking. That's how I got to school in the mornings, and that's how we got to the Boys Club a lot of times. After a while, instead of holding out our thumbs, we would yell at cars, "Going to town?" It worked. Sometimes people would stop because they didn't understand what four young kids would be doing standing out by themselves like that, and they also couldn't understand what we were yelling out to them. Other times they knew that four little boys, especially back in those days, were pretty harmless, and they would stop and pick us up and take us downtown.

Back to the downtown Boys Club, I was on the swim team and became a pretty good swimmer. I was fortunate to be part of a team that won the Junior Olympics as a relay team. I held a few records myself for long distance swimming, mostly 440 yard (400 meters) freestyle, 200 meter individual medley and 1500 meter freestyle. I went straight to the Boys Club after school every day and worked out. I might mention at this time that the reason I ended up a champion swimmer for a short time was by coming in every day and working out and practicing. I listened to my coach. I literally paid the price.

Anytime you want something badly enough, you must be willing to pay the price. Sometimes it's money, or sometimes it's just dedication and time. You have to be willing to sacrifice everything else and spend the time doing what it takes to be what you want to be. I usually swam from about 5 p.m. to 9 p.m. with a short dinner break. But I never had the money to eat, so I would go down to where my grandfather was working as the night watchman in the Boyle Building at 5th and Main, and sometimes he would give me a quarter, if he had it. That would get me a candy bar and a coke.

There was an older gentleman named Skipper that handled the pool, the towels, and the lockers. Occasionally, Skipper would ask me to run down the street and get him a hamburger for dinner. Of course, I was usually broke, but he would give me the money to pay for *his* hamburger. Instead of paying me to run the errand for him, he would always give me a free towel when I came out of the pool after working out for two or three hours. Man, those hamburgers smelled so good, I could have devoured three of them without even thinking, but I would always be faithful to bring them back to him untouched. Other than drooling for a bite, I survived. Skip would always charge the other swimmers two cents to get a clean towel, but I got mine for free until the last day I ever walked in there. I have yet in my life to pay for a towel at the Little Rock Boys Club.

The most important person in this period of my life was a man named Jimmy Miller. He was my swimming coach, and he worked at the Boys Club full time. In the summer we started going to a camp way out past the end of 12th Street. Most kids could only go for two weeks, but because of our family situation, we were eventually allowed to spend the entire six to eight week summer season at the camp. It was sponsored by the Kiwanis Club of Little Rock. That's where I really grew up.

My brothers and I would go straight to the Boys Club after school. That was our home until mother got home after working all day and half the night. That's when my relationship with my surrogate father began to really flourish. Jim Miller was like a father to me the entire time I was growing into a man. I was in that stage of a boy's life when he really needed a father or a role model that could teach him things about being a man. He was there for that entire period, from when I was about eight to sixteen years of age. Those are very important years for a boy.

I'll never forget the first time I met Jim. He was the lifeguard there at the Boys Club. I guess I was about eight when I went up to him and said, "Hey, Miller, could you please teach me how to swim?" So, he picked me up and threw me in the water at the deep end of the pool. When I came up gasping for breath, he said, "Duck your head and swim." It worked. That's how I learned to swim. He eventually became my swimming coach, as well as an executive and the head swimming coach at the Boys Club. He was also the camp director at the Kiwanis Boys Camp, and played the guitar, too. Yee Haw. I just had to learn to play the guitar.

Of course, mother never had the money to buy me a guitar, but one day I was looking through a comic book or paper or something like that, and I saw an advertisement that said you could go out door to door and sell Christmas cards to earn prizes. They had a lot of things you could get, depending on how many Christmas cards you sold, and they had a guitar in there for a certain amount of Christmas cards sold. I went for it.

When I wasn't working out at the pool, I would go out on the weekends selling Christmas cards door to door, mostly at night in the cold. I remember the cold well. It was bitter that winter, and I didn't have a lot of warm clothes. But, I did it. I sold enough cards to finally get it—I got my guitar. Now you talk about a happy kid; I could not wait until that guitar arrived. I didn't think it would ever arrive. It must have been eight to ten weeks before it finally got there, and when it did, I was in heaven. I put the cat-gut strings on it, tuned it up, and took it straight to Miller to learn my first chords.

But it wouldn't stay in tune. Eventually, after tightening the strings many times to try to keep it in tune, the neck started bending. I finally realized it was made out of cardboard, and I was so disappointed—you have no idea how disappointed. But I wasn't going to give up. Whenever I was at camp, and Miller (that's what everyone called him) wasn't playing his guitar, I would pick his up and practice on it. I learned at least three or four songs and started to get pretty good for a kid with no guitar to practice on. Finally, my mother realized the talent was there and went into debt to buy me an inexpensive acoustic guitar that would stay in tune, and it was all downhill from there.

There was another little incident that had a lot to do with shaping my life. When I still had the cardboard guitar with the bent neck and no strings, I was sitting out on my front porch one day while it was raining. It was one of those days when it just rains all day and never lets up. Right across the street, sitting on her porch, was the cutest girl I had ever seen. I wasn't even aware that she lived there until she came out on the porch that day and was just sitting there in a swing like I was.

We looked at each other, realizing the attraction was mutual (for 11 year olds), so I went inside and got my cardboard guitar. I started acting like I was playing it. Of course she couldn't hear if I was playing or not, but her eyes got real big, and she really locked in to what I was doing, or thought I was doing. It was then that I, being the insecure child I already was, realized I could get girls to pay attention to me simply by playing a musical instrument. I was never very outgoing, was always a loner, and shy. I didn't know how to approach girls, and it became a real hang up for me.

When I realized I could get girls' attention as a musician, it made me even more determined to become a musician to satisfy my need for attention and companionship. Of course, my mother loved me, but the oldest always gets the least amount of attention, especially when the mother's gone most of the time. I was a very lonely kid, needing love to the point where I would do anything to get people to like me. As far as the little girl on the porch across the street, nothing ever materialized from that encounter. I have no recollection of ever even meeting her or talking to her. She must have been more a vision of what my future could be, as far as getting attention from women. I never pursued her that I can remember.

So many things happened while I attended camp every summer until I was a senior in high school. I learned leadership, accountability, how to interact with kids that had different kinds of personalities and problems, and how to deal with kids from all kinds of home situations. I learned counseling, encouragement, and how to fill the void that was prevalent in a lot of kids that age that weren't getting attention at home—just like me. I guess you might say I learned a lot about myself through all the other kids simply by getting involved in their lives and being a leader to them. They looked to me for things that were missing from their lives, as I was trying to fill the voids in myself as a young person, too.

We had five cabins at the camp, and each cabin had about twenty-five kids in it. Each cabin had a cabin leader and an assistant cabin leader. Of course, there was also the camp director, Jim Miller, and a staff consisting of an assistant camp director, sports director, and a real doctor…a genuine MD. After about three or four years, I became an assistant cabin leader, then cabin leader, and eventually program and events director. We had miles and miles of woods, mountains, streams, and a creek that flowed right through the middle of camp. The creek was our swimming hole. We had swimming twice a day, usually for about an hour, and we used the "buddy system." You had to have a buddy to go into the water. Every five minutes we would blow the whistle and yell, "Buddy up!" You had to find your buddy immediately, grab his hand, and hold it up high. It worked, amazingly; in the thirty or so years we swam in that creek, we never lost a kid to drowning.

Chapter

2

Something happened in junior high school that really set the precedent for my safety while going through the 7th to 12th grades. I had a kid come up to me one day in the 7th grade and tell me that the school bully had told him that he was going to whip my ass the next time he saw me. So I told the messenger to go and tell the school bully to meet me out in the breezeway at exactly 3:35 p.m. I knew who the bully was. He was a kid just a little taller than me, who weighed about 40 lbs. more than me. In an actual fight, he probably would have taken me eventually, even though I was pretty scrappy.

I didn't want to go through my entire school life fearing other guys that were going to threaten me for various reasons or try to prove their masculinity by jumping on me. So, when the school bell rang at 3:30 p.m., I got my books, put them in my locker, and walked right out the door to where mister bully was sitting on a resting spot in the breezeway. The seat he was sitting in was quite low, so I kind of towered over him when I first walked up to him.

"Are you the one that said you were going to whip my ass?" I said, and before he even had a chance to stand, I slapped the living hell out of him. He was so stunned; he didn't know what to do. So I slapped him again. Then I hit him with my fist just one time, but enough to give him a black eye.

"Don't you never, ever threaten me or any of my friends ever again, do you understand?"

He very humbly said, "Yeah." Then I just turned around and walked off. There must have been at least twenty-five or thirty kids standing around when it happened, because they had heard that there was going to be a rumble out in the breezeway right after school. They just stood there in amazement. They couldn't believe that I had gone up to the school bully and actually slapped the hell out of him and said what I said to him. They just couldn't believe it. When I turned to walk away, they cleared me a path as quickly as any path has ever been made.

What good did that do? The word got out to every guy in Little Rock in our age group that if you threaten Jerry Masters, you're in a heap of trouble, which is exactly what I wanted to accomplish. Even though I was scared as hell the entire time, I never let it show. I must have been shaking so bad you could feel it all over Little Rock, but I made my point, and I became known as a bad ass that no one wanted to mess with. That reputation stayed with me my entire school life, even through high school. Guys just wouldn't mess with me. They actually feared me physically.

I was scared half to death when I did that, but no one ever knew that. I've always been a person of peace. I hate strife and fighting and yelling, or anything that disturbs my peace, so I wanted to deal with that part of growing up once and for all and get it over with so I could have a good time and concentrate on other things, and not have the likes of that hanging over my head. You would be surprised at the young people today that go through their entire premature days living in fear of what other people might think. I just wanted to deal with that aspect and not have to worry about it anymore. I bluffed my way through it, but I obtained what I was looking for, and have looked for, my entire life. I just wanted to live in peace.

My three years in high school were pretty uneventful. I joined the Swing Band, which was a dance band made up of band students, with vocalists and a dancer thrown in here and there, and a little guitar player who didn't have a clue what he was doing for the first year. I was playing chords that I had learned from Miller and a couple of other guys at camp, and I started figuring out how to read the music they had for guitar. Not all of the songs we played had guitar charts, but on the ones that did, I started easing into them and figured out how to make the chords by just practicing and literally teaching myself how to play.

I did buy a book that showed how to make certain chords, and that helped a lot, too.

We played all the dances there at Central. We even made a trip to New Orleans once and played at the famous Roosevelt Hotel on Canal Street where the Johnny Long Orchestra was playing. They actually let us come up and play a set while they took a break. At that period in time, it was like playing the Waldorf Astoria in New York.

We also made several other trips out of town on a bus, and it really helped me learn a lot about big bands. I hung out with a great bunch of guys like Tackett, Herman Branton, Ralph Patrick, and Leonard Kyzer, who we called "the Animal." He was a big-boned guy with kind of ruddy skin, and he was always getting into fights at school. He just loved to rumble, but played a pretty decent baritone sax.

I played in the Swing Band my sophomore and junior years, and as the only guitar player I knew of at Central High School, I became quite well known while I was there. We had almost 3,000 students in our high school, as it was the only public high school in town at the time. I went to camp every summer until my junior year in high school.

When I was about to become a senior, my mother, bless her soul, really let me go. She released me of all my chores and all my responsibilities at home. She just practically said, "You've got one more year to go...go out and have fun." And boy did I! I started drinking beer and smoking cigarettes.

I'll never forget the first party I went to. After drinking a couple of beers, I actually had the courage to go up to a girl I was very attracted to (and had been for a long time), and I asked her to dance. She said yes! Her name was Judy. I thought she was going to be my soul mate for life at one time, but she ended up marrying my best friend while I was in basic training in the Army. I had been gone for less than a month. I probably loved her more than anyone I had ever met, but she had eyes for my best friend, and they were afraid to tell me. They figured that after I went into the Army, they could get together and it wouldn't affect me any longer once I got over the hurt. They were wrong.

I had always been shy. I was afraid of asking girls to go out, even to dance or date. But I found out that alcohol gave me courage, false courage, but courage to do things I had never had the nerve to do before. When I started drinking, I would get what I called at the time "liquid guts." I hung out with a great bunch of guys. Although I was a senior in high school, most of the guys I hung out with were juniors. I had skipped a year in school, the second grade, so age wise we were all about the same.

Most of us were from lower middle class neighborhoods, but a couple of guys were upper middle class. That was important at the time, because we always had a problem with transportation. Of course, it always worked out one way or the other. The sad thing about this particular season of my life was that I quit going to swimming practice. The smoking wasn't a great help either. I also quit playing music, believe it or not, but I knew I always had that in my "back pocket." I still played in the Swing Band in high school, and I made all the important swim meets, but I wasn't at a hundred percent, and it was obvious.

At one point during my senior year in high school, I developed a lump in my left breast. I thought maybe it was from swimming or diving, but our family doctor, Dr. William Snodgrass, a dear man, after doing some biopsies and such, determined it was a cyst and gave me the option of having it removed or not. The cyst was quite obvious, and it made me look like half a girl, so I elected to have it surgically removed.

At the time, I had a dear friend, a young Jewish girl named Vidie Levine, who was a complete delight to me and always made me feel welcome anytime I wanted to come over to her house. Her parents were also so nice to me every time I came over. They were just some of the best people I ever met as far as my friends' families. They were quite well off financially, but my social status made no difference to them. At one point, her brother, who had gone off to college, gave me some clothes that were too small for him. They were a bit weird in taste, but they were still expensive shirts and slacks.

When I was in the hospital, about two days after my surgery (and I had had no other visitors), in comes Vidie with her mother and her entire family, and the biggest bowl of matzo ball soup you have ever seen in your life. After having had hospital food for about two days, it was absolutely out of this world good. It was what I discovered later to be "Jewish penicillin." They must have stayed and visited with me all afternoon.

A couple of guys that I ran around with, George Lorenz and Donald Tuller, also came up and visited for a short while, and they brought me a few cigarettes and a couple of cans of beer. The surgery was not a fun experience, but I recovered and had a very long scar where they literally had removed my entire left mammary gland. As I get older, the scar is getting more and more prominent.

Also during my senior year, I needed some running around money, and Mother got me a temporary job working with her for a couple of weekends at Safeway. They had me slicing bologna all day long. I must have sliced 1,500 pounds of bologna one day, and guess what she put in front of me that night for supper? Yep, you're right, a fried bologna sandwich with lettuce, tomato, and mustard on white bread. I could not believe it. She laughed till she cried. She needed a good laugh, and I provided her one.

That was about the only work I did, with one exception. I worked at a service station for about two months, but just weekends. I changed oil and filters, and lubed cars. I also pumped gas and washed windows. That was back in the days when they actually had full-service gas stations. We would actually go out and pump people's gas, wash their windshields, check their oil, or anything else they might need. That was a very greasy job, but I learned a lot about the inside of cars, which came in handy all through life.

Chapter

3

While I was in the Army, Mother was able to buy a house at 512 Brown Street, right behind Lamar Porter Field. Ironically, after I left Little Rock in 1961, they built another Boys Club right across the street from Mother's house and behind right field of the major ball diamond at Porter Field. The reason she bought that house on that particular street was because, at the time, Terry and Dennis had started playing Little League and Pony League baseball, and she didn't want to miss an inning of their games. That's how devoted she was to us. Not only that, she never missed a single swim meet I was swimming at if it was in town. She never missed a stroke I swam.

I don't want to get too far ahead of myself, but I want to give you an example. One summer I was a sophomore in high school, and we had a swim meet at the largest pool in Little Rock. It was not a team swim meet, but an open swim meet, which meant anyone in the country could come and compete. I had entered myself in several competitions, but my real specialty was the individual medley. That's where you swim 100 meters (or two laps) for each the four basic strokes—backstroke, butterfly, breast stroke, and freestyle. It was a 400 meter event. I had already either won or placed in all the previous races I had entered, but this particular race had been totally dominated for years by a friend and fellow Boys Club Swim Team member, Jeff

Wilson, who had a swimming scholarship to the University of Texas and was a second year student there. No one thought I had a chance to beat him. He was older, stronger, more experienced, and had dominated that event for a long time.

As usual, my mother was right there, sitting on the front row, but she never sat down once the whistle blew. To make a long story short, I beat him at his game. I won the race to the delight of about 300 to 350 people sitting in the stands, and my mother practically climbed the fence separating the bleachers from the pool. It was a very proud moment for me, but more importantly, for her.

As soon as I finished high school, I had two choices. I could try and get a job, doing what, I had no idea, but my mother met a guy at her work place one day who was an army recruiter. He was recruiting for the Army Security Agency. He needed specialists in a particular area, and after reviewing my school grades and talking with my mother, he felt like I would fit in just right. I sure didn't want to go in and be a foot soldier or in artillery, or even a clerk. And if I went at it his way, even though I would have to spend three years in, I could be what was called "unassigned." In other words, I was in the army, but I actually worked for the National Security Agency, and I pretty much took all my orders from them.

They mixed us up with a sprinkling of "lifers," or career soldiers, for different leadership positions, but most of us were specialists. I went to school for a year at Fort Devens, Massachusetts, and I won't even talk about basic training except for two incidents. The first one was KP. This caught me after I had been in for about five to six days. I reported to the kitchen at 4 a.m. and immediately went to the rear where they gave this "specialist" pots and pans duty. Man, I washed pots and pans until two a.m. the following morning. I got two breaks, thirty minutes each. I think if you do your math, I washed pots and pans for twenty-two hours.

The second incident was an upper. I was in a company of about 120 men. The first time we marched as a company in a parade to honor a visiting VIP, I will never forget the pride that rose up in me when we marched past the reviewing stand and that visiting VIP saluted us. I felt like a real American Soldier. I knew that I was doing the right thing by serving my country, and was I willing to give my life for my country. It put a smile on my face that took three days to wipe off.

At one time during our basic training, we had a physical fitness competition. We had to do pushups, pull-ups on the bars, sit ups—with no one holding our legs, and then finally, a 100 yard dash. When we came to the 100 yard dash, I was tied for first place! Well, one guy beat me by half of a step. But it was fun to know I was still in pretty good shape to come in second out of a hundred and twenty other men from all over the country—and I got a weekend pass, to boot. One hundred and eighteen other men didn't!

After I finished basic training, I basically wasn't a soldier much anymore. I was sent to Fort Devens, Massachusetts, for a year's worth of training to learn how to receive and copy Morse code. It was fun while I was in school, but man, now I know why they call that part of the country "Little Korea." They have two seasons up there: winter and the 4th of July. We literally got snowed in on the second floor of our barracks one time. When I finished school at Fort Devens, I had learned how to use my ears and how to copy Morse code.

My duties, I was going to find out later, were to copy the communications between all of the Chinese army units throughout China, and literally keep up with their units as they moved about the country. But I didn't know all of that until I arrived at my destination. When I finished school, they gave me the choice of several places in the world to go. There was one opening in Hawaii, two for Okinawa, several for Africa, Germany, and Turkey. I took Okinawa. Ah, the tropical paradise of Okinawa. We called it "the Rock." I spent almost one and a half years there and then spent my remaining time in Petaluma, California. I also chose Okinawa for another reason. I wanted to take my best friend with me when I went overseas—more about my best friend coming up.

I want to talk for a minute about something that we all have had to deal with our entire lives, no matter where we have lived or were brought up. I was reared in a bigoted household, it grieves me to say, but I just never could buy into it. Somewhere in my heart, even though I knew no black people at all except the cooks at camp, I knew it was wrong. All my friends would call Negroes the "N" word and said they were dirty, stunk, were stupid and lazy. But I knew it wasn't right, so I just turned away from them when they would start in with that behavior.

When I went into the Army, I took my basic training just one hundred and fifty miles up the road from Little Rock in Fort Chaffee, Arkansas, just outside Fort Smith, Arkansas. I had my first experience and opportunity to follow my heart when I was placed in the same barracks with one black guy. His name was Alan Thornton, from Dallas, Texas. One day someone messed up the shine on his boots. They were real shiny and looked great for inspection, and someone went over when he wasn't watching and scuffed the toes up real bad.

Now this was 1957, the year of the Little Rock Central High School incident, and the very first try at integrating a Southern high school. It was the school I had just graduated from about a month earlier. Everyone knew that. Well, Alan immediately suspected me of being the one that messed his boots up, because he figured all people from Little Rock were the same as the ones out in front of the school trying to keep nine courageous black kids from registering for fall classes. Of course, they had been stopped by our "illustrious" governor, Orval Faubus, who at the time had called in the Arkansas National Guard to keep them out.

Well, that didn't go over well with President Dwight Eisenhower, so he sent the 182nd Airborne to Little Rock to keep the peace and assist the students in registering for school. There were hundreds of my "fellow citizens" out in front protesting, including my beloved mother, who was beside herself because she didn't want Terry and Dennis going to school with black kids. Even when I was overseas and playing in a jazz trio with a black piano player, when I sent her a picture of the trio, she buried it in the bottom of her cedar chest.

Now back to Fort Chaffee: I told Alan I was not guilty, but he didn't believe me. He gave me the dirtiest looks every time I saw him. Then one afternoon, I came back to the barracks to find my boots filled all the way to the top with water. I looked over at Alan, and he just nodded. I was determined to make this guy my friend, whether he wanted to be or not. We went ahead and finished basic training, and I was then sent to Fort Devens for Morse Code Intercept School, and guess who had the same orders? Not only that, guess who ended up in the same barracks with me? That's right, Alan Thornton.

One day while we were at school, we were up on the third floor of our school building when we decided to take a smoke break, and we all went out onto the porch. The porch was open, but had about a four-foot wall to keep people from falling off. I walked right up to Alan and said, "Man, after all we've been through together, getting all these same assignments, don't you think this was all for a reason, for both of us, and that we should be friends?"

He looked at me with a scowl, and said, "No, I don't like you, and don't like nothing 'bout you." I grabbed him by the blouse of his uniform, turned him around, leaned him over the ledge of the porch, and I said, "You SOB, you're going to be my friend or I'm going to drop your ass right off this porch and tell them it was all just an accident."

He was scared to death, and he knew I meant business. So he said, "Alright, alright, you win. You want to be my friend so bad, we'll be friends." That night we went out to a club and had a few beers and started finding out that we actually had a lot in common. He loved jazz, loved to read, was very intelligent (*that* we didn't have in common). At the end of school, if you remember, I told you there were only two assignments to Okinawa. I was number two in my class, and he was like number seven or eight. I could have gone to Hawaii, but it only had one position open, so I took Okinawa, which had two, and the two of us ended up going to Okinawa together. So we spent the majority of our army time as friends, and close friends. We were really good for each other, and we tore down a lot of barriers that we both had experienced as kids, and it was very rich for us both.

However, if I learned anything from that experience, it was confirmed while working with Malaco Records for twenty-four years, which you'll hear about later. There I worked with nothing but black artists, musicians, singers, choirs, and songwriters for a very, very long time under every situation imaginable. And folks, this is the bottom line—a white person will never, ever know what it is like to be black, especially in this country. That's a fact, not an opinion. We'll never know what it's like no matter how hard we try.

Following basic training, I was getting ready to leave for Fort Devens after a two week pass. Right before I left Little Rock, my mother bought me a brand new Gibson Les Paul guitar and Fender amp, bless her heart. What a wonderful woman she was. I could write a book on my mother. She was a trip. There was no one else in the world like her, and I miss her very much. I took the guitar and amp to Fort Devens with me and hooked up with some very fine musicians.

One friend that actually became my mentor musically was named Paul. I can't remember his last name, and it's probably a good thing. I'll tell you about that later, but he was a piano player, singer, lounge type guy—he was a pro. He taught me many things about chord changes; taught me so many standard songs, leaning toward the soft jazz standards. All I had been exposed to at the time were country music and jazz and big band stuff. As a kid, I had listened to country music on the radio late at night on WSM out of Nashville, and I had dated a girl in junior high school whose father played in a western band on the Louisiana Hayride. It was kind of the Deep South's Grand Ole Opry. But Paul and I hit it right off. He took the "country" out of me and made me a much "slicker" guitar player.

After I finished Morse Intercept School in Fort Devens, I was, of course, assigned to Okinawa, which was quite a ways from Fort Devens, Massachusetts. I received a two week pass at that time, and I headed straight for Little Rock on a train, which took three days and two nights and was not a lot of fun. When I arrived, things at home were just different. I tried to spend as much time as I could with my grandfather, who was extremely ill with sinus cancer. He had been a pretty heavy smoker most of his life, and by the time I got there, he already had a tracheotomy—that's how he breathed and talked, through the hole in his throat.

My grandfather was a wonderful man who loved his daughter and his grandchildren and was always there for us. He knew what my mother was going through and always helped the best he could. He was a night watchman at a large building in downtown Little Rock. I could always go down to visit him from the Boys Club about five blocks away, and he would give me a quarter for supper. Back then a quarter would go a long way; it would buy a candy bar and a coke. He was so very important to me in my life and I'll miss him a lot.

Eventually it was time for me to report to Fort Lewis, Washington, for my transportation to Okinawa, but I was in a pickle to get there. Why? I had three and a half days to get there, and that's a long, long way from Little Rock, Arkansas. I had no money, my mother had no money, and my whole family was flat broke. It was the story of my life at that time. My Uncle Selwyn Hays worked at the bus station, so I scraped up enough money to buy a bus ticket to Fort Lewis. When I left, I had a sack lunch, two one dollar bills, and about fifty-seven cents in change. That was it. I also smoked and had one pack of cigarettes. I'd forgotten to eat before I left and ended up eating the sack lunch before I was even out of town. Sure was smart, wasn't I? I lived on coffee, peanut butter crackers, and bummed cigarettes.

After a three day and three night bus ride, I was wiped out and hungry, tired from sleeping sitting up, and very tired of riding. I remember waking up my first morning in a barracks in Fort Lewis and looking out the window. I could see nothing but Mt. Rainier. It was snow-capped and just awesome. It took up the entire horizon as I looked out of my barracks window. It was one of the most beautiful waking views I had ever had in my life. Two days after arriving in Fort Lewis, I was on the USS Mann troop ship headed for Okinawa.

Chapter

4

There were supposed to be 5,000 Marines with us on the troop ship, but their orders were cancelled at the last minute. So there was enough food, not only for us, but for the 5,000 Marines as well. Needless to say, there was food galore. So how did I do? I stayed seasick for the entire trip and never had a bite of anything that I can remember. It never even entered my mind to go to the medics and get some Dramamine. I just roughed it out.

While we were at sea about twenty miles from the coast of Russia and Siberia, the ship chaplain summoned me to his quarters. He very gently informed me, via the Red Cross, that my beloved grandfather had gone to be with the Lord. It wasn't a surprise, but I knew that I was going to miss him very much. He had been an important part of my young life, and he had filled a void that no one else could fill. I loved him very much.

While on the ship, I worked in the dependants' lounge giving out coffee and hot chocolate to dependants—the wives and children going overseas to join their husbands and fathers. The rest of the guys were outside most of the time in the freezing cold, chipping old paint off the ship as prep for repainting. Someone had his hand on me the entire time, actually my entire life, but I'll talk about that later. It took us two weeks to make it to Okinawa, and my seasickness finally left the day before we got there. By that time, the ship's cooks were shutting the kitchen down, so I still didn't eat until I got off the ship.

My experiences on Okinawa were interesting, to say the least. I joined the ASA swim team, which consisted of one swimmer—me. We had a very small camp on the island. I became a member of the 8th Army Swim Team, and made several trips to Korea for Far Eastern Swim Meets. They included Army, Navy, Marine, and Air Force swimmers, and the competition was a bit overwhelming. I brought back several medals over the two-year span, but it was not easy.

The trips I made from Kadena Air Force Base were always "space available," which meant that I would get on anything with wings that was going my way in order to make it to my first destination, which was Tachikawa Air Base in Japan. From there, once again I would go "space available" to Korea. The pool we used for the meets was a state of the art, 25 meter pool located at the 1st Cavalry Base at the 38th Parallel, Panmunjom, commonly known as the most dangerous area in the world. This is the dividing line between North and South Korea, and where the alleged peace treaty was signed to stop the Korean War (after losing 52,000 American lives).

Where the pool was located you could see over into North Korea. There were North Korean soldiers up on the top of hills with binoculars, betting on our swim races. It was funny. There were a lot of hills in Korea. For some reason, I wondered how many of the North Korean soldiers either made or lost money by betting on me to win or lose against some of the best swimmers in the world. These meets were like tryouts for the Olympics, and I was not in very good shape at the time, even though I did work out occasionally at my home camp.

I probably made five or six trips to Korea. I really liked that country. We would always land at Kimpo Air Base, which at the time still had some bomb craters. Other craters had been filled with either concrete or asphalt not long before. The so-called peace treaty between North and South Korea was signed in 1953, I believe, so the craters weren't actually that old—maybe five years or so.

The trip up to the 1st Cavalry Base took only about forty-five minutes, usually by bus, and sometimes by chopper. Kimpo Air Base of course was just outside Seoul, the capital of South Korea (a wonderful country, and also a wonderful city, very crowded, but free). There was a story of a man that was driving down the streets of downtown Seoul. While he was driving, he stuck his left arm out to signal a left turn, and when he brought his arm back in the car, his watch was gone.

They had a place in Seoul called the "Moose Line." It was where the soldiers would go if they needed some company for the evening. Usually ten or fifteen dollars would get you a complete night with dining, dancing, and then what you originally went for in the first place. Or for about five dollars, you could get what they called a "short time," or just long enough to get the job done, and then they'd be right back out there, and you'd be on your way.

When you would go down to the "Moose Line," there would be women for blocks and blocks, all standing right next to each other, and of every shape, size, and height you could imagine. They had skinny ones, fat ones, and just regular ones. And after an hour or so in front of a mirror, they were all absolutely beautiful, and I'm not kidding. They had some of the most beautiful women I had ever seen, and there were literally hundreds of them to pick from. All you had to do was pull up in your jeep or car, or walk up and just take your pick.

In addition, you could buy an ounce of marijuana, some of the best in the world, for two dollars an ounce. Once, as I was getting ready to fly back to Japan, which was where we stopped and changed planes coming from Okinawa, I bought about twenty dollars worth of grass. I just stuffed my pockets as full as I could. Back then, no one knew what it was anyway, so it wasn't that dangerous. When I got to Kimpo to catch my flight back to Tachikawa, Japan, I was running late and I literally had to run out on the runway to get on my plane. As I was running, some of the bags of "whacky-backy" fell out of my pockets onto the runway, and I just kept running. I didn't have time to go back and pick them up. But believe me, I had enough to last me the rest of the time I had left on the "Rock." It didn't matter, because it was so inexpensive. It's unbelievable in this day and age with the price being what it is now, or at least what it was when I quit all that stuff.

Our camp, Sukiran, was about a mile outside a small town called Kadena. Most towns, really villages, on Okinawa, were full of bars, movie houses, restaurants, and other normal shops. They also had hockshops, where I occasionally had to go to hock my watch to make it to payday. I had to live on about eighty dollars a month, which cut into my social life quite drastically. I sent my mother the other half of my pay each month, so that will give you an idea of how much the US Army paid its soldiers at that time, even though I did have free room and board. I didn't hang out in the bars much at all, even though I did meet a young lady one night, and we became friends. I would "visit" her quite often, and our relationship was more than just "two ships passing in the night." I really enjoyed my time with her during the day when she wasn't working, and we had a lot of fun together. Her name was Heromi, and she was so beautiful. She was just the right size, and soft, and fit up next to me perfectly. I wish I knew what happened to her and where she is today. She was very important to me at that time in my life and filled a void that no one else could fill. I know she loved me, as I did her.

I went to movies a lot in my spare time. Since my guitar (which I'm still waiting on in 2009) wasn't available, I went down to the Special Services and asked them if they had a guitar I could use while I was there. They said they didn't have a guitar, but they had an upright bass—a bull fiddle some call it—the orchestras call them double basses. It was a good bass, a Kay, but I was a guitar player, or at least I thought I was, so I knew absolutely nothing about playing a bass. It was strange about my guitar playing. It was sort of like my golf game. I reached a certain point, and I just couldn't seem to get any better. But after practicing on the bass for a while, I started playing with a piano player that was a jazz player. A drummer friend joined in, and we soon had a pretty nice jazz-oriented trio, with a very green bass player.

With a lot of help from other musicians and listening to records from a totally different perspective now, I started to improve. When you know nothing, and then can play a couple of songs, that's improvement. After a while, we joined with a comedian and a vocalist, and we started going to different bases as a USO package entertaining the troops. Of course, to get off work, it had to be under the cover of the USO. Believe me, when you've been cooped up on "the Rock" for months with nothing to do but read and play poker, anything that even sounds like entertainment is fantastic from your viewpoint. And the more we played, the better we got, and as a result, the better I got.

We played for the Marines, the Navy, the Air Force, and at Officers' Clubs, NCO clubs, and just anywhere they needed entertainment. We would have jam sessions at the Air Force Enlisted Men's Club at Kadena Air Force Base, and every musician on the island would come. There were some great musicians there that just sort of came out of nowhere. I was truly amazed at the talent that would show up on Sunday afternoons. They would also give all the musicians free drinks as long as they played, which was a big mistake, because some of them would get so smashed they couldn't play any longer. That happened to me a couple of times, but I learned my lesson—fast—about drinking in the daytime. By the time I got back to the states about nineteen months later, I was a pretty good bass player, but I had to leave the bass back on "the Rock." So that was all of the bass playing I did until I was able to get my own once I got back home.

After thirty-six hours on a prop-plane with the seats turned backwards, a bottle full of sleeping pills, and three stops in Japan, Wake Island, and Hawaii, we finally landed at Hamilton Army-Air Force Base just north of San Francisco. I took a bus to Long Beach, just south of Los Angeles, where I spent some time with my Uncle Elwood and Nat Hays. I then hopped a train for three days and nights to Little Rock, where I was met by my mother and some close friends. I had lost most of my hair by then, and when my mother saw me get off the train, she started crying. Worse things could have happened, and if that was all I brought back (or didn't bring back) from the Far East, then I felt like I was doing well.

I started looking for a used bass around town and finally found an old one that was black. I had no idea what kind it was, but it was mine, and it was a start. I noticed it didn't have much volume to it, and I heard something rattling around on the inside, so I finally got it out. It was a short, round piece of wood, so I whittled off the end and used it for a peg. I played the darn thing for almost a year before I finally found out it was the sound post. But I had the strongest chops in the country, and I could play hard, and my playing improved dramatically. With the strongest chops of any bass player I knew, when I finally got a new Kay bass, I could rattle the walls with my playing. What a difference a sound post makes in an upright bass. It's kind of like swimming with combat boots on until you get into competition. You take the boots off, and you can fly.

Well, I could flat play an upright, and you could hear it, and the tone was beautiful and definitive. Of course, by then the word got around town that I was back and playing bass, and all of a sudden I became the most sought-after bass player in Little Rock and the surrounding areas. I once played with a big band that Bill Whitworth had put together: five saxophones, five trumpets, three trombones, piano, guitar, and a drummer named Buddy Rogers, who eventually became my very best friend and remains that even today. What a great drummer he was. We were a rhythm section personified. The two of us

were tight as a rope. It was at this period in my life that I met the
mother of my son, James Michael.

Gaylon Mulkey, an old friend from high school who had just
gotten out of the Navy, and I started going out every night drinking
beer and just seeing what kind of trouble we could get ourselves into. I
was working at the Arkansas Democrat newspaper, and Gaylon was
working at Gus Blass, a department store in downtown Little Rock. We
would go to different clubs or bars, depending on how the action was.
We played shuffleboard a lot and shot pool, which I was a master at,
because at the Boys Club I became very well-versed in the art of
playing eight ball.

We went to a club one night, just he and I, and I saw this
adorable little lady out on the dance floor, barely five feet tall, with a
ponytail hairdo, and cute as cute can be, with the cutest little booty in
the state of Arkansas, just dancing her cute little booty off. I knew I
had to find out who this lady was, and I did. I started visiting her when
she baby-sat for her sister, Judy. Her name was Jeanne, without a doubt
the cutest, sweetest lady I had ever met. And she still maintains those
virtues to this day, I might add. We decided to get married, for some
reason. I have no recollection at this time why, but I just all of a sudden
asked her if she would like to get married.

There were several things that had had happened in our family
that I would not want to go into, but it was obvious that respect for the
covenant of marriage was not taken that seriously from what I
observed when I was growing up. When reality started creeping in and
I thought about what I was doing, I started realizing that I was not
ready to get married. Marriage is a commitment. It's a covenant that
you make between your wife and God, and it can't be taken lightly.
You are making a contract that should never be made unless you intend
to live up to it, "till death do you part," as it says in the vows.

I didn't want to quit music, and I didn't want to be tied down. I
just wasn't mature enough to handle the responsibilities of marriage,
but I didn't know how to tell her. I didn't have the courage; I just
hadn't grown up enough. Even though I didn't want to get married, and
I knew I was making a mistake, I just couldn't stand the thought of
breaking her heart. Things were so far along in the preparations, and
our mothers were ecstatic over the idea of us finally settling down. The
church was already decorated, and all the things were in place. So I
went ahead and got married, thinking that things would somehow work
out, that once we got into it, I would get used to it.

I had a day gig working first at the Arkansas Democrat in national advertising, and I eventually went to work for a food broker for a while, but I just could *not* stay away from clubs, and music, and anything that had anything to do with either. I was hooked on them. I enjoyed every aspect of playing at night, meeting women, drinking, and the whole thing that went along with being a musician. It just simply was my life. I had known it would be since I was five years old.

When my life kept easing that way, I eventually became apathetic to my responsibilities as a husband and father, and as much as Jeanne tried to hold on, I came home one day and they were gone. My wonderful son, Mike, was about six or seven months old. I also learned another valuable lesson from all of this. I had always assumed that the opposite of love was hate. But it's not, its indifference. It wasn't because I didn't love Jeanne and my son; it was just that I didn't want to be tied down. I cared for her, but it turned to indifference, not because of her, but because of my attitude and my desire to be free.

I couldn't hold on to the brokerage job, and I couldn't stay out of clubs, so eventually they left. I just didn't want to be married. But I also didn't want to hurt her. I knew all of that when I got married, but if I had stopped the wedding and been completely honest then, all this other, much deeper hurt, wouldn't have happened in the first place. I'd always heard that sometimes people are more important than truth, but in this instance, that was not the case. I knew I had hurt her deeply, but I was so selfish, I just had to have my way.

Chapter

5

I first started playing with Charlie Rich after we met at a club in Little Rock. He always called me the best little or best "G.D." bass player in the world. I played with Charlie for quite a while on the road. He would always call me when he needed me, and I would find us a drummer and guitar player, and we did a lot of weekend gigs for a year or two. As a matter of fact, Charlie was the first one to introduce me to amphetamines. We were both real tired on the way to Columbus, Mississippi, and Charlie handed me a little blue pill and, man, I was flying for the rest of the day and night too. I was even able to drink beer continuously, and it seemed like I never got drunk.

I started smoking pot when I was in the Army, and like I told you earlier, I could buy it on the street corners in Soul, Korea, for two dollars a bag (which was an ounce) in 1958, so drugs weren't totally new to me. But this was a whole different thing, a whole different trip, and I loved the feeling it gave me. I hadn't smoked pot after I came back to the states, so I had been pretty much drug-free since 1960.

We played clubs all over the South. We even played clubs sometimes that seemed like they were out in the middle of nowhere, and they would have chicken wire up in front of the bandstand. There would be so many people in a place, and I had no idea where they had come from. They would sit at long tables in groups and literally order beer by the case, as opposed to bottles or cans. It would get wild and wooly sometimes, especially when Charlie would play his big hit, "Sittin' and Thinkin."

They also brawled a lot—that was the reason for the chicken wire. But after a year or so of that, we moved up to the big time, a swank club on the bank of a lake in Hot Springs, called the Nite Liter. We had Buddy Rogers playing drums, and different guitar pickers, and then sometimes it was just the three of us. I was only playing on weekends and living with Buddy in North Little Rock in a small duplex. We drove back and forth from Hot Springs to North Little Rock, which only took about forty-five minutes.

I truly believe that Buddy is the best drummer I have ever played with in my life, and I've played with a lot. Not to mention, he was also one of my best friends in life, and I still talk to him quite often. There was a point where I didn't think I could ever play with another drummer, Buddy and I were so tight. It was like we were on the "same page" (I actually hate that phrase) all the time, no matter where we were playing or who we were playing with. Just the thought of playing with another drummer was actually frightening to me.

After a few weeks of just Charlie, Buddy and me, we were joined by a local musician who played the funkiest flute I had ever heard. His name was Edwin Hubbard. He was a hometown boy from a wealthy family, who had conveniently bought himself an apartment out on the lake and only lived a few blocks down from the Nite Liter. For some reason, Charlie started getting more and more into playing jazz, especially after he had downed a few drinks.

Most people came in there wanting to hear "Sittin' and Thinkin." It was about as country as they get, but Charlie might do it one time a night, during the first set, but then he would start "feeling his oats," so to speak, and start playing jazz. Well, this just happened to be right up our alley, music wise. We were all jazz freaks and loved it like nobody's business. The flute was what made the big difference.

I found out that Charlie had been in the Air Force, and had played in the Air Force Stage Band, or Orchestra, which was really a big band. They played all the Glenn Miller, Dorsey Brothers, Count Basie songs, and then started progressing to Stan Kenton, Les Brown, and Les and Larry Elgart. Then, when Charlie couldn't play at the Nite Liter, we started using an accordion player named Lee Allen. I have no idea where Lee came from.

Now before you start laughing, you've got to know something. This guy was, without a doubt, the most incredible accordion player I have ever heard in my life. He could sound like an entire band. He played the most incredible changes I have ever heard. I thought I could play jazz until I met this guy. He had been on the Vegas circuit for years, and was spit and polish, the most truly professional musician I have ever worked with, and in addition, he was married to a former Little Rock Central High cheerleader. They had met in Las Vegas and tied the knot. He could sing his butt off and play like an entire orchestra, all on that accordion. We sounded like a big band almost, but we flat jammed. I never in my wildest dreams thought I would wind up with a band that consisted of bass, drums, flute and accordion. But we were kickin'.

After a few months, we all realized we could never go any further than the Nite Liter in Hot Springs, Arkansas, so we took a gig at a new club in Memphis. Lee was married, but the rest of us were single, so we packed our bags and went to Memphis, permanently. After playing the new club for about two weeks, we started getting rave reviews in the *Commercial Appeal* by a writer named John Knott. He was as big in Memphis as Beale Street. Everyone in Memphis, especially in the entertainment field, hung onto every word he wrote, and he thought we hung the moon. We were a cooking band. But being a new club, the gig didn't last long, and we all had to start going our own way.

Lee went to work at Pepper Sound Studios making commercials for advertising agencies all over the country, and he was doing nothing but singing background. Edwin was wealthy enough that he didn't have to do anything unless he wanted to. His social status was a bit above ours, so he always ran with a different crowd. Buddy and I started playing at the Nite Liter in Memphis, which was one of the best known clubs in downtown Memphis. It was a beautiful, swanky club. We then found out that the Nite Liter in Hot Springs was a sister club to the Nite Liter in Memphis. They were both owned by the same man, Leroy Owens.

Leroy Owens was a gentle man, very hospitable, and he treated us like royalty because he knew that the reason his clubs lasted so long was because of the great music we were putting out night after night. He was paying us ninety dollars a week for playing six nights a week, four to five hours a night. That kind of pay wasn't very loyal, but we continuously packed it out. It was the only gig in town at that particular time for us. Charlie Rich would play with us occasionally, and along with a great sax player named Marty Willis, we were the house band.

I recall one particular night when Charlie was there, for some reason I got so drunk I passed out on stage with my head lying on Charlie's piano, and everyone in the band said I didn't miss one single note. They claimed I played as well then as I did when I was wide awake—that's how tight we were and how immature and stupid I was that night. I had, for some reason, been drinking that afternoon, and by the time I got there, I was about three sheets in the wind. I continued to drink when I got there, and about eleven o'clock I was gone off to la-la land, but I just kept right on playing. I never missed a lick.

After about a year of this, Buddy went off on his own, but as talented as he was, he didn't have a thing to worry about. I stayed at the Nite Liter for a while longer. Buddy and I had been roommates, but he had met his second wife-to-be, Sherry, a beautiful flight attendant with Delta. So we split all the things we had bought for the apartment, and he asked me to let them have the apartment.

About that time, I started dating Jerry Lee Lewis' sister, Linda Gayle Lewis. It was an experience I'll never forget. She lived with her mother in south Memphis, just a couple of houses down from Jerry Lee. Her mother was a wonderful lady, and Linda Gayle was a sweetheart. She was beautiful—strikingly beautiful, about three inches taller than I, and about five years younger than I was.

I moved in with Linda Gayle and her mother, and going up to Jerry's house became a daily affair. He was a very nice guy, occasionally, but pretty demanding. His wife, Myra, whom the whole world was told was his cousin, was such a distant cousin that probably most people in the country are as about related as they were. But the entire world, when you mentioned Jerry Lee Lewis, would say, "Oh, that's the rock and roll star that married his cousin." Most never talked about the fact that he was one of the very first icons in rock and roll music along with Elvis, Carl Perkins, Johnny Cash, and yes, Charlie Rich. All were discovered by my good friend, and most favorite person in the whole world, Sam Phillips.

Sam said (and he'd continue to say it almost every time I saw him years and years later after I became an engineer) Jerry Masters is the best "G.D." mixing engineer in music. He was my biggest fan. I loved him to death. His brother, Judd, was also Charlie Rich's agent and promoter for a long time. Sam's close friend Dewey had the South's first rock and roll radio station called "Red, Hot and Blue with

Dewey Phillips," on WHBQ, an AM station in Memphis. For years he was known all over the world just from his radio show, which was the first radio station to ever play an Elvis record. He helped make Elvis what he turned out to be. I guess the jury is still out on what Elvis really turned out to be, but he was the first; he was the darling of rock and roll, and had every woman in the country wrapped around his finger. And he could really sing nice, but not well, but that's just my opinion. I just wasn't, and am still not, a big Elvis fan. I appreciate what he did for music, but I didn't think he was that good of a singer. He just wasn't my cup of tea, I guess you could say.

Linda Gayle and I finally broke up after a while when I didn't want to get married, and I moved in with a couple of guys at the same apartment complex where Buddy and I had lived. While I was still working at the Nite Liter, I began dating a lady named Frankie, who was the hostess and hatcheck lady. She seemed to have a lot of class, very good manners, nice personality, and very friendly. She was just the right person to be working the door. We began dating, and even though we had had a spat or two, she became pregnant. I really did not want to get married, and I told her that, so being the irresponsible brat that I was, I thought it would just "go away." But guess what? Babies just don't "go away" unless you choose to destroy them. She did started talking about having an abortion, but that was something I flat wasn't going to let happen. Not on my watch. So I asked her to marry me. (Here we go again.).

There was something about her that drove me up a wall, but I couldn't figure out what it was. Still haven't. I even left her once, but when she mentioned abortion, I came back with my hat in my hand. We were pretty compatible for the most part, and I figured we would be able to maintain the status quo and have a good relationship. She was a Razorback fan, too, so that about did it for me. No problem, right? I didn't know at the time that marriage had a lot more responsibility attached to it than just living in the same house.

Now, you would have thought by this time in my life, especially after the disaster I caused in Little Rock, leaving Jeanne and Mike and all, that I possibly would have stopped for just one minute and said, "Jerry, does all of this sound familiar? Are you ever going to grow up and realize that simply being willing to marry someone does not a marriage make?" I could have chosen to just be a father, but that wouldn't have worked. Frankie wouldn't go along with that for a second. I also reminded myself about what causes babies, and wondered how I could have been so stupid and careless not to think about the consequences of having sexual relations outside the institution of marriage the way God planned it. I had a lot of learning to do at that point in my life, and I saw a pattern developing that could destroy me if I didn't start acting more responsibly.

Frankie was a native of Parkin, Arkansas, a small town across the river about twenty-five miles from Memphis, with a population of about 1,500—on a Saturday afternoon, that is. Her father, Sterling Melhorn, was editor and publisher of the *Cross County Times*, and was a real trip of a guy. I loved him to death, but I found out later that he had some major spiritual and biblical problems—and he was teaching Sunday school to hundreds of young people growing up in that town. He was a heretic, to put it mildly. It was dangerous and harmful, but a lot of kids grew up in that town believing that Jesus was not the Son of God, was not deity, was not crucified for our sins, and was not resurrected from the dead by the Father; and he taught those heresies for over fifty years. I felt bad for all the young people that grew up under his teaching.

Frankie's mother was a treasure to behold. We called her "Mama." She was one of the most endearing, loving people I had ever met in my life. She especially loved her grandchildren, and I came to find out many years later that love for a grandchild is unlike any other love in the world.

Frankie and I lived in an apartment in a ten-story building about a block from the Baptist Hospital there in Memphis, so she was within walking distance to the ER. The apartment was on the ninth floor of a high rise tower of apartments which had been living quarters for nurses there at the Baptist Hospital, but had been turned into rental units. It was the smallest apartment I had ever seen, much less had lived in. But it served our purpose, with me being out on the road so much and Frankie being pregnant. She could walk out the door and see the entrance to the ER from our front door. It was a good thing, too, because Frankie's water broke when she was only seven months pregnant, and she immediately walked down to the ER.

She walked down there at about 8:30 that morning, and Mandy was born at about 11 p.m. while I was playing at the club. I could hardly play the rest of the evening, but I had to go till 2 a.m., so I just sucked it up and finished the gig, then headed straight for the hospital. Mandy was born on October 26, 1963. She was a preemie and weighed less than three pounds when born. She had a pretty rough time for about the first thirty days. She had an ear infection and couldn't hold down milk of any kind. Frankie's milk never came in, and we even tried soy milk, but Mandy kept throwing up anything we tried to feed her.

She wasn't any bigger than a newborn puppy. She was so tiny that the only way we could tell she was crying or needed anything was by seeing her tiny hand up in the air coming from her crib. They had her in ICU for a week or so and then moved her into a regular room. I remember walking into the room, and even though she was in a baby bed, I could hardly find her she was so tiny. Charlie went with me to the hospital, too. He wanted to see her. He knew how much she meant to me, and he also knew the sacrifice I had made to make sure she was born.

At one point after we had walked into the room (it was about 3 a.m.), it was real quiet all over the hospital, and he looked over at me and said, "You know, Jerry, I've never had a Godchild. Could I possibly be her Godfather?" I looked very surprised. I said, "Chas, you most certainly can; we would be honored." So that night, Charlie Rich, my friend, became the Godfather of Mandy Leigh Masters. She was so beautiful, I couldn't believe it, and she was so tiny, you could almost hold her in the palm of your hand.

Something else happened the next day that was such a blessing to me. My mother and I had pretty much not talked with each other after the way I had treated Jeanne and Mike, and of course, Mother took up the slack of my not being there by keeping very close tabs on the two of them until Jeanne got a house only three houses up from where my mother had finally moved. Mother had bought a house out in the Geyer Springs part of Little Rock, at 5504 Western Lane, where she lived until she died in 1998.

So the day after Mandy was born, I called my mother, and it seemed like ages since we had last talked. She was pretty bummed at me, and I wasn't even sure if she would talk to me. I said, "Mom, I've got some interesting news. I'm not sure if you're going to like it or not." She said, "Well, what is it this time?" I said, "You've got a new granddaughter." She was totally silent for a minute, caught completely off guard; then she said (and I couldn't believe she said it), "I'll be in Memphis tomorrow." And then she said something I had not heard in a long time. She said, "You know, you've messed up a lot of people's lives here lately, but I love you. Thank you for calling."

I just stood there with my mouth open. There is nothing in the world more precious than the love of a mother for her children, except the love of grandparents; but that's a different kind of love, and we'll talk about that later on. She was in Memphis at 9:00 the next morning. It's a two and a half hour drive from Little Rock to Memphis, but for new grandmothers, especially with their first granddaughter, it's about an hour and forty-five minutes. I was so happy that the ice had been broken between us. My mother was always my hero, and the hero of a lot of people I knew in my lifetime. She had her problems, just like everyone else, but there wasn't a more respected woman in the city of Little Rock, Arkansas, than Marjorie Dyer Masters.

Chapter
6

I started going out with Charlie Rich on weekends quite often. I was his band manager, so every time we went out, I would have to find us a drummer and a guitar player. I started having a real problem with Charlie's drinking, and it started to be embarrassing at times...and depressing, too. We used several different people on drums and guitar, but after a while, Ace Cannon offered me a job playing bass with his band.

That's where I met Tommy Cogbill, one of the best musicians and even better human beings that I have ever known. Tommy, at the time, was Ace's guitar player (I didn't know he played bass at the time). Man, what a great bunch of guys, and what a great band we ended up having. Ace was also an accomplished saxophone player: alto, soprano, and tenor sax. He even learned how to play two saxes at once. It was so cool.

Later, much to my surprise, all of those guys except me, Fats, and Ace ended up being the rhythm section at American Studios working for Chips Moman. Tommy played more bass and was a sensational producer. They were cranking out hit records like nobody's business. They cut a record called "Memphis Soul Stew," and guess who was playing bass, and also pretty much set the standard for Memphis bass players and bass players all over the world...Tommy

Cogbill. If I had known when we were traveling together those two years that he could play bass like that, I never would have packed my suitcase and gone out with Ace. He was the "baddest" bass player in Memphis for years, not taking anything away from my good friend Donald "Duck" Dunn, who was the bass player with Booker T. and the MG's.

Duck used to come down to the Nite Liter with John Knott, the writer from the Commercial Appeal, and listen to me play before he became famous. Duck was so funky, but he couldn't walk in the same room with Tommy Cogbill, as far as I was concerned. I loved Duck, and he's my friend, but he couldn't play "Misty" at that time; it had too many changes. (*Smile*) Sorry, Duck. But he could flat get funky, and no one in the world could "lay it down" better than Duck. I wish I were getting his royalty checks.

Not only was Tommy Cogbill an incredible bass player, he was also a great record producer. He produced a record on an artist, Marilee Rush, called "Angel in the Morning," that sold a million and a half records at least, maybe even two million. Tommy could do it all. He was also one of my dearest friends, and I loved him very much. He was just a super guy in every way. There were so many great musicians starting to find their niche in Memphis, and we all were looking for that *right* gig, *right* group, *right* song, and *right* opportunity. After traveling for a couple of years with Charlie, Jerry Lee, Ace, and the Bill Black Combo for many thousands of miles (I thank Bob Tucker for giving me that opportunity), I was finally given my chance for the semi big-time, you might say.

Before I get started with Ray Brown, there were so many funny stories I could tell about the different things that happened with each group. Once while I was playing with Ace Cannon, we were playing a week's sit-down gig in Wichita Falls, Texas. We had been there several times before, and we always stayed in the same motel. Well, one night after our gig, or you might say one morning, about 4 a.m., the darned place caught on fire. The fire started in the rear of the motel (we never found out how), but the place was like a matchbox.

I was rooming with Fats at the time, and we were in bed asleep. Fats woke up and said, "Jerry, it's awfully hot in here, did you turn the heat up?" I mumbled something about it was kind of hot, so I picked up the phone and called the office and asked them if they could turn the heat down in our room. They controlled the air to all the rooms from the office, which I thought was kind of unusual.

All of a sudden, we saw the flames come roaring out of the back window. We grabbed everything we thought was valuable, especially the instruments we had with us (we always left most of our instruments in the club when we were playing week-long gigs; you could trust people back in those days, especially in Texas), and got the hell out of the place, still only half dressed. All of a sudden, Fats realized he had left his cuff link collection in there, at least that's what he said. But I knew what he was going back for, and I was relieved. Fats had a cuff link collection that included about seventy-five or eighty pairs of cuff links, but in reality, he had left his drugs in there. Or should I say *our* drugs.

We all shared what we had when it came to pills back then. What I'm trying to say here, with no bad reflection on anyone, is we lived on speed in those days. Amphetamines, black beauties, LA turnarounds, whatever you wanted to call them. We couldn't have done what we were doing to the extent we were doing it, without drugs. Now please understand, not all the guys I traveled with took these drugs. It was more me than anyone else. Whenever we would leave for a gig, we would always leave late at night or around midnight, depending on how far we had to drive. We would drive all night when there wasn't a lot of traffic, and we'd get there in the morning in time to hit the sack, sleep all day, and be ready for the gig that night, well rested and ready to go. But in order to stay awake all night and be alert enough to drive, I would take speed.

What was funny was that, with practically every group I went out with, no matter who, I would end up being the driver. I was a good driver. I could back a trailer anywhere in a second, and I could remember a place we had played before, and sometimes be able to drive right to it years later. I had a good sense of direction, knew most all of the highways out of Memphis and how to get wherever we were going, whether it be Texas, Florida, Indiana, Wisconsin, South Dakota, or Colorado; it made no difference. I knew how to get there the fastest way, and in all those years, by the grace of God, I never had one accident of any kind, never even a fender bender.

I must have driven at least a million miles in the ten years I was on the road. But I also have the abused body to show for it, too. I'll tell you more about that later. That was back in the days when bands, no matter how good or bad, did all their traveling by car. They loaded all their own equipment, set the bandstands up themselves, tore them down, and repacked everything after the gig was over. We didn't know what a roadie was. That word hadn't even been invented then. But we were literally, the original, "kings of the road."

One day in early 1964, Ray Brown, a Memphis promoter and booking agent, called me into his office and closed the door. He told me he had a proposition that could be very lucrative for me and possibly take care of my need for a steady income. Ray and I had been friends for quite some time, because he booked Charlie Rich, Ace Cannon, and all of the groups I had played with for years, so he knew me to be a responsible and dependable man with the ability to lead and be totally honest. He held me in high esteem, as compared to a lot of musicians he dealt with throughout his life as a premier booking agent. Ray was a dear man, with a big heart, and a good feel for business. I trusted him completely and knew that he would always shoot straight with me, no matter what.

Ray told me there was a record out that was burning the charts up and selling like hot cakes. It was a studio record called "Little GTO." It was a kind of surfing song. The artist on the record was Ronny and the Daytonas. The only problem was, there was no such group. The record was cut in the studio by John "Bucky" Wilken and Buzz Cason, two very prolific songwriters in Nashville. John's mother, Marijohn Wilkin, was one of the most well-known and successful country songwriters in Nashville for years. The record was a monster, but Bucky didn't want to take a group out on the road. He didn't even have a group, and he gave Ray the authority to put a "fake" group out on the road to help promote the record and keep the name, Ronny and the Daytonas, in the public's eye.

Ray asked me if I wanted to take a group out by that name and play gigs all over the country. He would pay me and the band a weekly salary, plus all of our expenses when were out on the road, plus they would buy us a brand new station wagon to carry all of our equipment, and I could drive the car personally when we weren't traveling. I had always wanted my own group, so I figured this was an excellent opportunity for me to not only have my own group, but have a steady income, which was hard to come by being a musician and traveling with different bands all the time. We usually got paid by the gigs we played, and if we didn't go out, we didn't get paid, no matter who we were playing with. So with this deal, we got a weekly salary whether we went out or not, and that was a dream come true as far as our families were concerned, and almost unheard of in the industry.

The first thing I had to do was start looking for musicians. I had to put a band together, and I was really spoiled after playing with such accomplished musicians for so long. I knew that the meager salary Ray offered would be a joke to the guys I had been playing with for the last couple of years, but, I had to start somewhere. The first guy to join the band was a guitar player named Gary McEwen. He was not only the first guy I hired, but he stayed with me throughout the entire thing. He was even one of the Hombres—more about the Hombres later.

Gary was married and had a beautiful wife, Carol, and two little girls, both very young. With Gary being married and having a family, I knew he would be solid, dependable, and a person of integrity. You could also tell he was very committed to his family and loved them very much. The next person was a drummer named Lee Cornei. He was so young, and so inexperienced, about all he had was the desire to be a star. He even got blisters on his hands from holding drumsticks for too long. That's how raw he was. He had a girlfriend that had the most beautiful long black hair. She said she ironed it every morning.

The next person I invited to join us was a very talented young man named Louis Paul. He was a very good rock guitar player and could sing quite well. He was just very immature, and as I later found out, had some minor mental problems as well. It was like having a platoon of raw recruits, and I was hoping I could mold them into a band. This was also about the time of the Beatle invasion of the U.S., and the whole country was Beatle crazed. And here was a bald-headed old bass player (I was 24 at the time), and a guitar player with short curly hair. Lee's hair was just sort of normal, but long hair was the thing at the time. Louis had semi-long hair, but he was letting it grow out, and I figured by the time we were ready to start touring, we would have at least one person on stage that looked half-way like a Beatle.

At first we were supposed to be called just "the Daytonas." There simply wasn't anyone on earth named Ronny. But as we started touring, everyone kept coming up to the band asking, which one was Ronny. When Louis fronted the band (he almost had to be the one), he kept giving everyone the impression that he was the leader of the band, which would make him "Ronny," so I just let him have fun. After a while, everyone started coming up to me and asking if they could be Ronny for one night. So I let them have their little fun and fifteen minutes of fame, but it started to be a contest. Everyone wanted to be

"Ronny." It was so funny to have one of your group come up to you in private and ask, "Jerry, can I be Ronny tonight?"

Then, the bigger the record got, newspapers and magazines started catching us on the road, and I didn't want just anyone speaking up for the group as a whole, so when they would say, "Which one is Ronny?" I would say, "I am!" On a couple of occasions, someone showed me a picture of Bucky, and I had no idea where it came from, but I tried to convince them that the picture was me. That was not easy, since the picture was of Bucky Wilkin, and he had enough hair for three of us. To be honest, the entire situation started to become a pain in the royal *wazoo*.

We did a five-week tour called, "The Johnny Rivers Memphis Special," and we had a big Trailways bus with the name of the tour on the front. We had the wonderful instrumental group and California icons, the "Ventures," Bob Bogle, Mel Taylor, Nokie Edwards, and Don Wilson. We also had "Chad and Jeremy" (Chad Stewart and Jeremy Clyde), an English duo with a big hit at the time, "Yesterday's Gone," and Johnny Rivers, of course.

Johnny only had two musicians backing him, a drummer and a bass player. They were excellent musicians. The bass player, Joe Osborne, was a nice guy, but the drummer was on a trip. He was very unfriendly. Once, when I was in one of my "not so good" moods, they made some kind of remark about us and our Southern heritage, so I asked them, "How does it feel to just be a sideman?" They went ballistic. I thought they were going to kill me. Both were a bit larger than I, but they couldn't catch me. In spite of the fact that we were all stuck together on a single bus day after day, and always having to interact, it was a fairly fun trip.

We always opened the show, followed by the Ventures, then Chad and Jeremy, then Johnny. We started in Texas, went west all the way to California, all over the west coast, the Midwest, and ended up with our final concert in Memphis. It was a trip, literally and figuratively. We played Reno and Tahoe. We were all over the country, playing at least six nights a week.

We did have about three days off in Wisconsin. The motel we were all staying in at that time also had Bobby Vinton and his band. They were playing a sit-down gig there for two weeks. One afternoon a couple of the Ventures, Bobby and I, and a few guys from his band, were out in a field there by the motel playing touch football. Bobby and I were on the same team, and at one time I threw him a pass and he caught it wrong and broke his thumb. He had to go to the emergency room and was in such pain he barely made the gig that night. So my claim to fame for that tour was the fact that *I broke Bobby Vinton's thumb.*

I might also mention that at the time, the Ventures were playing some new instruments that Bob Bogle and Company had designed called Mosrite basses and guitars. Bob let me use his bass on the tour for a couple of nights, and I ended up using it for the rest of the tour. It was a sweet bass, handled real well, had good balance, and great tone and style. That following Christmas, I got a pleasant surprise when I received a brand new Mosrite bass in the mail, black with silver hardware, as a gift from Bob and the rest of the company.

They were a very good bunch of players, and their personalities were just as special as their playing. It was such a great pleasure to tour with them and become friends. Chad and Jeremy were equally as nice, but they sort of kept off to themselves, and Johnny was a bit spoiled to be perfectly honest. We were all in a restaurant once, and Johnny had one of his band members go to the front and have Johnny paged so everyone would know he was in the establishment. That was kind of tacky, but we all had our moments, you might say. It was one of those tours that said to me: I'm really glad we did it, but I wouldn't want to do it again, at least not that way.

After we got back from the tour, I realized that Louis Paul was a problem child, and I needed someone with more maturity in the band. So I added a new rhythm guitar player, Jim Vincent, and let Gary front the band as lead singer. Jim only played acoustic guitar, which wasn't quite powerful enough, but he did sing harmonies, so he paid his way for a season. But we needed more power as far as guitars in the group. Even though I spoke for the group, I let Gary handle all of the other microphone duties.

Eventually, Jim left the group, so we added a keyboard and guitar player who ended up being the best friend I've ever had in this world—B.B. Cunningham, Jr. He not only played keyboards, but he was a good guitar player, too. For some songs we did needed two guitars, so B.B. made us almost a five-piece group with only four people. He was extremely versatile because he also sang quite well—as good as anyone else we had used on vocals. His voice was deep and rich, his pitch was excellent, and his attitude was fantastic. So that took some of the lead singing duties off Gary and allowed him to concentrate on playing rhythm guitar. We also added a new drummer,

Johnny Hunter, an old and dear friend who had also played with Charlie and me on numerous occasions.

Johnny was one of my dearest friends and had been for quite some time. I knew his parents quite well, also. Johnny's mom and dad were really special people and loved their son very much, as did I. This is the group that ended up being the Hombres: B.B. Cunningham, Jr., Gary W. McEwen, and John William Hunter. We toured until around 1966. With B.B. and Gary and Johnny, we started really coming together as a good band. But we sure got tired of playing "Little GTO." We must have played it a thousand times over that two years, and we just got tired of being someone else, and tired of playing "GTO." We wanted, needed, and deserved our own identity after all that time.

Chapter

7

We had a gig to play somewhere in north Texas one Saturday night, and we decided to make that our last road trip. We were all sick of the road, sick of setting up and tearing down, sick of wondering if anyone would show up for our gigs, sick of wondering if the promoter was going to have the cash to pay us, sick of driving, and sick of living in motel rooms. We stayed in a motel one time somewhere up in Nebraska that literally had three or four wood steps that you stepped up on to get into the room. It had wooden floors, a pot bellied stove for heat, and quilts on the bed with feather pillows. It was the only motel within a hundred miles, so we had to go for it. Actually, it was sort of a pleasant change for us, and I liked it a lot.

We once had to play a gig on one night, then get up the next morning and drive across the entire state of Iowa, then get up the next morning and drive across the entire state back to where we had originally played the night before. And at that particular time, the winds were coming out of the north at twenty-five to thirty mph for about five solid days. When we made the first trip west, I ended up with a sore shoulder and arm from trying to hold our station wagon on the road from the constant winds coming out of the north, and could hardly play that night. Then the next day, I did the same thing to my other shoulder and arm driving back across the state, because the winds were exactly the same the next day as they were the day before. And you wouldn't believe it, but at the time, we carried the four of us, our luggage, our instruments, including Johnny's drums, our amps, guitars, keyboards, and our entire sound system in one 1966 Chevrolet station wagon. You might have said, "had band, will travel."

This was in 1966. Today when a band goes out, they take four or five eighteen-wheelers just for their instruments and stage set ups, lights, sound, smoke, the whole nine yards. Even if they can't play or sing, they've got the stuff to make people think they can. The band usually flies from gig to gig. My, how things change.

When we decided to call it quits on the road and change our name to the Hombres, we were taking a big chance. We had no idea what we were going to do as a band. But someone much bigger than us (of the divine nature) was looking out for us, and had been the entire time. We were truly blessed to get what we called a sit-down gig in West Memphis, Arkansas—Woo Pig Sooie, just across the river from Memphis. But it might as well have been in Memphis, because after a while, the word got out. We were getting tighter and tighter, rehearsing more often, and after a few weeks we were the hottest band in town. People would literally line up outside and wait for seating in a lounge that sat about 125 people, plus standing room only.

On Thursday, Friday, and Saturday nights, you couldn't get in the place unless you had reservations or got there early. It was a lounge in the rear of one of the best Mexican Restaurants in the South at the time. It was called Ponchos, and the lounge was called the El Toro Lounge. The bandstand was up behind the bar. We also had a local singer who was popular all over Memphis for his antics and his singing. His name was Charles Turner. Charlie would come on, sing a couple of songs every couple of hours, and walk around in the audience carrying a basket, which he used to hold his tips. He was making more money than we were, but we were just happy to be playing, becoming tighter and tighter as a band all the time.

The local entertainment writers constantly referred to the Hombres as the "best of the best" bands in town, and the El Toro Lounge in West Memphis was place to go when you wanted to go jukin'. Many people would go up front early, eat dinner in the restaurant, then have tables reserved back in the lounge. When they were through eating, they would just walk back to the lounge and make a night of it right there in one building. And they had the best cheese dip in the entire USA. No doubt. Chips and dip. I wouldn't dare go home without a sack full of chips and dip.

Frankie and I and the kids had moved to Parkin, Arkansas, Frankie's home town, about a year and a half earlier. Also, not long after Mandy was out of the woods, Syndy Sharp, Frankie's daughter by her first marriage, moved in with us. Syndy had been living with her grandparents since Frankie moved to Memphis, and she was about five or six years old when she moved in with us. I thought we were going to be alright as a family until I really started to get to know Syndy. Then I knew we had a major problem, and there wasn't a thing in the world I could do about it except just try, try, try.

After being raised by her grandparents, she was spoiled rotten. She was accustomed to getting anything she wanted anytime she wanted it, and I wasn't about to let that be our lifestyle when I was trying to teach them about growing up and loving and caring for each other. She was so spoiled that when Mandy had her first birthday, Syndy threw a fit over Mandy's gifts. Syndy insisted on receiving gifts as well, even though there was no reason for her to receive any. She was a proverbial "brat," from the word go. We rented a couple of different houses, and then ended up buying one when our first record came out. The problems got worse and worse with Syndy, and it got to where I couldn't even spend time with my own daughter without having to include Syndy in everything I did. I got so sick of it that I got to the point where I didn't even want to go home at night.

By working in West Memphis and living in Parkin, I was pretty close to home. Parkin was about twenty miles west of West Memphis, yet I would stay at the club every night as long as possible drinking and carousing, sometimes just standing out in the parking lot until the sun came up, talking with other musicians. Because of our popularity, they came by the numbers, almost every night. Then I would sleep most of the day until it was time to go to work that evening.

We worked the El Toro from 9 p.m. till 2 a.m. six nights a week. The pay was not that great, but after getting off the road, it was a blessing from God and we all knew it. We had so many dignitaries that came to hear us; one in particular was the founder and CEO of the Holiday Inns of America. What was so unusual about it was the fact that he had never gone out to a nightclub in his life, but he had to go see the Hombres. His name was Kemmons Wilson, and he was an icon in Memphis and the entire world-wide hotel-motel industry.

Memphis was the world headquarters for Holiday Inns of America, which was the biggest hotel-motel chain in the world at the time. But it was such a surprise to everyone involved that he finally went out jukin' for the first time in his life. He was nearly sixty years of age, and he went to see the famous Hombres over in West Memphis. And because of his visit, they took a picture of us in front of the Holiday Inn in West Memphis that said, "Welcome Hombres," and put it on the front page of the Holiday Inn monthly magazine that went out all over the world.

Another top-notch guy that used to frequent the club to see us was Donald "Duck" Dunn, bass player on many of Stax Records' enormous hits over the years, and he also played with Booker T. and the MG's. Also, his compatriot and partner in crime, Steve Cropper, would come. He was one of the most premier guitar players and song writers in the world of R & B, also a member of Booker T and an established producer himself, along with Isaac Hayes. Steve wrote, along with Otis Redding, "Sittin' On The Dock Of The Bay," which was an enormous hit for Otis. Others that came to see us were The Memphis Horns, with Wayne Jackson, Andrew Love, and Jack Hale, a funky Memphis-style horn section that were also icons on the Memphis and world music scene for years and years. They were also my dear friends, especially Wayne Jackson.

Wayno, as I would call him, would come over to the El Toro after we'd get through playing at 2 a.m., and we would all stand out in the parking lot smoking, drinking, and shooting the bull and telling "war stories" and jokes till sun up the next morning. Don't ask me how I stayed awake all that time, but you might say that I had a lot of pharmaceutical help, especially when I was on the road, starting with Charlie Rich, through Ace, Jerry Lee, Bill Black, the Daytonas, and then the Hombres. It became a way of life for me. I would get what I called "sufficiently wired" before every gig, and it just became the way I lived. I couldn't have made it without the help of pills. And the pills would cause me to drink a lot to keep the edge off the amphetamines. But it was all for a reason, which you will find out about as you continue to read this book.

We continued our stance at the El Toro, and even though it was starting to be a drag, it was a job. Then one day, out of the blue, our dear friend and record producer, Huey Meaux from Houston, Texas, called us up on the telephone and said, "Are you guys sitting down?" We said yeah, and he said "I've got some great news for you…. You guys have got a hit record!" We all just kind of sat there for a second. He said it was number one in Flint, Michigan, and number one in some other major market that I can't recall at the moment. He said that it was starting to get airplay in every major market around the country, and it was a SMASH. It was called "Let It All Hang Out."

You see, something I neglected to mention was that during our little experience of being a fake group, once B.B. and Johnny came into the group, and we started getting so much better as a band, Ray Brown decided we should go down to Pasadena, Texas, and record with his good friend Heuy Meaux. We were so naïve at the time, we didn't know who Heuy was, and we had no idea what was going on, but we figured we could cut some songs, kind of like GTO, and continue our little fraudulent lives and also cut our own record. We had some fairly decent songs, but I'm really lying, we didn't have anything that I thought was even worth burning tape on.

But we headed to Pasadena anyway, which was a suburb of Houston with oil derricks all over the place, and we did our usual thing, which was to leave at about midnight the night before, drive all night, and get there in time to get rooms and rest before our recording session that evening. It was going to turn out to be one of the most famous trips of our lives, and it's still as alive this day in 2009 as it was then in 1965.

We were still on the road at that time, so this was going to be just a stopover in Pasadena to humor our booking agent and his friend Heuy Meaux. Then we were going on to play a gig the next night in nearby Beaumont, Texas. So, it was about 5:30 a.m., the sun had just come up, and we were on Highway 59 South between Texarkana and Houston. We came over the top of a hill, and lo and behold, there was a huge "chicken wreck" at the bottom of the hill. It seems this truckload of chickens had crashed into a bridge abutment, and all over the place were dead chickens, live chickens, half-dead chickens, smashed chickens—it was just a chicken mess. It appeared the truck had rolled a couple of times, but the driver was alright, just shaken a bit.

Well, all the guys were asleep, but "Mr. Amphetamine Jerry" was wide awake, and I said, "Hey guys, wake up, we done got us a chicken wreck down here." Everyone kind of half opened their eyes, and B. B. says, "Well, just let it all hang out." I thought about that remark for a few minutes, and I said, "You know what guys? That would make a great title for a song. We could come up with some sort of riff, kind of like the guitar riff on "Gloria," write some verses that make absolutely NO sense whatsoever, and let the hook be "but just let it all hang out."

I could just hear it in my head. It seemed like the chicken wreck was just the epitome of our lives for the last several years. It seemed like all the suits were just throwing us bones while we were out there working like dogs using our gifts to make our families comfortable and have things all the people with "regular" jobs gave their families. We were tired of always having to "go in the back door" of places we worked, while all of our contemporaries were going in the front door because they wore suits to work. This would be the perfect outlet for us to prove that we deserved one big break so we could reward our friends and families for enduring so much hardship with us being gone all the time and bringing home nothing but peanuts for pay.

And we did exactly that. The four of us each wrote a verse. Johnny came up with an intro that he got from a Red Engle record from the 40s, "I preach my dear friends...." We each wrote verses and tried to make sure that no verse made any sense whatsoever. The entire idea was for people to forget about all the protest songs going on due to the war in Viet Nam. It seemed like everyone was becoming a prophet or an intellectual or were trying to prove something with the songs they were writing, and we just wanted something people could dance to, jump up and down to, or whatever gave them a thrill.

Even my current wife said that when she first heard it driving out to Pensacola Beach as a teenager, she had to pull over on the side of the road and get out and dance. There were countless towns where pastors and teachers and parents would sit down and try to find something evil or dirty in our lyrics, but guess what? In the music business there is no such thing as "bad" publicity. That's exactly what we were trying to do. Mess their heads up so the kids could have some fun with it. It was merely a FUN SONG meant to HAVE FUN WITH.

I must admit that the verse about the man walking upside down and the TV being on the blink was about two of the guys who were experimenting with smoking grass. They would literally sit in front of the TV after the gigs and watch the dot when you turned the TV set off and see things that made them laugh for hours. I was enjoying their having fun, but we never did that sort of thing on gigs. We did NOT get stoned when we played. Maybe a beer or two, but that's all.

When we got to the studio, we told Huey that we wanted to cut a fun song, just for the heck of it. Then we would do the serious recording for him. Well, when we put it down and listened to the playback, I knew it was a HIT RECORD the moment I heard it back. It just had that magical feeling that hit records have, that makes you want to hear it over and over and over again. Huey thought it was a joke. I knew it was a hit, and I told him so. A year and a half later our producer realized we knew what we were talking about. We knew how to make records if people would just let us. Only one city kept it from being a multi-million dollar #1 record, and that was New York City. I guess it was just too funky for the Big Apple.

We went ahead and cut about ten half-assed "surfing songs" (none of us had ever even been in the ocean except me and B.B.), and I can't even remember the names of a single one of them. We then bopped on over and played our gig in Beaumont and went home. We had a hit record sitting in the can for a year and a half, and nobody believed in it but me. And I soon forgot about it, just like everyone else.

Chapter

8

By the time Huey called us, Ray Brown was going ballistic with the booking. He was asking from $5,000 to $15,000 a night for us, depending on the venue. Huey wanted an album immediately, and our days at the El Toro were numbered. We started making plans to go on the road again, but this time under much different circumstances. As the record started getting bigger and bigger, we would fly out of Memphis with nothing but our instruments and our luggage. Johnny would take nothing but drum sticks and maybe some cymbals occasionally. No more driving all night, no more sleazy hotels; we would get our money, half up front and the other half before we even went on stage.

There was just one problem with this new situation. I HATED TO FLY. I had flown thousands of miles on many occasions when I was in the Army, and since I had to fly what is known as "space available," I flew on just about every plane the air force had in its arsenal, except fighter planes. I'm surprised they didn't stick me on one of those a few times. One thing is certain; there can be no more vicious thunderstorms in the East China Sea than anywhere in the world. Once I was flying from Tachikawa, Japan, to Okinawa in a prop C-46, or C-47, the military version of a DC-3, and that plane would get knocked sideways, almost upside down, drop a thousand feet, then get knocked back up two thousand feet, and this went on for at least two hours. When I got off that plane, I kissed the ground and swore I would never get on another airplane again. I had a fear of flying that has stayed with me even to this day. But I did what I had to do. And at times, I simply had to get on the plane and go. I was your basic white-knuckle flyer.

Here's just one example of how flying affected me. We had two gigs one week-end, one in Fort Wayne, Indiana, and one the next day in Pittsburgh, Pennsylvania. It was only about 200 miles from Fort Wayne to Pittsburgh, but we had to meet the next night in Indianapolis because our families were flying in to meet us for a weekend of fellowship. We had been gone so much, we thought it would be a good idea for them to come up and spend some time with us and kind of see what it was like being "stars" now.

We chose Indianapolis, Indiana, to meet because it was the spot for our next gig a few days later. Indianapolis was only a short drive south of Fort Wayne, so we figured why drive from Fort Wayne to Pittsburgh, then turn right around and drive all the way back to Indianapolis. We could just charter a plane to take us to Pittsburgh after the Fort Wayne concert, and then drive a few miles south to Indianapolis when we returned the next day. That made perfect sense to me. We had very few driving engagements normally, but we drove this time because we needed our entire line of equipment. It was a rare occasion.

We were getting spoiled by then. We requested a twin-engine plane from the charter service for the four of us, and they agreed. That night a huge storm came through Fort Wayne that just battered the town relentlessly with rain and high winds, and there was a cold front right behind it that made the temps drop at least twenty-five to thirty degrees from what they had been earlier.

When we drove out to the airport the next morning, we were informed by the charter company that the twin-engine plane had been blown off the runway. It had a bent propeller and was stuck in the mud. They had tried to have it removed, but with no luck, so the owner, who was also the pilot, informed us that he had a single engine STOL (short take off and landing) plane, called a Helio that could accommodate us for what we needed. Since we had little luggage and just our instruments, he thought we could get all of our stuff on the plane and have plenty of room for everyone, as long as one person didn't mind sitting up front with him.

We obliged, and off we went. I was wondering why it was called a Helio, and I was curious also what STOL really meant, and I found out in a hurry. We couldn't have used more than a hundred feet, if that, of runway space before our wheels were off the ground. I couldn't believe how quickly we were in the air. So they got the Helio, obviously, from helicopter, and STOL spoke for itself. That was just the beginning of this saga.

We left our car, a Cadillac Coup Deville, I might proudly mention (my very first Cadillac), with a trailer full of equipment on the runway at the hanger where the charter service was located. By the time we had climbed to about three or four thousand feet, the turbulence became quite intense. It was quite unnerving. It was some of the fiercest turbulence I've ever encountered in my life, with the exception of the trip in Japan, and we were not enjoying it at all. I was sitting there sucking on a Coors Light at 10 a.m., everyone else was holding on for dear life, and Gary, our brave little soul all by himself in the rear seat, was barfing into his hands. When I asked the pilot if he had anything in the likeness of a barf bag, he said no, so Gary had to hold his partially digested breakfast in his hands until we landed in Pittsburgh an hour and a half later.

I was an "old pro" at flying, even though I hated it, but this was the end of the road for me. Never, ever again would I get on an airplane. And do you know what's really funny about all of this? I love airplanes. I love to watch them. I know what the model number is of most of the WW2 fighter planes and bombers, even today's most popular choices for flying, and the commercial aircraft as well—but I hate to get on them. Still, this is just the beginning of this story. It gets worse, if you think that's even possible.

We played the gig that night, then went to our rooms, got some rest, and were up bright and early the next morning headed for the airport for our return flight on the Helio. I looked up at the sky and felt the wind. It was still brisk, and there was still some pretty heavy cloud cover, but it was broken clouds, so I knew the storm was breaking. Still, I just couldn't do it. So, I saw the guys out to their charter, paid the pilot (for his room that night too), sent them on their merry way, and I told them I would see them in Indianapolis in a few hours.

I already had rooms booked for us and our families, including the kids. Then I went down to Avis and rented me a nice, big, floater (a large sedan that floats down the road), and I hit the highway for what should have been a five to six hour drive to Indianapolis. I figured we would all get there about the same time. But there was just one small problem in all of this. After I got about forty miles out of Pittsburgh, I reached down into my bag to get something, and I heard a rattle that I didn't want to hear...it was the keys to my car. My car was sitting on the runway back in Fort Wayne, waiting for the others to fly in from Pittsburgh and drive it to Indiana, but I was the ONLY person that had keys to the car.

I had always hidden a spare key to all of my previous vehicles under the hood in a magnetic box, but when I got my first Caddy, I didn't get a chance to do the same. So when they arrived in Fort Wayne, guess what? They couldn't drive one inch. I was breezing down I-70 as they were standing on the runway one hundred and fifty miles north of me, after a beautiful, totally non-turbulent, perfect flight from Pittsburgh, wondering how they were going to get to Indianapolis with a car they couldn't even get into. Why didn't they have cell phones back then? Not that it would have done any good. But I had no idea what to do.

When I reached the Holiday Inn in Indianapolis, I pulled into the rear parking lot and saw my car, motor running, with the ignition hotwired by our illustrious drummer (a former juvenile delinquent) who grew up in a hard part of Memphis, John William Hunter, bless his heart. I was so glad he had stolen cars in his youth, because, otherwise, they would still be waiting for me. We all got a big laugh out of that one, but it was an experience I'll never forget.

It was also fun to see the kids after their first plane ride. I didn't dare tell them what a chicken their dad was as far as flying, and thank God my compatriots kept my secret to themselves and never embarrassed me by telling anyone else. I just did not like the sensation of flying.

We had another flying incident that was just the opposite, and this time I even got to fly the darn plane myself for a few minutes. And this was promotion at its best, as far as promoters go. The outfit that booked us for this trip really had their acts together, because they pulled off not just a double, a triple, or a "four-ble," but a "five-ble" dose of Hombres appearances in two different states in one night. (Those are strictly "Jerry words"; you won't find them in a dictionary anywhere.) It was just incredible.

We started out doing two appearances at a club called the Red Rooster in downtown Pittsburgh, Pennsylvania. Then we went to one of their sister clubs, all the way across town and did another appearance. Well, we thought we were through for the night. We only did about three songs at each club, and then the promoters had whisked us out of the first one, into a Land Rover, and had speedily driven us to the next Red Rooster. After that, it was about 9:30 p.m., and we thought, "Man, what an easy night."

The guys then put us back in the Land Rover, took us out to the airport, put us in a Cessna Skymaster, which is what most pilots call a push/pull twin-engine plane. It has one engine in front and another behind the cabin. While one engine pulls us forward, the other engine literally pushes us forward. It's a cool aircraft, and believe it or not, the weather was ideal for flying—not a cloud in the sky, high barometer, no winds aloft, and guess who flew the plane for about thirty minutes? If you're thinking, "No, you didn't," well, you're wrong. I flew an airplane for the first time in my life, and it was more fun than a barrel full of people. I loved it.

I could feel the control, the way the stick controlled the up and down maneuvers, plus turning by simply banking the plane as opposed to turning the plane. It was so cool. Do I want to do it again? Nah. It was okay for a change of pace, but it's not always that pleasant up there, and your entire surroundings and conditions are controlled by the wind direction and the barometer readings. When the barometer starts descending, the pressure is starting to get low. When low pressure starts meeting high pressure, things change, and they can change in a hurry when you're up there in the clouds. That's what killed JFK, Jr. He just wasn't aware of the changing conditions, and things kind of crept up on him. He lost sight of the horizon, and when that happens, and you don't have an instrument rating, you're in a heap of trouble, my friend.

So, they flew us to Uniontown, Pennsylvania. It was about fifty miles southeast of Pittsburgh, and we did a fifteen-minute show, got back in another Land Rover, and headed back to the airport. We then set our compass for Altoona, Pennsylvania, ninety miles northeast of Morgantown, did a fifteen-minute show, then went back to the Cessna and set our compass for what I thought was home or Pittsburgh. But NO, we went to Morgantown, West Virginia, about a hundred miles southwest of Altoona. I was in shock. It was 2 o'clock in the morning, and we were headed to another town, in another state. We walked into another Red Rooster, and there were 7,000 young people waiting anxiously for the Hombres, those boys from Memphis that had that big hit, "Let It All Hang Out."

Well, that was all we played, but it lasted over seventeen minutes. Instead of ending it after about three minutes like we normally do, on the end we started vamping on the changes, and B. B. started playing free, just wailing his butt off on a B-3 organ, soloing. And then Gary started playing a solo, and he just couldn't hit a wrong note. We grooved like that for a long time; then Johnny and I broke it down with a drum solo (which means no one else played but Johnny; the rest of us just stopped). He must have played for over five minutes, but we were so tired and so relaxed, that we just couldn't stop, and we couldn't hit a wrong note.

We were in a groove we hadn't been in for so long, and we couldn't stop. I came back in on the bass with Johnny and started doing some jazz licks from my old days. I ended up playing the start of "Hang Out," then B. B. and Gary came back in on the chorus, and we finished the song. The crowd went berserk with joy. It was the first and probably the only acid rock version we ever did of a simple song like ours, but it worked, and we ended the night on a very high note, no pun intended.

We then were whisked out to the Cessna and landed in Pittsburgh at 5:30 a.m., just in time to get two hours sleep before our plane left for Memphis at 7:40 a.m. What a night! And, they paid us for each gig, which turned out to be a pretty lucrative evening for four poor musicians that God chose to bless after all those years of pounding the pavement wanting to someday be rock stars. We had finally made it.

But you know what's sad? I wasn't a bit happier or more at peace being a big rock star than I had been when I was making fifty dollars a night for just a weekend with another group. There was still something missing; I didn't feel fulfilled. I just felt empty, like there was still a huge void inside me that should have been filled by accomplishing what I'd wanted all my life. I should have been one of the happiest people in the world, right? I wasn't, not one bit. We'll talk more about that later.

Chapter

9

We continued to tour, and of course, the record didn't stay on the top of the charts forever. They always say (I've yet to figure out who "they" is), "You're only as big as your last record." Another old saying was, and this fit us to a T, "One record acts are a dime a dozen." Just think back to so many of your favorite records over the years. I'll bet you a hundred dollars that you can't tell me the name of the group for 90% of them. You only remember the song, usually the opening two lines, sometimes the name of the song, or the hook, or the chorus. But usually you only faintly remember anything about songs and records that had such a big influence on your life and the memories they created: when you heard them, where you were, what you were doing, who you were going with, or who you broke up with. Things like that. There was an old saying I used to always tell people. I don't know who to give the credit to, but it stuck with me all my life. It was, "One day you're nothing, the next day you're a star, but the day after that, nobody knows who you are," and it's the absolute truth. It's unfortunate, but it's true.

We did go in and cut another album. We cut it at Ardent Studios in Memphis. They were the only ones in town at that time that had an eight-track studio. WOW, eight tracks. Think of all the possibilities. We had cut "Hang Out" on a three-track, actually, so we had one extra track. I think we ended up putting some cymbal crashes on the extra track, because Johnny had forgotten some during the live cut. We also, I think, doubled the background vocals on the vamp. Once again, I can't remember. All I know is, IT WAS A HIT.

Our second album was kind of lame. We had a couple of fairly decent songs in there, but we were trying to establish ourselves as up-to-date, legitimate recording artists, with different effects, and panning things back and forth and all that, but the bottom line is, we didn't have any songs. What few half-way decent songs we did have were just stupid. One of them was "Take My Overwhelming Love and Cram It, Straight Up Your Heart." This is not a reflection on B.B. or Gary or Johnny. It's just that we were trying to copy some of the acid rock stuff we'd been listening to, and we just simply had our heads on backwards as far as I'm concerned.

There just wasn't another "Hang Out." We were trying to stay in that same genre, but it just wasn't commercial. We did have one song that started getting a bit of airplay, but the record company didn't have any records in the stores, and when people tried to go out and buy the record, they couldn't find it. I don't think the album itself ever even came out. We had worn ourselves out trying to compete with good songwriters, and we all had different ideas about what we should be doing. The bottom line is, we didn't have a producer. We needed a good, professional producer that would call the shots, find us songs, say yes and no when needed, and find us some songs that we could work up in our genre. There just wasn't a genre for that kind of song.

We needed someone to take *us*, as a group, and get the very best out of who we were. In this business, it's all about songs. Good singers and good bands are a dime a dozen, but it's all about a good song. You take a really good song and put anyone that can sing on it, and it's going to be a hit if it's handled right. So we decided to shut it down. B.B. and Gary wanted to do studio work with a record company that B.B.'s dad owned. I wanted to keep the group together and just work sit-down gigs, because I loved to play bass. Johnny just wanted to stay high and search for peace.

He finally found his peace in 1974 when he took a .357 magnum, put it to his head, and pulled the trigger. He had abandoned his beautiful family and great wife, Bobby Ann, and had gone on his search for Edgar Casey, or whoever else was supposedly prophetic at that particular time. He was looking for his own personal messiah, while all the time the real Messiah was knocking at his door—but

Johnny wasn't home. He took every possible drug he could get his hands on, moved into a trailer over in West Memphis with some young girl none of us knew, and finally one day just ended it all. I miss him very much. At the time, Johnny was one of my dearest friends, but somewhere along the way, he left us all mentally and went off on his own trip. The only problem was the fact that the trip he was on was a dead-end excursion.

I got a job playing bass at a couple of different clubs, and I was driving back and forth from Parkin to Memphis. I had to let my second Caddy go back, and I borrowed a '65 Mustang from my brother Dennis. Eventually he had to come get that back from me because I couldn't make the payments. Things were quickly falling apart then. After I realized we weren't going to stay together as a group any longer, I knew I wasn't going to be able to make a decent living just playing bass, so I had to do some thinking and checking around for opportunities.

The first club I played at was called Buster's Hernandos Hideaway. After about four or five months of playing to an empty club, I took a job with a kid that played rhythm guitar and half-way sang. We started being the house band at a club called the Whirl-A-Way Club, out on Lamar Ave., and it had a drive-in movie right next door. A lot of times I would go outside when we were on break, and I would stand there and watch the movies. Even though I couldn't hear the sound, I tried to read their lips.

I also might mention that Johnny was also playing drums with us at the Whirl-A-Way at the time, but he would never spend time talking with me or anyone else. When we would take breaks, he would just go off somewhere inconspicuous by himself, and I don't know what he did. I just have no idea what was going on in his head; he wouldn't talk, he would just said hi. He would smile with that Johnny Hunter smile I knew and loved so much, and we would laboriously play from 9 p.m. till 2 a.m. six nights a week.

On the weekend, we would have special guests that would come and do a couple of shows a night. One particular special guest was Gary McEwen's mother, Gwen. She was a comedienne and a moderately good singer. The singing was mostly taken care of by Sheila Hern, a young, exceptionally beautiful, former Miss Memphis and runner-up in the Miss Tennessee beauty pageant in 1967. She was a very good singer, had great pitch, and would sing with the band every set at least three or four songs. I introduced the young beauty to Bali Hi

Wine. It was very inexpensive, yet strong enough to take the edge off the amphetamines I was taking at the time. Strangely enough, she ended up married for a season to a friend of mine, Robert Gladney, who played tenor sax at the club for a while and was the father of her daughter, Allie.

Sheila and I, in addition to being lifelong friends, also had a mutual friend who was a very famous disc jockey (they call them announcers now). His name was George Klein, and he not only played our song every thirty minutes of every day, and called our names out individually every time he played it, George was also very tight with Elvis Presley. He spent what little time he had off out at Graceland hanging out with Elvis. In addition, he had Sheila on his Saturday afternoon TV dance parties, as a guest hostess and whatever he needed her to be.

All the people in the music business, even though Memphis was a large city, were knit together into just one big family. Everyone knew everyone else, or knew about them before eventually meeting them. It was a good feeling for us. We took care of each other and were always prepared to come to the aid of any other Memphis artist or musician that needed any kind of assistance. Memphis was home to me for about eight years, and I loved every minute of it.

Elvis's bass player was a gentleman named Bill Black. Bill was a genuinely nice person and had his own group that was extremely successful called the Bill Black Combo. As a matter of fact, if you remember, I toured with his band a lot, thanks to his road manager, Bob Tucker. I'm going to tell you a humorous story about the Bill Black Combo in a second, but first I want you to know what Bill did for me personally. It was instrumental in my becoming what I ended up being until just the last few months.

Bill had a studio of his own in Memphis called Lyn Lou Studios. He named it after his daughter. It wasn't a real busy place, but they did do quite a bit of production there on various artists, mostly in the evening hours. The studio was managed by a record producer, Larry Rogers, also a guy I had known for years. I went over to Bill's one day and asked him if I could borrow his studio occasionally during the daytime, between the hours of 9 a.m. and 6 p.m. just to practice if there was nothing else going on. He thought I meant practice bass or something, I don't know, but my intentions were not anywhere close to that. Since I was determined to stay in the music business, and I knew that I wouldn't be able to make a living playing bass (I just wasn't that good), I decided I would teach myself how to engineer records. I had sat with Tommy Cogbill over at American Studios when he was recording Neil Diamond, and I'd even done a few punches on a horn session with him.

American Studios was owned by Chips Moman, and these guys made Memphis history with the number of hits they cut in just a short season. I went over and hung out on a daily basis for quite a while during my lull after the group broke up, just to get a feel for the studio surroundings. I was so broke at the time, I had to ask Chips to loan me thirty-five dollars so I would have enough money to get back to Parkin one evening. That's how bad things were at that season of my life. Even though I was working the clubs, the pay was inadequate to pay for the house we had bought in Parkin, along with the groceries and utilities. We were just flat broke.

American Studios had one of the finest rhythm sections in the world at the time. If you remember the song, "Memphis Soul Stew" by King Curtis, that was Tommy Cogbill playing what turned out to be the standard for bass players at the time, and it was cut at American. The guys cut so many hits for a while; I wouldn't even know where to start to name them. If I started to list all the hits that were cut by musician friends I came in contact with in my life, this book would be larger than the Bible.

They set the standard for music at American Studios for a long, long time and were one of the best-kept secrets in town. Chips Moman even used a Rolls-Royce for a fishing car. He put mud tires on it and would drive it anywhere he liked to go fishing, no matter how rough the terrain. He was quite a character, but real, big-hearted, benevolent, and deserved every penny he earned. But everything happens in seasons, and eventually their season came to an end, and the majority of the pickers moved to Nashville, where they are still in great demand for sessions.

Tommy Cogbill died in a VA Hospital in Nashville on December 2, 1982. Just a few of the songs Tommy played bass on were "Sweet Caroline" by Neil Diamond, "Kentucky Rain" and "In The Ghetto" by Elvis, "Cry Like A Baby" by the Box Tops, "Natural Woman" and "Chain of Fools" by Aretha Franklin. Those are just a very small sample of the hits Tommy alone played on, not to mention the hits the rest of the guys played on with Mike Leech playing bass.

Tommy Cogbill was considered one of the top five bass players to come along in the last century to set a standard for bass players. He alone was one of the best-kept secrets in the American music scene. As a matter of fact, Jaco Pastorius, who was considered "the best bass player who ever lived" by Bass Player Magazine, listed Tommy as one of his biggest influences.

One last thought about Tommy Cogbill. As long as he and I played in Ace's band together, about two years, I find it just incredible that I was allowed to play BASS with one of the finest bass players in modern American history standing by my side playing guitar, and he also one of my dearest friends in the entire world. I thank you, Lord, for the special blessing of allowing me to be part of this man's life. He was a very special man, and I miss him very much. He did ride his bike, a Harley of course, down to Muscle Shoals once just to say hello to me back in 1974, which was a special, special treat.

I knew I had the feel for being a mixer, because I knew what a band was supposed to sound like in order to sound good. I had also been in quite a few other studios and was familiar with the protocol and layout. I had played in a few bands where the guitar player was too loud or the keyboards weren't loud enough, and knowing about how a good band should sound, I knew I could pull it off if I could just figure out what all those damn knobs did on the console. It seemed like there were a million of them. But after studying the console for a while, I noticed that all of the channels from top to bottom were the same, except for the master section. I also knew that "up was always louder." I assumed that that was the rule, only to find out later that there was one exception to that rule (I'll tell you about that later, too).

So, I played at the club on Sunday night till 2 a.m., drove the fifty minutes to Parkin, got up early the next morning, and was at the studio on Chelsea Blvd. at 9:30 a.m. I put a radio out in the middle of the studio, put a microphone in front of the radio, and plugged the microphone into the wall. Remembering which input I had plugged the mic into, I then proceeded to go into the control room. I figured that within thirty minutes I would simply pull up a fader, and the sound of the radio would come through the speakers in the control room. My friends, "it were not 'dat simple," as they would say down South.

I worked till about 6 p.m., then took a shower, got dressed, and went to the club; and I was back at it the next morning. After two weeks, TWO WEEKS, I finally got sound to come through the speakers in the control room. It was a miracle. I turned every knob in that room for two weeks and finally got the right ones in order. The next thing I had to do was figure out how to get that sound to the tape recorder. It never entered my mind to put the eight-track Ampex tape machine on input. But after a while I started getting into it. I was becoming an engineer, and it was the thrill of my life.

After a while I went out and found a band of young kids that had been practicing in their garage and I asked them if they wanted to "make a record." They went bananas. I brought them into the studio every day and tried all kinds of microphone placement techniques and different guitar sounds, and after a while I thought I had it down, at least on that particular equipment. I was a full-fledged beginner recording engineer. Hallelujah! But I was also a tired engineer after keeping those kinds of hours for week after week after week. The only days I had off were Mondays. I was really worn out and not exactly sure what to do from there. I knew my big break was coming one day, but little did I know how it was going to materialize.

Chapter

10

About the Bill Black Combo story I was going to tell you, we had a pretty big band with the Combo. One of the reasons for it was the fact that we carried two guitar players, plus a sax player, plus we took a roadie, our good friend and compatriot, Bill English. His main function, besides helping to load equipment, was to help with the driving duties. As I mentioned earlier, it always seemed like I would end up driving, no matter which group I was playing with. I just had a knack for being safe, having a good sense of direction, and also the ability to drive in all kinds of weather conditions.

We had to go to Rapid City, South Dakota, for a four-night gig. That's a long drive for a four-night gig, but we had another job to play on the way up there. That helped financially, and it was in the same general direction. Our booking agent, Ray Brown, was very famous for occasionally throwing into his bookings what we called a "killer jump." That meant that the distance to drive from one gig to the next took one day and one night. He would look at us and spread his fingers about two inches apart, and say, "But it's only that far on the map." The only problem was the size of his map as compared to the sizes of our maps.

So we had the first night in Springfield, Missouri. That was on a Saturday night. Then we had the rest of Saturday night and all day

Sunday and Monday to make it to Rapid City, which is as far west in South Dakota as you can go without ending up in the Black Hills, and you can't drive to Rapid City, SD the way the "crow flies." So we left after the engagement that Saturday night in Springfield. I did some zigzagging to get on Interstate 35-N and head for Sioux Falls, South Dakota, so I could then turn west to Rapid City, which was the entire length of South Dakota. That's a lot of driving, considering driving to Springfield, playing a gig, then packing up and driving all night and all the next day. So I was about whooped. I finally had to give it up, and I summoned Bill English, our substitute driver/roadie to take over.

We were in Council Bluffs, Iowa, and we had to get off the interstate for the change. Bill took over the driving duties, drove about six blocks, missed the turn-off for the highway we were on, did a U-turn onto a one-way street, cut through a service station, almost killed six people pumping gas, pulled back out on the street, once again going the wrong way on a one-way street, missed another turn-off, and finally pulled over, got out of the truck, and handed the keys back to me. I forgot to mention that we were in a nine passenger GMC pulling a trailer. I got out and looked in the back of the truck, and everyone was still zonked completely out, so I got behind the wheel and proceeded north on I-35. I got to Sioux Falls, South Dakota, about 2:00 a.m., then proceeded west on I-90. We were only 335 miles from Rapid City, but there was one minor problem; it began to snow, heavily.

Now, that truck sat a little higher than a car, but it was snowing so hard, I couldn't see more than fifteen feet ahead of me. I had not slept in two and a half days, and I was so tired I was hallucinating. People started waking up and talking about all of the buffalo in South Dakota, as if they were running wild all over the place, even the highways. I didn't know if they were or not. By the time we had driven about half-way, the snow was at least four feet deep, and it continued to come down hard and heavy. I could tell where the highway was supposed to be by watching the telephone poles, and I just pretty much "held it 'tween the ditches," as I sometimes say, and kept on moving.

One important thing about driving on snow is to never stop; try to always keep moving, if you can. Once you stop, you lose your momentum, and it's hard to get going again. That's when you start "slippin' and slidin', peepin' and a hidin'." (I just had to throw that in there.) At one point, just before daylight, I thought I saw a live buffalo, and it was running right along beside us, but it kept getting closer and closer, and it appeared to be on a collision course with the truck. After a few minutes, I realized it was simply a giant bale of hay.

By the time we reached Rapid City, there was not only six to seven feet of snow on the ground, but a layer of ice on the roads. But the next day, it warmed up enough to melt most of the snow. We played our four-night gig, and I was rested up enough that I even got a chance to drive down south of Rapid City and view Mt. Rushmore. It is absolutely awesome.

At the beginning of this saga, I mentioned that we always took two guitar players with us. I thought I would quickly mention the reason for that. Bill always used on his records what he called a pencil guitar. It was usually Reggie Young, a premier guitar player in Memphis, and now in Nashville. He would play the chords of the song as usual with his left hand, but with his right hand he would take a pencil and tap on the strings with it. That gave the rhythm section a more unique sound. Bill's records were always instrumentals, but if I were to mention some of the hits they had, I'm sure you would remember some of them: "Smokey," "White Silver Sands," "Josephine," "Honky Train," "So What," and "Tequila," just to mention a few.

Bill always used a tenor sax as his lead instrument, and guess who did all of those recordings? Do you remember the sax player I mentioned that played with us at the Nite Liter in Memphis? His name was Marty Willis, and he could play any song that anyone requested. He had a great ear, great tone, and was just a fantastic sax player. He also was a dear friend, and continues to be at this time.

So the year was 1969, and I was getting so tired of playing the Whirl-A-Way, I just didn't feel like I could play another night. Then one day I got a call that altered my life considerably. Another guitar-playing friend of mine, Travis Wammack, who had a minor hit during the 60's called "Scratchy," called me from Muscle Shoals, which was a small town in northwest Alabama. There was a studio in Muscle Shoals, and it was owned by a record producer named Rick Hall. The studio was called Fame Recording Studio, and I had heard that it was fast becoming THE place in the country to record. At the time, I had no idea why it was so popular, but I was soon to find out. Incidentally, FAME came from Rick's original studio which was across the river in Florence, so he called it the Florence Alabama Music Enterprises. Hence, FAME.

Travis said that Rick wanted me to come down and play bass with his rhythm section for one of Fame's artists, Clarence Carter. Clarence was a blind recording artist that was somewhat successful up to this point, but was soon to have the number one hit in the country. Little did I know, but this was going to be my big chance for accomplishing the second major goal of my lifetime, to someday become one of the top recording engineers in the world. I had already accomplished goal number one, to be a rock star, to no avail, so I figured if I could accomplish my second goal that would finally give me the peace and joy I had been searching for my entire life.

They offered to pay all my expenses and hotel and food while I was there, along with session pay for playing, so it was going to turn out to be quite lucrative for me since the finances were hurting big at that time. Muscle Shoals was due east approximately 140 miles from Memphis, plus the twenty-five miles from Parkin, so it was about 165 miles, or about a two and a half to three hour drive for me. In this particular case, it was about a two-hour drive, as I was very much excited about this opportunity, yet I was also scared to death.

I was used to playing on sessions for strange people, plus I was playing differently at this time than I had been with the Hombres. One thing I learned from Tommy Cogbill was to play with my fingers. Even though I had played upright bass with my fingers, when I switched over from upright bass to electric bass, I, for some unknown reason, started playing with my thumb, of all things. I have no idea what led me to play that way, but it was the most comfortable at the time. After a while, I started playing with a pick, like a guitar player, and I played that way all the way up until I started playing in clubs when the group broke up.

All the advice that Tommy had given me was starting to bear fruit and starting to make more sense. When I started playing with my fingers, I finally felt like a real bass player. It was so much more comfortable and so much easier to do the thing I had been unable to do before. It was just a whole different feel, a more natural feel. I had borrowed the studio's Fender Precision bass for the session. I was playing another kind at the time, but it was not a good recording bass. It sounded good in clubs, but not in the studio. I knew that, so I borrowed the Precision just for this session.

The song we were going to record was on The Chairmen of the Board's album, and the name of the song was "Patches." We started cutting the track on a Monday morning. Once we had the track sheet and all the musicians in place, we ran through the song a few times, and then we recorded the track for the first time. I thought it sounded and felt pretty good, but then we cut it over and over and over. In order to get a good sound in the studio, I had to play real hard to get a lot of punch out of my notes. I was accustomed to playing a bass with active electronics, so the sound was plenty loud, but with the Fender Precision, it didn't have active electronics, so I had to play much harder to get a good "studio" sound.

After about fifteen cuts, my fingers were starting to get very sore, almost to the point of bleeding, but I just kept playing. The intro to the song, which I was playing up very high on my keyboard, wasn't as hard as the low notes, but it still hurt. We finally took a dinner break about 5 p.m., and when we came back we were all so tired, we decided to come back and try again the next day. Needless to say, the next morning my fingers were not in good shape, but I had to keep playing. This was my big break, and I had to grit my teeth and bear it, no matter how much it hurt. I was afraid I would start getting blisters, because if the blisters burst, it would be curtains for me, but God was faithful and gave me the grace to make it through.

To make a long story short, we cut the track for three days and ended up using the very first track. That's the way it usually works. So by Wednesday night, Rick Hall decided which track he was going to use and he paid us all and told us we could go home. He did want to keep Clayton and Travis for some overdubs, but the rest of us could go home. But that wasn't anywhere near the end of this incredible piece of producing, marketing, and what a record company really has to do when it thinks it has a hit record.

As I was packing up and standing out in the hall, Rick walked by and said he was thankful that I had come down and that I had done a really good job. It was then that I mentioned that I needed a job full time, that I was sick of clubs and wanted to do studio work full time.

He said he really couldn't afford to hire me as a bass player full time, that it wasn't practical because he didn't do that many sessions at a time. So I interjected, "But I'm an engineer, too." That caught his attention. He said, "Oh you are, huh?" When I spoke in the affirmative, I gave him the impression that I was a real veteran at the board, so he thought for a second, then he said, "Well, I'll tell you what then, I'll pay you $100 a week if you want to go to work for me full time." I immediately said, "I'll take it."

He said to get my family together and move on down, and he'd somehow help find us a place to live. I was in heaven. I was in absolute full-time-music-business heaven. I immediately called Frankie and told her to start packing, and she was in the packing mode by the time I got home about four hours later. It was late Wednesday evening when I got home.

Now, to continue on about the record, you're getting ready to hear about a miracle job of record marketing and promotion. Monday morning, as we were packing and getting ready to move, I was in the living room, where we actually had no furniture except for our stereo, and I had the radio on tuned to WHBQ in Memphis, which played all the top records all the time. I just was lying around in dreamland, when all of a sudden I heard this bass line that I had been playing all last week, and here comes Clarence singing, "I was born and raised down in Alabama on a farm way back in the woods. Oh, I was so ragged folks used to call me Patches..."

I just sat up, and my mouth dropped open. I couldn't believe it. How did they do that? I heard later that The Chairmen of the Board had heard we were going to cut "Patches," and it was the second best song on their album, so they rushed to try and get their version out before we got our version out.

Now, the previous Wednesday afternoon as Rick and I were saying goodbye, Carol buzzed down and told Rick that Jerry Wexler, the President of Atlantic Records, was on the phone. We shook hands, and he hurried upstairs to his office to take the call. Moments after I left Fame, Rick went in and did his overdubs with Travis and Clayton. He had the horn section on standby, and had Harrison Calloway come by and get a copy of the track to write horn parts to. He had Carol Little, his beautiful and wonderful secretary, call and ask Jimmy Haskell, Rick's favorite string arranger in Los Angeles, to start writing string parts, as he would receive a copy of the track, via Fed-Ex, in the morning. He did Clarence's vocals that night. On Thursday he recorded the background singers, and then did the horns with the Muscle Shoals Horns. Rick got on a plane that night, flew to LA, and cut the strings in Los Angeles Friday afternoon. Then he flew back to Muscle Shoals Friday night. He then started mixing all Saturday morning and night, and by Sunday morning the master mixes were in New York at Atlantic Records where they mastered it.

They made enough single 45's for every major station in the country, had plane tickets for all of the production team and record promoters on their staff, plus some independent ones, and Jerry Wexler himself, the President of Atlantic Records, even took some of them to major stations on the east coast. They all flew out to their assigned destinations on Sunday evening. So Monday morning, every major radio station in the country had an Atlantic promo man or executive sitting on their door steps waiting for them to come to work, handed the record to the morning man on the air, and it was an instant smash before noon that Monday morning.

It sold well over a million and a half records and was number one on the charts for several weeks, plus, it was the biggest record to ever come out of Muscle Shoals at that time. It took the entire country by storm. That was my introduction to big-time records and the record business at its best. I also, over the course of my career, had the opportunity to see record companies at their worst, going all the way back to the Hombres second record. But this incident was a major coup d'état, if I ever saw one.

We moved down to Muscle Shoals, which is in the northwest corner of Alabama, with all of our belongings in the back of a big ole bean truck that had no top, and wouldn't you know it, the rain started to fall, ever so gently, just before we arrived in Muscle Shoals. The truck and driver had been loaned to us by Frankie's Uncle, Harry Melhorn, who was a prince of a man, a local cotton and soybean farmer, and friend to this day.

I'll never forget the house we first lived in. Linda Hall, Rick's wife, had literally gotten on her bicycle and ridden around the surrounding neighborhood for several days and found us a rental house that met our every need. It was so sweet of her. It was a bit downhill from what we had been living in, but it fit us just right, so it all worked out beautifully. You can't be choosy when you're trying to live on only $100 a week with a wife and two children. I would never have had the time to do what she did in her spare time, and she had three boys to raise at the time. It was definitely above and beyond the call of duty.

The house was only three blocks from the studio, so to get back and forth took hardly any time at all. We only had one car then, a 1966 Chevy station wagon with absolutely no bells or whistles, and about 85,000 hard miles on it left over from the Daytonas days. That had been Frankie's transportation when I was driving those big Cadillac's all over the country. Rick also let me drive one of the promotion guy's cars that wasn't being used until I could figure out a way to get us a second car.

You can't afford a lot of extras when you've just been one of the biggest rock stars in Memphis history not a year and a half earlier, but now you're making only $100 a week, before taxes, and paying rent, utilities, food, school supplies, etc. How we made it was only revealed to me much later in my life, and you'll hear about that later. Somehow, we always had everything we needed.

Chapter

II

I was doing a bang-up job for Rick and he knew it. I'd only been there a few weeks, and we had a session coming in from out of town, and I was called on to engineer it because it was a rental session. That means it wasn't for Fame records, and it wasn't one of Rick's artists. It was a young man from Dallas, Texas, named Bobby Patterson, who later became a promo man for the record company I ended my career with in Jackson, Mississippi. Bobby was a small man in stature, but he could sure sing R & B music. To be perfectly honest, I was scared half to death. I had to take everything I had taught myself at Lyn-Lou, and reapply it to Fame's control room and console, and I had to do it fast. It was not easy. But once again, when I pulled up that first fader and got the guitar sound to come through, I then saw how to get it over to the tape machine, and it was downhill the rest of the way.

That first sound coming into the control room was the best sound I had ever heard in my life. Once we got to working, I really started getting into it. I never once told a single soul until I started writing these memoirs that Bobby Patterson's record was the first actual recording I had ever done in my life. If those musicians and, most of all, the artist had known what a greenhorn they had sitting up there in the control room, it would have been bad news for me and possibly the beginning and end of my career as a recording engineer.

We ended up with one of the best sounding records ever done at Fame after I got through with it, and not a soul knew what the real story was until now. And even better, Bobby Patterson walked out of Fame Recording with an album he could be proud of. Bobby and I were to meet years later, but under totally different circumstances. Neither of us ever forgot that week we spent together when I did my very first album at Fame Recording Studios in Muscle Shoals, Alabama, the start of what turned out to be a stellar career.

I learned more from sitting with Rick Hall, listening to him, watching him, assisting him, and also engineering for him, than any one person in my entire life. I also learned a lot about how to treat people and, in some cases, how not to treat people. Every morning I would bring a breakfast sandwich to work wrapped in tin foil, and I would lay it on an amplifier back in the amp room to keep it warm until I was ready to eat it. It was usually a bacon and egg sandwich, with cheese occasionally, but it was always so good. I just couldn't eat in the mornings until I was good and awake and had a couple of cups of coffee. Rick walked in one morning while I was working and eating my sandwich, and he said to me, "What're you doing, boy?" I said I was just eating my breakfast. He said, "I don't pay you to sit here and eat on my time, boy. You eat your breakfast before you come to work, do you understand?"

Needless to say, that didn't go over too well with me, but I needed the job, so I said nothing. But just between you and me, I continued to do the same thing for several more months. Even though Rick had his moments at times, he still had a heart of gold, and I love him and respect him to this day. Funny though, a week later as we were working, he looked at me and said, "How much am I paying you?" When I told him, he gave me a $50 a week raise, which was like a million dollars at the time. So he always used to come through when needed.

We cut some giant records while I worked with Rick, not including "Patches," which was still on the charts. One of them was the Osmonds. The Osmonds were a talented group of young boys from Ogden, Utah, at the time, and their father always traveled with them and was with them every minute of every day. He and I became good friends over the course of their recording debut at Fame. George Osmond was also a very courteous and gentle man, easy to talk to and communicate with. Donny Osmond, the very youngest, was only about seven or eight years old at the time. Our first record with them was

"One Bad Apple," written by George Jackson. We followed that giant single with another solo single by just Donny Osmond called "Sweet and Innocent," also written by George Jackson.

There was one incident that happened right after we had released the "One Bad Apple" record (which was on MGM Records incidentally) that was quite humorous and was soon known all around the national music grapevine. It seems that Barry Gordy, the owner and president of Motown Records, was driving down a freeway in Los Angeles when the Osmond's record came on the radio. Now, the Osmond record sounded exactly like the Jackson Five when we got through with it. Donny was the Osmonds' answer to Michael Jackson of the Jackson Five. Well, Mr. Gordy heard "One Bad Apple," pulled off on the side of the freeway and used an emergency phone (this was way before cell phones obviously), called the record company, and angrily wanted to know who the hell had cut a record on his group, the Jackson Five, without his knowledge.

The story got around the entire record business that Rick had really pulled one on Motown Records, who never seemed to find any kind of love for the music coming out of Muscle Shoals to begin with. However, several years later, they signed a deal with a couple of Muscle Shoals producers (friends of mine also), Terry Woodford and Clayton Ivey, at another studio in town, and they very calmly put on their sign, "Wishbone Recording Studio," and below it they put "A Division of Motown Records." This was several years later, but I thought I would tell you about it now because of the irony that Motown never gave us any credit for the great records that had come—and were to come—out of a little one-horse town in northwest Alabama.

We also recorded other big artists while I was at Fame. I had the pleasure of playing bass on several more records including an album by Liza Minelli. Mickey Buckins did the engineering. We also had a beautiful artist named Candi Staton who cut a single that sold a lot of records, a cover of a country song called "Stand By Your Man," which we did R & B style. I also played bass on Candi's record. We did single recordings on Bill Medley of the Righteous Bros. Bill was allergic to air conditioning, so guess what? Yeah, every time he came into the building, we had to turn all the air conditioners off, and it was right in the middle of August. With no airflow whatsoever, and no air movement for what seemed liked weeks, we must have lost at least fifty pounds each in just sweat. I would go home every night just soaked through to the skin in sweat. And he didn't give a rat's "rear end" if we were sweating or not.

We also did a single on Wayne Newton, who flew in from Las Vegas on his private plane and brought an entourage of people with him. I had to reserve every single rental car in town just for his staff. That's what being a big Vegas star can do to you. We also did a single on Bobby Hatfield, the other half of Bill Medley's Righteous Bros. package. We did a record for Paul Anka, who had written "My Way," but he wasn't the first to record it; Frank Sinatra had. I asked Paul why he didn't record the song first and have a big hit like "the Boss" did, and he said, "Jerry, people do what Frank tells them. Even though it was my song, once he heard it, it was *his* song. Period." Even Wayne Newton was going into the studio to record it, and for some "unknown reason" he didn't. (The "unknown reason" was the two guys in dark suits and sunglasses that walked into his producer's office and told them Frank sent them.)

We also did recordings of Andy Williams and Mac Davis, who wrote a lot of his own songs. Mac came in for a session once, and Rick listened to a few of them and then said, "Mac, I like your songs, but they don't seem to have any kind of a hook to them—you know, something that really grabs you and makes you want to hear it again, a hook, you know?" So Mac says, "Alright, Rick, I'll go back to my room and see if I can come up with a hook that will make me a hit." He came back the next morning, and we recorded his new song, "Baby, Baby, Don't Get Hooked on Me," and it sold over a million copies. Rick got his hook, and Mac got his hit. Rick was a great record producer, if not one of the greatest.

While I'm at it, I need to also tell you that the name, Muscle Shoals, was known as both an area and a town. There were four towns all situated next to each other, but it was called the Muscle Shoals Area or The Shoals. Unless you had lived there for a long time, the only way you could tell which town you were in was either by the signs between the towns or the Tennessee River which separated the largest town, Florence, from the other three burgs, Sheffield, Tuscumbia, and the actual town of Muscle Shoals City (the youngest of all four cities).

A very narrow bridge carried traffic back and forth across the Tennessee River, and there were rumors all over town, the entire fifteen years I spent there, that there were people that had never crossed that bridge. Some said it was because the bridge was so narrow, which was true, but others said it was because there were just certain people who lived there that simply would not drive across the bridge—because they had no need to. I must say that the four lanes of the bridge were very narrow, and there were many wrecks on the bridge simply because of that fact.

Just east of the bridge was a huge dam, and just below the dam was a rocky area that was called shoals, which contained thousands of mussels which were bivalve mollusks and were edible, but I wouldn't recommend them as part of your meal, not these days anyway. I'm sure the Native Americans feasted on them regularly, but I'll pass on the mussels in the Tennessee River. This particular dam, Wilson Dam, was a part of TVA (Tennessee Valley Authority) and also had the world's largest inland lock that took barges of various minerals and such (pushed by tugboats) that ended up in New Orleans. The Tennessee met up with the Mississippi River and Ohio River near Cairo, Illinois, then proceeded south to New Orleans. I might also mention that the Tennessee River, at one point before it gets to the Mississippi River, goes north before it intersects with the Ohio and Mississippi Rivers. It is one of only two rivers in the world that go north, from what I've heard.

Tuscumbia was the birthplace and home of the great Helen Keller, the deaf and blind lady who lived a miraculous life and made great strides in her quest for life in spite of her infirmities. I've heard that when you lose one sense completely, your other senses become much more sensitive and stronger in order to make up for the loss of the one. So, you can imagine what Helen's mind and heart were like with the losses she suffered, yet she conquered, very eloquently. She was a miracle lady and made history with her many, many accomplishments.

So, Fame Records and Rick Hall became my chance for basic training in the recording studio business, and I couldn't have had a better teacher, not only in what and how to do various things, but also a lot of what not to do that alienates people from wanting you sitting behind the console when they're making records. I always believed that, being an engineer, you had to know about music, but being a musician was even better, much better. I also taught, in my later years, that being an engineer was half technical and half relational. It was the relationships you developed with different artists that made them want to not cut records with anyone else but you sitting behind that console. That became the case with a lot of artists I eventually worked with, more specifically with Paul Simon and Bobby Wommack. But we'll talk about all of that later.

As an engineer, you just became one of the band, but you were sitting in another room blending what they were recording into an acceptable creation of the wonderful world of music. I've always felt that music is one of the major arts in the world that has broken all barriers between people of different tastes, beliefs, politics, religions, bigotries, language barriers, or anything else that can come between one man (or woman) and another. The language of music has opened many doors that otherwise would have been shut tighter than a drum, and it has opened up opportunities for communication when all else has failed.

It can, by the same token, be used as a weapon to lead young people, who are so influenced by music, down the wrong path simply by taking a beautiful melody or great-feeling, up-beat tempo and putting a lyric to it that presents ideas that can destroy lives and bring torment to families—especially families who never actually sat down together with the children at an evening meal on a regular basis or set up a line of communication, with mutual respect for each member of that family, so that problems could be met head-on before they ended up in totally ruined lives or even death.

I'll talk about why music is so powerful later on in the book. One other thing I want you to know. As I mention so many people in this book that they were "good friends," it's probably one of my weaknesses as a writer but, it is also the truth. Most people that I connected with in this business either ended up as dear friends or as people that I just couldn't connect with for some reason. So I just wanted you to understand why I use the expression "good friend" all through the book. It's also probably a reflection of my insecurity caused by a neglected childhood (smile). What a bunch of crap that is. Let's keep going here. You're going to love this next anecdote.

This was a classic episode which unfolded while I was at Fame. We were working with Liza Minelli, and we had finished recording her rhythm tracks, which I played bass on and Mickey Buckins engineered. We started overdubbing the horns, her lead vocals, background vocals, etc. She wanted me around and involved, so I just picked up the engineering duties for the rest of the album. Once, Liza, Rex (her husband at the time) and I wanted to go grab a quick sandwich. We figured we would take a chance and go get a Big Mac at the McDonald's just around the corner from the studio.

As the three of us walked in, there was a young man sporting his little McDonalds's hat working behind the counter. When he saw us walk in, he ran from the front counter and went to the back of the store. Another worker came out to take our order, but the first young man kept peeking around the corner from the back of the store at us. The lad had a bad case of acne, but he was still interesting looking. Every time Liza would look up, he would duck his head back around the corner where we couldn't see him. He continued to do that for a while, and we were starting to get a kick out of his antics.

Finally, after about ten minutes of playing hide and seek, he jumped out from behind the back wall, looked right at Liza, pointed his finger at her, and with a Southern drawl, said, "Mea Fair." You had to have been there to appreciate how it went down. He said it again, "Mea Fair." He thought Liza was Mia Farrow. He knew she was a celebrity, but he couldn't figure out exactly who she was. That was why he kept peeking out and looking, and then the light came on, but not very brightly, obviously.

All three of us almost fell on the floor laughing. It was so funny we ended up practically crying by the time we got back to the studio. We could hardly eat from laughing so hard. So innocent was he, and so caught up, but he just couldn't figure who she was, so he figured she was Mia Farrow. Very, very funny and helped get us out of the funk we were in from working so hard for so many days with no relief. He had no idea how he charged us up with his innocence and his curiosity. That one will stick with me for the rest of my life, just like most of the other things I have shared with you up to this point, and we've got some 'doozies' yet to be told. Just keep on reading.

Chapter

12

One day while Rick was out of town, I got a call from some guys over at another studio that I had heard a lot about, but had never met. They were from Muscle Shoals Sound Studios, and they were Jimmy Johnson, Roger Hawkins, Barry Beckett and David Hood. It seems they were Rick's original rhythm section, the ones that had cut many great records for Rick. A couple of them had even worked on Aretha when she had made a short but embarrassing trip to Muscle Shoals a year or so before I got there. They were premier studio musicians who had decided to leave Rick and Fame and start their own studio so they could get what they felt like was their due on the records they were being a very big part of. Aretha had come to town, but following a very ugly incident between Rick and Aretha's husband, Ted White, they left town after just one session and were never to return again. I'm not going to go into the details of the incident, but it was totally unnecessary and equally unfortunate.

So the guys called me from "Sound," which is how I will refer to it from now on, or MSS. They wanted me to do an edit on a quarter-inch two-track stereo master for them, which I had quickly become very quite good at. We used single-edged razor blades to either remove unwanted sections or replace certain sections of a mix from another mix. We would sometimes do fifteen or sixteen mixes of just one song.

We later used computers to mix so that we could perfect the mix and only make one quarter-inch master. Then later on we would make a digital copy of the mix, as opposed to a quarter-inch copy on analog tape.

The guys from Sound had an edit they wanted me to do for them, and I was literally scared to death. These guys were the kings of Muscle Shoals music. Their studio was bound to start taking off when they got all the equipment and the right people in place, and they knew it. They were gold and platinum just waiting to happen. I was so nervous when it came time to do the cut, that, just to make sure, I kept rocking the tape back and forth to make sure I was in the right place. All of a sudden these guys started realizing I was nervous, and started laughing at me acting as if I weren't sure. I felt very foolish, but I think they knew I was just nervous since I had never worked with them, and the last thing in the world I wanted to do was to make a bad cut.

They were all grinning like Cheshire cats while I was rocking the tape, and finally I looked up and saw them all smiling. It sort of broke the ice between us, and I openly confessed I was nervous. We all got a big laugh out of it, and I made the cut and it worked perfectly. You couldn't tell there was a splice if you listened to it for the remainder of your life. So we all talked and chewed the fat for a few minutes, and they asked about my past and how I got to the Shoals; then we parted ways. Inside me, I wanted to go over and work with those guys so bad, but I didn't dare hint around about it or even mention it when they were there.

They had a guy named Larry Hamby working for them on the board at the time, so I figured my chances were pretty slim of making a switch. The feeling between the guys at MSS and Rick were lukewarm at best, so I didn't dare say one word to anyone about anything at the time. Two or three weeks later I got a phone call that, once again, changed the course of my career and was the catalyst for the incredible future that faced me. The only person that knew it was my Father up above, the Author and Finisher of my Faith, which I was to discover many, many years later.

The call, of course, was from Jimmy Johnson at MSS, and he asked if I would come over and check out their studio when I got off that evening, which at first was a little disappointing, but still, I was very excited about the opportunity. When I arrived, they were all there, and we sat down in Jimmy's office. They said that Larry Hamby, their current engineer, had expressed a desire to pursue interests other than music, and they wanted to know if I would be open to making a move from Fame over to Muscle Shoals Sound. The date, as best I can recollect, was July 1970.

I had been at Fame about a year and a half, and I was, in all reality, not overjoyed to be working there. Working at Fame, I had two adverse feelings. One was the same feeling I had concerning the time I was in the Army. I wouldn't give a million dollars not to have done it, but I wouldn't take a million dollars to do it again. There were times I thought, "I can't take this one more day," and there were also times that I thought, "I wouldn't ever want to work anywhere else." That's the kind of emotional rollercoaster ride I was on when I was working there. The way Rick treated me on any particular day determined which avenue I would go down that day. But sometimes the next day would be totally different. He would get on rampages sometimes where I could do absolutely nothing right. Other days I could do no wrong.

Needless to say, I took the job at MSS right there on the spot. I didn't even ask them if they were going to pay me, much less how much. All I knew was I wanted to be a part of what they were getting ready to do, and it was my job and had been since before I was born. I gave Rick two week's notice the next day, and I actually can't remember if I finished the two weeks or not. He might have told me to get my stuff and leave, but I just don't remember.

I'll tell you how excited I was. The weekend before I was to start, I went over to Sound, hoping there would be a buzz of activity going on, but it was closed. For some strange reason, someone had left the front door open. Little did I know that I would set off the alarm when I went inside the building. It was a silent alarm, I thought, but there was a very loud ringing going on out back that I wasn't aware of. So I was sitting up front in the "lounge" just waiting for someone to come by so I could tell them that I was the new engineer. I sat down on one of those black Naugahyde couches and just waited for a human being or a police officer or someone to show up. I'd never been so excited about starting a new job in all my life.

I then heard a voice coming from the studio, "Hello, is anyone there?" It was some guy I had never seen. He walked in and said hello, and I introduced myself and told him I was the new engineer and had just stopped by to look the place over. He asked me how I had gotten in, and I told him that the door wasn't locked. He was a bit strange looking, and he was not a bit impressed that I was the new engineer. He said he just lived down the street and heard the alarm and thought he would come up and see what was going on. He then introduced himself.

His name was Eddie Hinton. He was a guitar player, and eventually he and his wife, Sandra, became two of my dearest friends. Eddie was once considered as the original guitar player, along with head man Dwayne Allman, for the famous Allman Brothers' Band. But Eddie turned it down in order to be part of the Muscle Shoals Sound Rhythm Section, which would later become known worldwide from Lynyrd Skynyrd's "Sweet Home Alabama" as the Swampers, which they mention in the last verse. Barry, Jimmy, Roger, and David used several different guitar players throughout their long string of successful recordings, including my favorites, Eddie Hinton, Pete Carr, and Tippy Armstrong. But Eddie was the very first.

Later on in the mid-70's, Eddie did a solo album for Capricorn Records of Macon, Georgia, which happened to be the Allman Bros. Band's record label. After doing all of his recording in Macon, Eddie asked Phil and Allen Walden, the presidents of Capricorn, if I could mix the entire album for him at MSS and take it to Sterling Sound Mastering facility in New York for mastering. I was so pleased that Eddie had enough confidence in my mixing abilities and even let me oversee the entire finishing process until his record was on vinyl and ready for release. But I'm getting way ahead of myself here. I just wanted you to know who that strange guy was that walked into MSS that day when the alarm was ringing, and I ended up meeting a lifelong friend and one of the best guitarists in the world.

I might also mention that before MSS was founded, Eddie and Dwayne Allman were staff guitar players at Fame, playing for Rick, but it lasted a very short season. Dwayne was the very first musician to cross into Colbert and Lauderdale Counties with very long hair. No one around there had ever seen anyone like that, and he was not very popular with the locals, needless to say. Eddie passed away in 1995 and was buried in Tuscaloosa, Alabama. Sandra drowned in the Tennessee River in Sheffield, Alabama, just a few years later. I lost two very special friends. I needed them to live much longer than they did, but who said life was fair?

The guys at MSS also had a very lucrative publishing company, and to kind of break the ice and get things rolling, we did some demos on one of their prolific writers, "Prince" Phillip Mitchell, and also George Jackson, who was another Fame refugee. We used those demos just to get used to each other and give me a chance to dive into my job and get comfortable with the new equipment. When we first started recording there in 1970, we were recording on a Scully 8-track recorder and had an old Universal Audio console with those big black rotary knobs. I don't want to get into a lot of technical stuff in this book, but I just wanted you all to know what I started with. I'll eventually explain how we climbed the ladder in the technical aspects of my job. We were always "state of the art," right up to the industry standard, constantly.

That's one thing I so appreciated about Jimmy Johnson and the rest of the guys. They always took money that was left over after paying the bills and put it back into the studio. They didn't stick it in their pockets like most studio or company owners I've worked with since. I might also mention that shortly after I got there, we got a new console, a Dan Flickenger 24 in, 24 out console and a brand spanking new MCI 16-track tape recorder. Boy, was I in heaven, technically that is. Flickenger was from Detroit, and he brought an entire crew down from Detroit with him to install the console, while our local maintenance guy, Paul Kelly, and his assistant, John, were installing the new 16-track tape recorder.

At one point, everything seemed to stop working. The entire system just shut down and wouldn't work. The entire crew of "geniuses" had their schematics all strung out around the tiny control room and were talking in a language that no one could understand, trying to figure out why the darned system all of a sudden came to a screeching halt. After about two hours of every one just waiting around, including Paul and John, Paul says, "Wait a minute, Dan." He whispers something to John and then tells him to get down under the console, and Paul goes behind the tape machine. About six or seven minutes later, Paul sticks his head out from behind the tape machine and says to John, "Jiggle dat war over thur, John." John jiggles a wire, and all of a sudden everything comes to life, and the entire system starts working like a charm. You had to have been there to appreciate the humor in that. It was so funny that all the genius techs from the big city couldn't find the problem, and our little maintenance guy, who had rather been fishing down on the river, got his assistant to jiggle a wire, and it all came together like a charm.

I started getting introduced to big time recording within sixty days after I came to Sound. The first artist to walk in the door was Wilson Pickett. What a trip he was. Wild and wicked Wilson Pickett. The two producers, Brad Shapiro and Dave Crawford, didn't know me at the time, so I kind of let Jimmy get that session started. But after he started wearing out, I casually slipped in behind him and, even though a bit skeptical at first, Brad and David finally realized I knew what I was doing, and it no longer became a problem.

Our first chart record was "Don't Knock My Love." It was a good record for Pickett, and I got my first taste of the "big time," as far as established artists at MSS. A session not long after that, much to my surprise, turned out to be very historic for me in two ways. I got my first gold record as an engineer at Sound on the first release, and a platinum record on the follow-up single. The artists were the fantastic Staple Singers, featuring Mavis Staples with her powerful voice and Pop Staples on the most funky gospel guitar I've heard in a long time.

The first record, which went gold, was "Respect Yourself." It had the greatest laid-back feel I'd heard in a long time. Barry was playing a Wurlitzer piano, which had a soft but funky sound to it, and it was an instant smash. The follow-up record (I know you'll remember, because you still hear it all the time, even today) was called "I'll Take You There." And the hero of this song was that famous David Hood bass line. Mavis referred to him in the middle of the song as "Little David." It went platinum, which meant it sold two million dollars worth of records, not necessarily two million copies. But you still hear it in commercials, in movies, in TV shows, just about everywhere. It became a classic. You can't get away from that famous rhythm that the "Swampers" made.

Another thing about that session that was amazing was the fact that I sat next to an old friend for days and days, and I didn't know at the time he was an old friend, and neither did he. Does that make sense? I'm talking about the producer, Al Bell, who eventually became president of Stax Records, for which we were recording the Staple Singers in the first place. It was one of those times where we were doing overdubs. The person we were working with took a dinner break, and Al sent out and bought us big old thick T-bone steaks. Man, they were good. While we were eating, Al just asked me casually where I was from. I told him I was from Little Rock. Al said, "Well, what a coincidence, so am I."

To make a long story short, when I was in the ninth grade at West Side Junior High School on 14th Street in west Little Rock, Al was working less than a half block away at a radio station next to a bakery as a disc jockey at KOKY (I think). Being the jazz fan that I was, and playing in the Swing Band in high school, I had accumulated several jazz LPs. Even though I didn't have very many, the ones I did have were quite good, and not many people owned the LPs I had. I would always try and get albums none of my friends had so we could all swap around and not have to buy a lot of albums individually.

Al had a jazz show on KOKY on Sunday afternoons from 2 p.m. till 5 p.m. He also had a request line. I called in several times making requests, but he never seemed to have the songs that I requested. So one Sunday, I asked him if I brought down some of my records, would he play them over the air. He was elated, and I became a regular visitor to the station, always bringing just a couple of my LPs and adding a little spice to his collection, since it was sort of limited.

The station wasn't real powerful, only about 1000 to 1500 watts. With that little broadcast power, his show probably didn't get out much further than about thirty or forty-five miles, maximum. Even that far out, the signal wasn't that strong, so he had pretty much a limited audience. This relationship continued on until school was out, but I always looked forward to Sundays because of this particular radio show. (They don't call them disc jockeys any longer; they now call them announcers, just for the record.)

When I asked Al if he remembered that little thirteen-year-old white kid with a flat top that used to bring him jazz records on Sundays, he said, "Yes, I remember him well. He made my show much more complete with his collection." I said, "Well, you're looking at him." He just about fell on the floor. He said, "After all these years, you were the kid with the flat top?" I fessed up that I was the one. We really connected then, and our relationship lives on to this day, not to mention the historic records we recorded together. And after we finished that album, he graciously sent me a bonus check of $1500 that blew my hat in the creek and helped make up for the very modest salary that I was being paid.

Shortly after the Staple Singers session, Al came back to MSS and spent two weeks doing nothing but cutting tracks. When they got ready to go back to Stax in Memphis at the end of the two-week marathon, they had to bring a station wagon just to carry all of the 16-track masters back to Memphis. I think we cut something like 48 rhythm tracks, and we had no idea who the tracks were for. All we knew was they were great tracks.

We had another producer that would do that same thing, but more often. He was a producer from Detroit, Don Davis. He would come down for a week or sometimes two and do nothing but cut tracks.

Most of the time we wouldn't even know who the tracks were for. Don would go into the vocal booth and pretty much talk the musicians through the tracks. He would already know the keys, the chords, the tempos, and sometimes even the artist he "thought" he might use them on, but usually not.

Don always brought a very talented music director/ arranger/co-writer with him from Detroit named Rudy Robinson. Rudy was a super keyboard player, and person, in addition to being an arranger and songwriter along with Don. Another thing about Don Davis was the fact that he loved my bass playing for some reason. So every five or six songs, he would ask me to go out and play bass, and that meant I also would get a session pay for just that one song. It was much needed revenue for me and a lot of fun, to boot.

I played on one-track once, and about five or six months later, driving down the road, I heard a record that had already climbed the R & B charts to the top 10 and was starting to climb the top 100 in Billboard. It was by a Detroit group called "the Dells," and the song was "Give My Baby a Standing Ovation." And guess who was playing bass? I might also mention that one of the big hits that Don did, and we didn't know who the artist was at the time, was "I Believe in You" by Johnnie Taylor. Don Davis made a habit of coming down practically on an annual basis and doing his thing with us. It was a lot of fun.

When I was living in Memphis and scratching for every penny I could get, someone would ask me if I would play on some demos for ten dollars a song. Of course, I figured since they were "only demos," it would be alright to give away my "magnificent talent" that cheaply (smile). The only problem was that maybe a few months later I would hear that "demo" being played on the radio. They had ended up (or maybe had planned right from the start), getting a master session for demo pay. That happened to a lot of us in the early days before the union started looking out for its people.

But the union was actually a big flop as far as *really* looking out for its people. The executives would sit down at the Memphis union building all day long and take phone calls from people looking for bands. Then they'd give the gigs to their favorite bands— themselves. It just so happened that all the union officials worked in bands that seemed to be working every weekend, week after week. They were making a killing supposedly "protecting us" as members of the AFL-CIO. What a rip-off the entire union idea turned out to be once organized crime took over. It was a great idea until the Mob got in on the act; then it became corrupt from the top all the way down. There were no exceptions that I know of, except one man, and that was Tex Harmon, the president of the American Federation of Musicians' Union in Birmingham, Alabama.

Chapter

13

While we're talking about corruption, I just want to take a second here and bring up something that's been a 'burr in my butt' during my entire career. When I was offered $100 a week to come to work for Rick, I thought, well, it's a start. I figured that the more experience I obtained and reputation I began to build, eventually they would start paying me a salary in line with my abilities and professionalism—not to mention the fact that my just being there would bring in a lot of artists that could have just as easily stayed in Los Angeles or New York or Europe or whereever they happened to come from—but no. For the first three or four years I worked there at MSS, they were paying me $150 a week, plus time and a half overtime. I was bringing home some fairly nice paychecks with all the overtime I put in, sometimes sixty-five to seventy hours a week, but I had to half-way destroy my health to make a decent living.

For some reason, unknown to me, people in the record business look upon recording engineers as the "bottom of the barrel" workers—like they could just go out on the street and hire someone to do my job if I didn't want to do it. So many musicians, visitors, and artists would sit there and watch me work thinking that I was making thousands of dollars a day doing what I was able to do. The speed with which I would work and the magic I could do to records to make a "silk purse out of a sow's ear" was just astonishing to so many people. They just would not believe it if I told them how much money I was being paid, or you might say, not being paid. And it turned out to be that way throughout my entire career. I hate this word, but we were and still are the "niggers" of the music business, and if you know the real meaning of this word, it has nothing to do with race, and all my black friends know that.

When I was working at Criteria Recording Studios in Miami, one of the best studios in the entire world, I was being paid $6.50 an hour. SIX DOLLARS AND FIFTY CENTS AN HOUR! I was doing what very few people in the world can do, at what many considered the top studio in the universe, and that's what I was being paid. If I went in and worked eight hours on a session, you do the math. And there were no guarantees of sessions, ever, only when the business would come in. Some weeks, I had NO sessions. And it's hard to live in Miami, Florida, making $6.50 an hour. I honestly don't know how I made it, but there was Someone up there that was looking out for me and taking care of me, making sure I always had exactly what I needed. It sure did take me a long time to realize that, but we'll talk about all of that much later in the book.

Another thing, too. It seemed like every place I ended up, whether it was with the Hombres, or at the Whirl-A-Way, or in Muscle Shoals, or Miami, or Birmingham, or back in Muscle Shoals, or in Jackson, Mississippi, there was always success of one sort or the other. Fame had its best days when I was there, MSS had its best days when I was there, Criteria had its best days when I was there, and Malaco had its best days when I was there. That was not a coincidence. It wasn't because *I* was there; it had nothing to do with me. It was because I was sent to these places when they were getting ready to reach their peak. Coincidence? I don't think so.

Now, I don't want to take ANYTHING away from the rhythm section that most artists came for; that *was* most of the reason. The thing that was so great about Barry, Roger, David and Jimmy, as a rhythm section, was the fact that they weren't clock watchers. They were there for one reason, and that was to cut a hit record for that particular artist, no matter who it was. They really cared. They would spend ten or twelve hours a day cutting a song and only charge two sessions in some cases. A session was only supposed to be three hours, but they didn't care. They wanted to cut a hit just as badly as the artist. However, they (the Swampers) began to realize that they were cutting hits for others, and they wanted their share, so they began to demand a percentage of the royalties on every record they cut. They were willing to negotiate, but they always got a piece of the action, or they wouldn't play.

What about the rest of the guys that were JUST AS BIG A PART OF THE RECORDS? Nada, nothing, not one thin dime. Paul Simon considered me part of the success, as did most of the artists that came in there, but not enough to pay me. It seems like I spent my entire career trying to get what I thought I deserved for the successes going on around me, but it never happened. That's the world for you, I found out later. That's the nature of man. However, I did get bonus checks from Paul Simon, Al Bell, and...duh...that's it.

Recording artists also came to Muscle Shoals because it was so out of the way, and they could relax and not have to worry about groupies and such. They enjoyed the peace and quiet, plus with it being a dry county, there was nothing to do but make records. There were no bars or clubs until after I left. So as far as I was concerned, the combination of everyone that worked there doing what they did best and doing it from the heart was, in fact, the heart of what was Muscle Shoals Music, including the secretaries, the song writers, even the guys that came in at night and cleaned the place up. It was a place, with a season, and it was the right people at the right time with the same goals that made it world famous for so many years. You can ask anyone in the music business, anywhere in the world, if they've ever heard of Muscle Shoals, and 95% of the time they will tell you, "Oh, yes."

I remember Jimmy telling me once that there was going to be a young high school student coming in occasionally just to observe and try to pick up on what was going on and decide what he wanted to do with his life. It was a young man named Steve Melton. Now, our control room was really small. I've been in single spaced restrooms larger than our control room. There was enough room for about four or five people, including the engineer, comfortably. Otherwise, it was very crowded. Off to the right was a small room where we kept our power amps, tapes, etc., and it also doubled as a shop for the maintenance man, Paul Kelly. I mentioned him earlier. He was the best; he was the 'jiggle that wire over thar' guy. The only problem was that whenever something would break down, we'd have to go down on the river and try to find him, 'cause he'd be down there fishing. This was BCP (before cell phones). He was small in stature, yet large in heart, and he was our guy, and we loved him like no other. He worked for the radio stations in town on the side, either that or he worked for all the studios on the side, we never figured that one out.

So, Steve would come in every afternoon after school, and stand over in the amp room and write on a notebook. He never said a word to anyone for at least a year. The first time he opened his mouth and asked me a question, it scared me half to death. He hardly ever asked questions; he just took notes, and I would let him sit at the console and study the various knobs. He occasionally asked what something might mean, but most of the time we didn't even know he was there. To make a long story short, Steve turned out to be the Chief Engineer at Muscle Shoals Sound, and also one of the very best engineers in the world. He remains one of my very best friends in the entire world to this very day that I'm writing these memoirs. I even talked to him yesterday.

Another young man that came along a few years after Steve was Greg Hamm. Greg was the son of the owner of one of the most successful heating and air-conditioning companies in the area. He also had the most gentle spirit of any man I've ever known in my life. Nothing bothered Greg. There could be a war going on out in the parking lot, and Greg would be just as peaceful and unconcerned as a dove. He also turned out to be one of the best engineers in the country, but after getting married and realizing what it takes to continue in our business, after all was said and done, he decided to go back and help his dad and brother run their successful company. But Greg could flat mix. He could make a silk purse out of a sow's ear with any combination of sounds better than anyone I knew, except maybe Steve.

I also want to give these two guys credit for bailing me out of so many situations where I needed to get up and run because of some domestic situation or personal need. They could slide in the chair behind me and NO ONE would ever know the difference. They were absolutely THE BEST OF THE BEST. I thank God every day for what those two guys meant to me then and what they continue to mean to me today.

We boogied along for a year or two, continuing to cut various styles of R & B with the likes of Bobby Wommack, Luther Ingram, who had a multi-million seller, "If Loving You is Wrong, I Don't Wanna Be Right," and Tommy Tate's "School of Life," and a great pop artist from San Francisco, Boz Scaggs, who did an album, "Dynaflo." I might mention that I came in on my vacation and mixed for him only to have him forget to put my name on the album credits for engineering and mixing. On my vacation! That was the thanks I got. Things like that kind of confirm what I said before about people's attitudes about engineers.

We had a visit from J. J. Cale, and Leon Russell, who ALSO left my name off his album, but at least he sent me a gold record as a way of saying I'm sorry. He also sent the studio a gold album, and he didn't forget to pay the musicians or the studio bill. So there we go again. Pride, isn't it awful?

We did an album on a group from England known as Traffic. It was led by Stevie Winwood, who was talent personified. He played the piano and recorded the lead vocals at the same time, which was rather unusual in studios. So I closed the piano lid and put masking tape across the ribs of the inside of the piano under the lid and clipped two tiny Sony ECM-50 mics on the low strings and one on the high strings. I got a great stereo piano sound, plus, it kept the lead vocals from leaking into the piano mics just in case Stevie might want to re-do any of his lead vocals or maybe just punch in a few lines. It gave us great separation as far as sound was concerned.

Traffic had Jim Capaldi playing tambourine and contributing to the vocals; they also used David Hood on bass and Roger Hawkins on drums. All of the band sat up in a circle right out in the middle of the studio. We cut the entire album in about six days, including the mixing. After we cut the tracks, we added some sax and flute parts with Chris Wood, therefore keeping it a very simple, yet soulful, album and loads of fun. The credits on the album say it was recorded in Jamaica, but that was because the record owner, Chris Blackwell was trying to avoid some sort of legal ramifications, so he put on the cover that it was recorded and mixed in Jamaica. I wish it had been. That would have been fun.

The group then went on tour for about two months and took Barry along to play keyboards while Winwood played a Hammond B-3 organ. They also took Jimmy along to oversee all of the live sound. It was supposed to be a rock group, but it sure sounded like jazz to me, all of the time. Not far out jazz, but improvisational enough to be called jazz, if that makes any sense. I guess you would just call it free-form music at its best. I'm sure they all had the time of their lives.

Shortly after that, we got a session that changed the entire genre' of what Muscle Shoals was all about. We were always pretty much considered a Rhythm and Blues studio, at least mostly down-home music. But we got a call that turned out to be the start of an entirely different season where we proved that we could do any kind of music there is and make it commercial. We also proved to the whole world that we were not just a bunch of rednecks, but people that knew how to make records, regardless of their style or genre', and we turned the heads of every music person in the business. We cut an album on Paul Simon. Even today, Paul says it's the best album he recorded in his entire career.

In the space of about three months, we created some of the largest selling records and most popular songs in the history of Muscle Shoals, and we blew the hats off the entire music industry. All of a sudden we were considered a real recording Mecca for all those who wanted to make music. Artists started coming to Muscle Shoals from every corner of the globe to make music with a bunch of semi-country boys in Alabama. I also ended up making friends for life with Paul Simon and his eminent producer, Phil Ramone. And shortly after Paul's success, we achieved another milestone. We cut the only record that Simon and Garfunkle ever did together after they split, "My Little Town." They haven't recorded together again since. It sold 1.8 million records, but that's a whole different story that I'll tell you about later. It's a classic.

By the time Paul and Phil got there, they had already cut and finished a song in England called "American Song." I loved that song. I always used it as a closing song when I designed, built, and ran a disco right before I moved to Miami. Much to Paul and Phil's amusement, we had been having problems with our roof leaking after a serious rain shower, and it was leaking in the control room right over the Flickenger Console we were so proud of. A major roof job would have shut us down for a few days, so until then, to keep the water out of the console, we went to the store and bought a huge supply of Kotex Napkins, extra large, extra absorbent, and thumb tacked them in a line all along the ceiling above the console where the water was dripping in from. After a few hours of water coming through and being soaked up by the Kotex, they turned a bit brown in color, and they looked, uh.... uh, they looked "used."

It was quite a sight, and had not Paul and Phil been professional enough to see through minor problems like that, they would probably have packed up and left. But they got quite a kick out of it, and it didn't take much time making the gossip circle in the music business. Before long we became quite famous for being the "tampon-enhanced studio" down in Alabama.

We cut quite a few tracks, and with Paul having bursitis in his left thumb, he couldn't play guitar for long periods at a time. So in some cases, I would get Paul's acoustic guitar parts out of the way before anything else and then edit those in later. If he had the acoustic intro, I would do seven or eight intros and then splice them together and put them on the front of specific songs when needed. At one point during the album, we took a break from the guys in Muscle Shoals, got in a rental car, and drove down to Jackson, Mississippi, to do an overdub with a Funeral Band from New Orleans called the Olympic Brass Band on a song we had done called "Mardi Gras." For some unknown reason, Paul thought that all rhythm sections in the South were as good as the guys at Sound. Man, he was in for a shock. So, we also cut a track while we were at Malaco in Jackson. It was "Learn How To Fall."

I had the opportunity to rekindle some old friendships while we were there in Jackson: Tommy Couch, the owner of Malaco, and Wolf Stephenson, the engineer and vice-president at Malaco. It was so good to see them, and they were so gracious to us for coming. They had made numerous trips to the Shoals just to see exactly what we were doing, in hopes of taking some of that knowledge back to their studio and attempting to do what we were doing. Unfortunately, it doesn't quite work that way, but we did cut a few of the songs they brought with them, but, with other artists. As far as Paul, we worked pretty much all day the first day, acclimating to the atmosphere, the equipment, getting set up for the horns, etc.

At dinner time, Tommy asked us what we wanted for dinner. It appeared he was either going to cater some food or send out for dinners for all of us. Paul expressed he would prefer chicken, and Phil was in the same mode, so I just went along with the crowd, and we all went for the chicken. When we got ready to cut the track, after finishing the horn overdub, Paul's hand was starting to give him fits, so he told Phil and me that he wanted to go ahead and get the acoustic guitar intro over with. So we did about seven or eight cuts of the four bar intro, which was just Paul's guitar by itself. I figured, no problem, we'll just throw that intro together and then attach it to the basic track once we got it cut. We just had one problem once we got ready to start editing. They had no two-inch take up reels.

When you start editing, you get different pieces on separate empty reels and label them, then set them aside and select the next section, and so on, and so on, until you've got the whole intro. Then you just make the correct cuts with a razor blade and splice them together. Now, we were not dealing with bars here or phrases; we were sometimes dealing with a single note from one cut and another note from another cut. But with no take up reels, we were in a pickle with no place to put the pieces. So Wolf suggested that we get a bunch of reels of new tape, which had just a tiny bit of space on the front, and use them for take up reels. Well, these bad boys are heavy when they are full. I would say a full reel of two-inch tape weighs at least 18 to 20 pounds.

So, we started putting pieces of Paul's guitar solo on the end of new rolls of tape, and started building a solo until we got a good intro. Then Paul would say he didn't like a particular note or two, so we would have to go back and listen to all of the takes we had recorded until he found a couple of notes he liked. So we would take the old piece out, put the new piece in, put the machine in play, and Paul would listen and say either yea or nay. We continued doing that until we got an intro that Paul liked. It took us eleven (11!) hours of picking up and putting down, and undoing splices and doing re-splices until we got the final results that satisfied Paul Simon.

The tape looked like a mummy when it ran across the heads of the machine, because it was just about all splicing tape, which is white, and the recording tape is black. I have never been so tired in my life. But the real kicker happened about forty-five minutes after we ordered dinner. Tommy Couch came walking into the studio and said, "Your dinners are here." Then he handed us each a sack with our "dinners" in it. Now we were expecting nice dinners with baked potatoes, salads, etc., but that's not what we got. Tommy handed one of the top entertainers in the history of music, his producer, and me boxes of Kentucky Fried Chicken and a roll of paper towels. I couldn't believe it. But at that stage of the game, it didn't matter any longer. I was so tired I would have eaten the leather off a baseball. Paul just looked at Tommy and seriously said, "I deserve better than this!" Mr. Couch just shrugged his shoulders and didn't say a word. But I'm sure he knew that he would never live that down. So, after our "gourmet" meals, we finished our track at Malaco. We already had our horns on Mardi Gras so we headed back to Muscle Shoals.

Paul had also cut a song in New York with just himself on guitar and the Dixie Hummingbirds singing background. The song was "Loves Me Like A Rock," and it also turned out to be a giant hit. So when we got back to Muscle Shoals, we had Barry make a chord sheet of what we already had with Paul's guitar and the Dixie Hummingbirds, and we actually "under dubbed" the rest of the instruments. That's what I call it when you have a song partially recorded and then cut the rhythm section last. It's very rare to cut a tune that way, but in this case, it was incredibly successful. I thought it was going to be difficult for Barry, Roger, David, and Jimmy, but man was I wrong. They nailed that thing in about two hours, and it was a smash hit for Paul. The Swampers were just an amazing group of guys, no matter who was playing lead guitar, whether it was Eddie, or Tippy or Pete. It always clicked, with one exception.

Paul's album, "There Goes Rhymin' Simon," came out and just burned the charts up, and Paul still calls it the best album he ever did. About a year later, he returned to try and cut some things for a new album, but for some reason, it just wouldn't happen. We couldn't get a single track, no matter what kind of song or what. Also, Paul was suffering from what writers call writer's block. He just didn't seem to be able to write a song. Everything he tried would fall apart, and it was just a bad season for him. I felt so bad. But there's a season for everything, and it just wasn't the time for Paul to do another project in Muscle Shoals for a while.

Chapter

14

I'd like to share a funny thing that happened a couple of years later that involved the other half of the production of the Paul Simon record. My good friend Phil Ramone, is one of the most respected producers in the country, even today. He's received tons of Grammys for his productions, and has produced artists like Billy Joel, Kenny Loggins, Barbra Streisand, Barry Manilow, Frank Sinatra, Bob Dylan, and Gloria Estafan, just to name a few. Phil really knew what he was doing, but when he was in our house, he showed me the utmost respect and let me run the show. I'll always be so thankful for that professional courtesy he showed me.

When we were cutting the track for "My Little Town," at Phil's request we were running our tape at twice the normal speed, because we didn't have any noise reduction, and Phil was the type that insisted that his records be as quiet as a church mouse, so to speak. No tape noise of any kind, even though the way we normally recorded, our records were perfectly quiet and had no tape hiss, because we kept the machines clean, lined up, and adjusted continuously to make sure we were getting the best possible recordings. When we recorded normally at Sound, we would run our tape machine at 15 IPS (inches per second), and we could get at least five or six, maybe seven songs or cuts of the same song on one roll of tape.

You have approximately thirty-four minutes of recording time at 15 IPS. But Phil wanted to run the machine at 30 IPS, which is twice as fast, and you only have about seventeen minutes of recording time, so we could only get three cuts on a roll and have just a little tape left over at the end. The faster the tape machine is running, the quieter the sound on playback.

We had been cutting on the track for about an hour, but we just never could get that magic cut, the one where you know without a doubt that that's the one. After every three cuts, I would back the tape up to the top, start over, and record over the ones we had tried before, which is normal. We would keep certain tracks if they were real close, but we were trying to save tape, which saves a lot of money.

We started again, and we had two cuts that were really good, but not quite there. Then we cut one more, and I knew the one after that would be the one. I knew the musicians were right there, and any time wasted would have ruined the feel they had and broken the groove they were in. Besides that, Barry Beckett started counting the next cut off, and I knew as well as Barry did that this was going to be the one, and so did everyone else.

So, instead of killing the groove and taking the few minutes it would take to switch tape, or take the time to rewind the tape all the way to the top, I just reached over and switched the tape recorder to 15 IPS. They cut the track, and that was the one—the one we had been looking for the last two days of trying. We had our song, we had that basic track, and it was magic, without any doubt, and everyone knew it. But it was 15 IPS, which really wasn't that big of a deal, at least to me.

After we listened back, everyone was elated that we had finally got it. Paul and Artie were just thrilled, and so was Phil. Then I very sedately told Phil that it was 15 IPS, and he went ballistic on me. He was screaming and yelling at me and said, "I can't believe you cut that at 15 when you knew I wanted it 30. It's going to ruin it!" I said, "Phil, it sounds just fine. It has no noise. It's the best I've heard these guys play in a long time. You've got yourself a big hit here, man." Phil then said, "Masters, I'll never forgive you for this. That was just irresponsible." I said, "Phil, I know these guys; I can read them like a book. I knew they were right on top of it. If I had stopped and changed tape, or had even taken the time to back the tape up, they would have lost their groove, and we wouldn't have a hit like we do now."

He went outside and started pacing, and I went out and tried to pacify him and encourage him. As our conversation continued outside, I said, "I'll tell you something else, Mr. Ramone. If this record is a hit, I'm not ever going to let you forget it." "How could a record cut at 15 IPS be a hit, Mr. Big Shot?" he said. I answered, "Phil, have you seen the charts for the last four years? Have you noticed all the hit records from this studio in the top ten practically every week that we cut at 15 IPS?" He looked at me and said, "Well, we'll see." It eventually sold one million, eight hundred thousand records. That's 1.8 million, if you need it in numbers.

A few years later, I was working with Johnny Rivers at Criteria in Miami, and Phil was in town, also at Criteria, recording and producing one of my favorite groups, Chicago. One day he stuck his head in my control room and said in a very sarcastic tone, "Hey Masters, don't forget that 'up' is louder!" I in turn said, "Hey, Mr. Ramone, don't forget "My Little Town"; and besides that, if you'll take a drive out to Tommy Dowd's house, you'll find out real quickly that 'up' is not always louder. So once again, you're wrong, Phil!" I got him big time, and he knew it.

Tommy Dowd had an MCI 500 console in his house with reverse faders. When the fader was pushed all the way up, it was off, but when you started to lower the fader, the music became louder. It was just the opposite of most every other console in the world. I had busted the chops of the biggest record producer in the world, and we laughed about it the entire time he was in Miami. Every word that was said was in jest. He was a bit miffed at the 15 IPS, but he knew it didn't make that big a deal eventually. It was the magic in the players and the vocals of Simon & Garfunkel that made that record sell 1.8 million records. It wasn't what speed the tape was running at. And besides that, it turned out to be the only record they did together after they broke up, and we got to be a big part of it. It was just one of a thousand episodes of my life in the music business that made it all worthwhile. It was the talent, the camaraderie, the fact that music is such a powerful medium and so much fun.

When I'm sitting behind a console painting a picture with music, there's no better feeling in the world for me, and I give the Lord all the praise for allowing me to pursue this career. He went before me, opened doors for me, and blessed the work of my hands and my heart. You would be very surprised at the number of people in this world that spend their entire lives doing something they get absolutely NO enjoyment from. It's just a job to feed their family. But to do what you love most your entire life, and get paid for it, is without a doubt a true blessing from my Creator, and I will spend the rest of my life thanking Him for it. I'll never forget the first time someone asked me to come play my guitar in the studio. I actually could NOT believe it when he said he would PAY me to play. I couldn't believe that someone was willing to pay me to do what I loved more than anything in the world. It was just inconceivable to me.

One last thing about tape speed: like I said, if you have a hit record, it doesn't matter what the tape speed is, or who was playing on it, or whatever. I once did some rough mixes for Jerry Wexler on one of his artists that he brought to MSS. Before he left to go back to New York, he wanted me to quickly make a fast mix of every song we had done. That way he could listen when he got home and make decisions on the rest of the production from those rough mixes. It was late at night and I was tired, and I just flew through the entire album of songs. I would go about half-way through the song and then print it. When he decided to finish the record and mix it, he was going to mix it in New York with one of his hot engineers at Atlantic. But for some reason, they couldn't ever get the sound and feel that I got on my "rough" mixes a few weeks earlier, no matter how hard they tried. He ended up releasing the record and making the master from the mixes that I threw together for him that night, at 7½ IPS I might say, when I was so tired and wanted to go downstairs and get me a beer. So it sometimes doesn't matter what the technical aspects of a record are if they have that magic that can only come from the omnipresence of our Creator.

We mixed every song on "There Goes Rhymin' Simon" at MSS, and when we first started, the first song we mixed was "Kodachrome," which turned out to be a giant record for Paul. After I got what I thought was a pretty good mix, Phil made a couple of suggestions which didn't make a lot of sense to me. And then Paul made a couple of suggestions that also didn't make a lot of sense. Pretty soon the fairly good mix I had started began to sound like doo doo. I realized we were simply OVERMIXING the song. They were trying to do things to the mix that just weren't necessary, and they were killing it. So I stopped, asked them if they would kindly make a quick run down to McDonalds and get us all some breakfast, and when they returned about forty minutes later, I had the song mixed. When they walked in, they knew it was good, and they never made another suggestion, other than minor ones, the entire rest of the time. Even when they got back to New York, Phil went into his studio, which he knew better, and tried to remix some of the songs I had mixed. He finally confessed that he couldn't improve in any way what we had done in that little hick town in northwest Alabama, with or without the Kotex on the ceiling. He would put my mix up and try his best to better it in his studio, and he couldn't come close. The album was a classic, and still is even today. Roy Halee, out in San Francisco, mixed a song on that album that was very good also, so I can't take all the credit for one second. It was a combined effort of a lot of people that made that classic what it was.

Another season that was a lot of fun was the multiple Bobby Womack sessions we did. Bobby was a regular at MSS. He was one of the fastest, most talented, determined, prepared, and gentlest artist we ever worked with. As with a lot of the artists we worked with, Bobby and I became great friends—a friendship that lasted and is still alive today. Bobby trusted me with his life, as I did him.

Bobby Womack was one of the all-time greats of R & B music, without a doubt—an icon when it comes to soul music. We could do a complete album on him in three days if we didn't have so much fun doing it. He would do guitar licks, then add a harmony guitar, then another one, sometimes another one. Then he would do the same with vocals. He was a "stack" king. That's why he had such a unique sound. A lot of soul guitar players couldn't figure out how he got those guitar sounds, but I had the opportunity to show them on many occasions during my career. I knew them by heart. And just like Don Davis, Bobby liked my bass playing. He would always let me play bass on at least one song on every album he did at Muscle Shoals Sound. And what a pleasure it was.

One song in particular I remember playing on was "The Look Of Love," which I think was a Karen Carpenter song. What a groove we had on that song. Another song he did, which was written by Paul Anka and recorded by Frank Sinatra, was "I Did It My Way." The reason this particular song became so popular was because it was quite long. And the reason it was long was because at the end of it they started vamping after the last chorus. In other words, they kept the song going, but Bobby quit singing and just started talking. He was talking about his life, how he ended up to be who he was, how he loved recording in Muscle Shoals, and at one place he started talking to me, personally. He was talking about the fact that so many people that he loved were just as responsible for his success, because they helped him along the way, being available to him and offering their services to him with no strings attached. And he talked about how it made him feel to have those kinds of people around him.

At one point in the song he said, "And the little engineer who said, 'Bobby, if I can't help you, I'll just put my hat on and get on out of here.'" Then he said, "Isn't that right, Jerry?" What an honor to be included in his testimony that he put to music, and it got a lot of airplay too. Everywhere I would go, when people found out who I was, they would say, "Oh, you're the little engineer with the hat." When I got my first gold record, I started wearing a hat called a Gambler, and I put a gold star on my hat. Then when I got the platinum album on "I'll Take You There," I put a silver star on my hat. But as I said, I was really honored by the way that Bobby included me on his record verbally.

One last thing about Bobby. When we would get through with the album, Bobby would leave all the multi-track master tapes with me, give me the freedom to mix all the songs and sequence the songs as to where on the album they would appear. Then I would take the master tapes to New York's Sterling Sound Mastering Facility, and I would have my friend George Marino master the album. After that, I would get on a plane to Los Angeles, they would pick me up at LAX, I would hand the album to Bobby personally, then usually stay with him at his house for a few days in Hollywood. It was always a very generous and fun trip for me, and thoughtful on Bobby's part, in spite of the fact that I did a lot of flying for a few days. Especially the flight from New York to LAX. That was a six-hour flight, I believe. So I deserved some wings for that assignment, for sure. But it was worth it, needless to say.

Another artist that came to Muscle Shoals, which I shared the recording duties with Steve Melton on, was Bob Seger. We did several albums on Seger there in the mid-70s, which included the singles "Night Moves," "Mainstreet," "Katmandu," "Beautiful Loser," and many, many more. What was so interesting about the Bob Seger hits, though, was what happened with his biggest hit of all, "Old Time Rock and Roll." Usually when we had a day off after spending several weeks on an out-of-town artist, we called it "a day at the beach." Then sometimes after we had chilled for a few days, we would bring our best songwriters in like George Jackson, "Prince" Phillip Mitchell, and others if they had a really good song that we thought deserved the attention of the much-used Swampers.

On one occasion in the early 70s, we cut a demo with the rhythm section on a George Jackson song called "Old Time Rock and

Roll." It was not only a great song, but the track we cut on it was killer, to say the least. We all felt pretty good about the song, so we kind of held on to it and saved it for someone we thought could really kill it, or do it really well. "Old Time..." was one of the demos I happened to do, if I remember correctly. If I didn't, Steve will kill me. The reason I mention that is because Bob Seger ended up buying that demo track from us. It didn't come cheap, and it ended up one of the biggest records in popular music today, "Give Me That Old Time Rock and Roll."

Chapter

15

About that time, something happened that had a huge impact on my life. We were a very close knit family growing up, with all we had all gone through and Mother having to work herself half to death to keep us alive. Jimbo was the baby of the family, as I told you earlier in the book, and he and I were cut out of the same mold. The two of us had more of my mother's genes, and Dennis and Terry had more of our dad's genes. Therefore, Jimbo and I seemed to be closer, shared the same traits, had the same skin type, same overall body frame, and even thought alike more than Terry and Dennis.

Jimbo went into the Marine Corps in the summer of 1967. This was right smack dab in the middle of the Viet Nam war. He was a grunt Marine, hard core, not an ounce of fat on his body, and he could literally take a running jump, run up the outside of our house, grab hold of the roof and be on the roof in seconds. He would be sitting at the dinner table, and suddenly, out of the blue, he would let out a loud Hoo Rah, which is kind of a Marine's way of firing himself up on the inside and preparing him for anything that came at him. He was a true front line, fighting machine, grunt Marine.

He spent two years in Viet Nam. He was sent to 'Nam right after boot camp, and had the misfortune of being at Khe Sanh in January of '68 when the entire outfit was encircled and trapped by the

NVA (North Vietnamese Army) for seventy-seven straight days. The last report I heard, the battle of Khe Sanh was 20,000 to 30,000 NVA against 6,000 Marine and Army personnel. At the end of the battle, the NVA had lost 15,000 and we had lost approximately 1,600. That 1,600 counted Americans and South Korean forces.

He recalled going out on patrol, and in one particular instance, was the only one of his eight-man squad to return alive. He had ended up fighting for his life with only a bayonet. He was wounded quite seriously after defeating the enemy, and was sent to Australia for a few weeks to recover from his wounds. He was shot up pretty good, had shrapnel wounds all over him, including in his skull. But being a true patriot, he returned to Viet Nam for another year of duty, at his request. He was U.S. Marine through and through.

When he finally returned home in early '72, he was a physical, mental, and psychological mess, and the shrapnel wounds in his skull caused him to have periods where he couldn't control his body movements. After a couple of years of rehab and therapy, he finally got his life, physically and mentally, back together. Then he met the lady of his life and was in the process of getting married for the first time when he was tragically killed. His car, a brand new one he had recently purchased, had rack and pinion steering that he wasn't used to, and he lost control in a curve, skidded off the road in the rain, and hit a tree head-on. He was killed instantly.

When they called me and told me, I was in shock and disbelief. I immediately got in my car and headed for Little Rock. My mother was devastated. It's one thing to lose a child, but when you lose your baby, it's different; and she had lost her baby after all he had been through and survived. He comes home, gets his life together, makes plans to start his life with a wife, a job, everything a person could need, and gets killed in a stupid auto accident. My mother never, ever recovered from Jimbo's death. Neither did I.

People came from everywhere. Our house was so full of people that loved us, you couldn't even walk from one room to another it was so packed. I went back into his room, quietly closed the door, and started looking through his personal belongings. Not surprisingly, his clothes fit me perfectly. I started packing everything that was his and put them in the trunk of my car, which the studio had just bought me as a bonus for all the hard work I had done in the last five years. (That was the extent of my rewards for the years of brutal, long, exhausting work. But I hold no grudges with the guys at MSS.)

Jimmy Johnson's wife had been driving a 1973 baby blue Mercury Cougar at the time. I had always admired that car and wanted one just like it. Out of the blue, Jimmy called me into his office one day and told me to go to the Lincoln-Mercury dealer just a couple of blocks down the street from the studio and order me a brand new 1975 baby blue Mercury Cougar. Now, in those days you could buy a brand new car with all the bells and whistles for around $3,500 tops. What I didn't know was that they had changed the entire body style for '75, but also raised the price about $2,000. The Cougars then looked like the small Lincoln Continental Mark II. They were beautiful.

But let me finish about Jimbo first, and we'll come back to the car. I was back in Jimbo's room packing all his stuff 'cause I didn't want anything of his lying around to remind Mother of him, if at all possible. Then it hit me, and it hit me like a ton of bricks. My baby brother, Jimbo, was dead, and I literally went to pieces. I started sobbing, and I just couldn't stop. Various people would come in and hold me and love on me and tell me everything was going to be alright, but I just could not get it together. I hardly even remember the funeral. They had to almost carry me in and then carry me out. I couldn't walk or talk or do anything. I was just completely devastated. I couldn't stop crying, and I was still sobbing when I got in my car to go back to Muscle Shoals. I had never been so bent out of shape in all my life. One person that really tried to console me was Theresa "Peanut" King. She was right there with me and supported me. Frankie did nothing.

Something else happened to me when I was driving back to Muscle Shoals that night, and it was just supernatural. There was an intense thunderstorm occurring as I was driving east on I-40 headed for Memphis. It was about 7 p.m., and I was about twenty miles east of Little Rock when all of a sudden I saw a huge lightning flash, and the sky was filled with a giant rainbow at night. Every time the lightning would flash, which was about every ten seconds, the rainbow would still be there. Then something very spiritual happened that I can't even explain, but it was like Jimbo's spirit entered my heart and blended in with my spirit. At that moment I felt like I was living my life for him and for me, together. I would wake up in the mornings, and by the time I had my coffee and started to get ready to go to work, it would hit me again, and I would start crying. I thought I would never get over it. The grief was just overwhelming. It was like the grief just wouldn't go away. John Wyker was someone who noticed my grief, and he helped me cope in a way that you'll hear about in a minute.

During that time, I met Kathy. I went into Central Bank in Sheffield one afternoon to make a deposit. I usually went through the drive-through, but for some unknown reason I went inside, and when I walked up to the teller, I saw her. She was the most beautiful woman I had ever seen, and I knew she was the one I had been looking for my entire life. And what was strange was the fact that she felt the exact same way. When I left there, as soon as I got back to the studio, I picked up the phone to call her, but her line was busy. Why was her line busy? Because she was trying to call me at the same time. We both knew right from the start. The first time I looked into her eyes, we both knew. I told her I must see her immediately, and we got together that very afternoon. There was just one problem. We were both married to someone else.

When I told you about the time I was in Jimbo's room and I went to pieces, and various people came in to try and comfort me and hold me and love me, well, Frankie never did anything to comfort me. She didn't even ride in the family car with me to the funeral. I just don't think that kind of love was a part of Frankie's and my relationship. Frankie wasn't into me as a person; we just had a child together and sort of played marriage for thirteen years. But I fell flat, head over heels in love with Kathy.

We would meet down at our other studio in Sheffield, just a few blocks from the bank as soon as she would get off work every day. It was called Studio B. We didn't use it very often for recording, so it was almost always vacant during the day. Kathy and I were not intimate for at least six months for several reasons, but mostly because we were trying to do right, even though in our hearts we had already done wrong. We knew what we were doing was wrong, but we just had to be together. I just had to be with her every moment I could, and I had to hold her. When we weren't together, I felt like all of me wasn't there. We were just meant to be together, and after about six months, we started becoming intimate. We just couldn't help it.

God, I loved that woman so much, I didn't want to live without her. But I still was grieving for Jimbo. Whether these two things were related, I really don't know, but they had nothing in common, and my grief still haunted me. One thing that was helpful was the fact that Kathy had lost her older brother just a couple of years before, so we talked about that, and it helped me put things into perspective. But I had to try and live for Jimbo and myself at the same time. It's like I was living two lives. I would talk to him and tell him what we were going to do today, and tell him to come on and get ready. It was just insane. It bordered on necromancy, and I knew that was evil, so after a while I stopped all the pretending. It was just surreal, yet it was as real as real can be to me.

Kathy and I continued getting closer and closer, and as we met everyday, we made plans to be together forever. I felt like she was the one I had been searching for my entire life, and she appeared to feel the same way. She would even call me from her house when her husband was there and talk to me. Her husband must have thought I was a girl friend or her mother, or something. We talked about getting divorces as soon as possible and moving out of town, because she was afraid of what all her friends and her mother would think. So we agreed on Miami.

Frankie and I decided to get a divorce, because I finally discovered that the opposite of love isn't hate, but indifference. I just became totally indifferent with Frankie, and we never could get it together in a lot of areas. She never really protested the divorce. The only thing she said about the whole thing was right before they left. She said, "I don't want to do this." That was it. Unfortunately, I never had the courage to confess to Frankie about my adultery, so it was my indifference that eventually drove her off. We had been married for thirteen years, and I simply wanted to be with Kathy, and I didn't care what price I had to pay.

Frankie had already gone to Memphis, pretending to go visit her mother in Parkin, and had found an apartment in Marion, Arkansas, which is about half-way between Memphis and Parkin. She was only fifteen minutes from Memphis, and her brother's ex-wife had found her a job in Memphis. I'm trying to tell two stories at the same time right now, but in all reality, it was even more complicated than that.

I was dealing with so much at the same time that I was about to lose it. I was burned out as far as recording, still dealing with Jimbo's death, in love with a married woman, married myself, and it was getting to be more than I could handle. When Frankie and I divorced, I gave her everything in the house, her car, and agreed to give her half the proceeds from selling our two-year-old house. I had built it for $19,800 and sold it two years later for $38,800. It was a very nice house, because it was built by a friend of mine. He put a lot of extra things in it, yet it still cost less than $20,000. That's quite a profit we split, but she deserved every penny, and I also sent her child support every month.

Just a short time before Frankie and I agreed to divorce, a good, good friend stepped in nonchalantly and practically saved my life, from an emotional standpoint, and he put me on the road to the most fun I had ever had in my life. John D. Wyker—"Lightning" I called him—the most real, down to earth, Quaalude taking (at the time) eccentric with a heart the size of Lake Michigan. He realized what was going on with me and told me to meet him down at the city dump in Sheffield one Saturday afternoon. Yes, the city dump of Sheffield. I was sitting in my car when he came riding up on a dirt bike. He had bought a Suzuki 185 trail bike and had stripped it clean all the way down to nothing but frame, engine, fenders, wheels, and handlebars, and had put a big sprocket on the back wheel and a knobby tire for more traction. It would go anywhere and almost climb a tree.

Like I said before, all of this was happening before Frankie and I had agreed to get a divorce. She was still trying to figure out what was wrong with me, yet she really didn't care. She just didn't want her comfortable life to be interrupted in any way. At least that's the way I saw it at the time. She had a new car, we had just built a brand new house, had new furniture, and the family was really sitting pretty. Mandy was in the sixth grade, and Syndy was in junior high school. We looked like your all-American family, with one exception. The head of the house was getting ready to check out of the whole thing, mentally and then physically.

So "Lightning" (he had done so many 714's that he moved extremely slow everywhere he went) handed the bike to me and said, "Take her for a spin." They had a trail that went down through the woods and then down by the river, up the river bank for about a half-mile, then through more woods, and then back up to where our "camp" was. It was about a half mile in length, but you had to do a little climbing and maneuvering, then climb a short hill as you approached "camp." That was not easy for a beginner. I did pretty well at first, but when I came to that hill, I got about half-way up, and the bike came out from under me. I fell back down the hill in the middle of a bed of very sharp rocks at the bottom of the hill, and the bike fell on top of me with the engine running wide open. I picked myself up, had a gash on my shoulder that was quite deep, and other scratches and abrasions, but I was still alive, and I turned it around and made another run at the hill and made it.

The thing that I noticed was that while I was on that bike, trying to keep it upright going through all those obstacles, gullies, trees, and boulders, and then climbing that hill, I had not thought of one single thing except how much fun I was having—although I always thought about Kathy. If my mind had started to wander, or I had started thinking about all the things that were bothering me, I would have been hurt really, really bad. When you're riding a dirt bike through the woods at forty-five or fifty miles an hour, and you make a mistake, you get killed real easily. And the thing that would cause you to make a mistake would be taking your mind off exactly what you're doing and where you're going every moment. I found, not only a way to get everything out of my mind (except Kathy of course), but also a way to have my first childhood, finally, after thirty-six years.

From the time I was eight years old, when my father left my mother, I was stuck with responsibility until my senior year in high school, but that only lasted a year. I had to study to graduate, then I was in the Army, then I was married and had a son, then I was married again and had a daughter, and all this time I was working a job. I never got a chance to have a childhood. So I went down and bought me a toy and went out and played in the dirt. It mentally saved my life, and I give all the credit to my good friend John D. "Lightning" Wyker, from Decatur, Alabama, and also the leader of a group "Sailcat" that had a hit record called "Motorcycle Mama" in the summer of 1972. Thank you, John. You helped save my life.

Chapter

16

One habit that I got back into when I went to work over at Sound was smoking grass. Of course, I smoked some in the Army, but not very often (marijuana). It seemed like so many people were doing that in those days, and those that would come there to record would always offer us some, and even some that worked there were into it. It made sessions a lot more fun and it helped me stay relaxed and able to concentrate. That's a pretty good excuse isn't it? We could get it so easily, and we would go out in the woods right beside the studio, where there was a pine tree, the only tree on the vacant lot. We had to walk through some high grass to get there, so we would walk through the grass in order to smoke some grass (smile). With the high grass all around us, no one could see us, and we never, ever smoked in the studio.

One thing we didn't need was a raid by the police or a news story about how all those dope-smoking musicians over at such and such studio got caught with drugs. We would lose our lease on the building and end up having to shut down, plus end up in jail, too. The people in that town were very conservative, and simply would not understand. They probably had us doing it in their minds anyway, so we might as well go ahead and imbibe. But we were too "hot" (as in successful) to be too stupid, so we were very, very cautious with our every move. At first we would wait until late afternoon or dark when we were beginning to tire before we would start smoking, but after a couple of years we were starting the day, sometimes as early as 10 a.m. under the pine tree.

Then Tommy Wright, our studio photographer, walked in one day with some psilocybin mushrooms. They were minor hallucinogenic. He had gone out in a cow pasture and picked an entire bucket full of them (they grow out of cow manure). Then he boiled them and added some Kool-Aid to them. He would bring several jars of mushroom cocktails to the studio, and it would start to be fun city for quite a few hours. As a matter of fact, I did an entire Rod Stewart album while blasted on mushrooms. The album was "Atlantic Crossing," which had several hit singles on it like "Sailing," "Don't Want To Talk About It," "This Old Heart Of Mine," "First Cut Is The Deepest," and "Tonight's The Night." We did a lot of Rod's records for a few years. Tom Dowd would bring him as his producer, and he was courteous enough to let me do the engineering, even though I was stoned on mushrooms one, maybe two days.

Mushrooms were relatively harmless as watered down as they were, and they were good for helping us stay awake, especially for late night sessions. They kind of put a smile on your face and made you very mellow, yet wide awake. They were pretty harmless, but the juice tasted terrible. I was always totally in control of my faculties and never made mistakes or anything like that. I wasn't that blasted, just laid back and felt good and alert. I had been known to continue to take an amphetamine occasionally also, so drugs were a big part of my life at that time. But when I was with Kathy, I always wanted to be as straight as I could. I didn't want any kind of cloudiness in my mind when I was with her. She was so beautiful, and I just couldn't keep my hands off her, and she was the exact same with me, which should have been a tip off early on, but I was so smitten that nothing in the entire world mattered but being with her at that particular time. I was totally, blindly in love, I guess you could say. I would have given up everything in my life for her, and I thought she felt the same.

Just before the idea of Frankie and I divorcing started to materialize, I started riding dirt bikes on a regular basis. I bought a TS 185 Suzuki Trail Bike just like the one Wyker was riding. I stripped it down also, just like Wyker did, taking off everything that I didn't need. Other than the frame and the motor, about all I needed were the fenders. Had to have those to keep the mud off my back and my face, or I would have taken them off too. I mean the damn thing had turn signals, a headlight, a speedometer, and a couple of other things that we simply did not need. It was made to ride down the road and then occasionally ride off-road if we wanted to. But we wanted to make it a simple tree climbing, mountain climbing dirt bike. And for beginners, it was the perfect bike.

When I first bought it, I came riding up in the driveway at home. When Frankie saw it, she completely went bananas with anger because I hadn't discussed it with her. I didn't care if she approved it or not. That's the kind of person I had become. That was also when I decided to shave my head, completely. I went to the place where I normally got my hair cut and told them to just whack it all off. I was in a total state of rebellion by then. Besides, every time I came back from the woods, my hair was so long and thin that, when I washed it, it just stuck out and made me look like Bozo the Clown. I was sick of it.

I was turning into a person no one knew any longer. Frankie wasn't part of my life any longer; she just didn't know it. Now that I look back, she might have even loved me, in some strange way, just a little. But I was totally indifferent toward her, and had been for quite some time. On the weekends, I would leave on my motorcycle and wouldn't come home until late Sunday night. I had a rack on the rear bumper of my Cougar that held a small motorcycle. I put it on there on Friday nights and was up early on Saturday mornings (after taking a hit of "speed"), and I would not come home for two days. How anyone could have loved me at that time in my life I'll never know, but Kathy did, and I know my precious twelve-year-old daughter, Mandy, loved me very much. I was her "daddy" and that would never, ever change, and she knew that for a fact. And it hasn't changed one bit, even today.

The city dump didn't last long at all. We started going up to a place just across the Tennessee line, northwest of the Shoals, called Bruton Branch. It was about fifteen miles south of Savannah, Tennessee. It was what you could call a Disneyland for dirt bikers. It was right on the Tennessee River, just before Pickwick Dam, and was miles and miles of trails and power lines with hills. Right in the middle was what we called "The Big Hill," and it was responsible for several deaths over the years from people trying to climb it in jeeps, motorcycles, and dune buggies. But only dirt bikers could make it.

I must boast in one thing, and that is the fact that I was the only one of the "Out To Lunch Bunch" that was able to climb it. But it took me almost a year to accomplish it. It was so steep, it was almost straight up, probably about a 75 degree incline, with nothing but loose dirt, jagged rocks, and the biggest obstacle, right before you got to the top, slate. I did so much riding out there, and went out there so much, that I began to know every trail, every rut, rock, incline, decline, every way to just about anywhere. I was so fearless at that time that I even went out and rode the trails at night, without any light of any kind except the moon. I didn't care if I lived or died at that time. I would say that only my hope for being with Kathy kept me going at that time. However, the longer we went, the less hope I had, but I'll explain all that later.

I went from Bruton Branch to motocross courses. The first time I ever rode a real motocross course, I literally thought I was in heaven. I'll follow up on the motocross part of my life later, too. We've still got a ways to go before that season of my life. Incidentally, the members of the "Out To Lunch Bunch" included Wyker "Lightning" and myself of course. (The name they gave me eventually was "Captain Audio," because I was always leading them, either on a ride, or simply getting everyone together to make the trip up there.) Other members were my good friend and one of the best writers in the world, Dick Cooper, or "Chain Saw," now an accomplished record producer and engineer. David Hood and Roger Hawkins, two of the Swampers, would come out and ride with us occasionally. And also Billy Powell, who was Wyker's paper boy, and was the one that really inspired this entire thing to begin with by simply delivering Wyker's paper on a dirt bike and got Wyker interested originally.

Billy was the one that actually taught us all about riding these darn things in the first place. He just set the example, and we followed him. Then we each picked it up and developed our own bike and style of riding. Due to my mental state, I was more interested in all this dirt bike thing than anyone, simply because I needed the distraction. Some more riders we had were my friend Chuck Killen, who owned the only motorcycle shop in Florence or Muscle Shoals, and B.J. Malone, who worked for the railroad. My extraordinary engineer and close friend Steve Melton eventually got into it, for a while, anyway. Another one was a young man who was also walking in Wyker's footsteps with the Quaaludes, Jerry Crump, whose father owned the largest and oldest Chevy dealer in the Shoals area. That pretty much made up the "Out To Lunch Bunch."

The only problem with Jerry Crump was that, even though he was wealthy enough to buy all brand new everything from bike to gear to equipment and everything else, he would always go out for only one ride, then ride back into camp, fall off his bike and stay passed out on 'ludes' for the rest of the day. When we would get ready to leave that night, we would wake him up, and he would go home with all his brand new expensive stuff still not even dirty.

By the same token, we had people that would always come out and join us socially, especially one of the best photographers in the state of Alabama, Tommy Wright. He took a lot of photos, at least at first. Then he decided he wanted to go out on a ride with us once, and he ended up breaking his right leg, severely. I'm pretty sure it ended up a compound fracture, but we didn't know that at the time. We were about seven or eight miles from camp, and it was starting to rain. The only way we could get him out of there was for me to ride him out on my bike with me. The muddy logging roads were getting so saturated by the rain that our tires started sinking into the mud, and we couldn't steer. All we could do was try and keep our bikes upright by wiggling our front tires just enough to keep our balance, which wasn't too hard unless you had an extra person on there with you, which was my case.

We kept falling over when I would lose my balance, and every time we would fall over, it would be on Tommy's compound fractured leg. We must have fallen fifteen or sixteen times before we got off the logging road and into the woods where I could stay upright. It was the most painful trip Tommy ever made in his entire life, but he never once complained about my riding. He just hung on and was a real man about the entire thing. His leg was in a cast for three months, at least. They had to do surgery on his leg, and he still has a slight limp because of it.

Meanwhile, back at the ranch, or Muscle Shoals Sound, we continued our track factory kind of life style. Peter Yarrow, one third of Peter, Paul and Mary, came in the summer of '75, about the time people were having to wait in line to pump gas, if it was their day to get gas. The economy was in a slump, and Peter, trying to take advantage of the situation, did an album called "Hard Times." My life, needless to say, was becoming a total disaster, and it was starting to show in my work. Peter and I didn't necessarily get along too well, and the frame of mind I was in made things even worse. I finally had to turn the session over to Steve, who by then was even better than I was. He could certainly get better guitar sounds than I could the first time he sat down behind the console. He'll have to write his own book to explain that, but he was like Gang Busters behind that console. I have no idea where he got it. I guess it just came natural to him, because he turned out to be the best. He and Greg were both just dynamite as engineers, and I had all the confidence in the world in them. As a matter of fact, they were becoming so good, I was afraid no one would want me to even engineer for them again. But Peter's LP never did anything.

The following year, he brought a young lady down to record, and she was so beautiful. Her name was Mary McGregor, and she did a record called "Torn Between Two Lovers." It turned out to be a monster record, sales wise. I had to use the vocal booth for one of the guitar amps, and Mary wanted to do her vocal live, so I had to put her in the bathroom. As small as it was, there was no other choice. Now we had, without any doubt, the smallest bathroom in the history of bathrooms. It was about five feet deep and maybe four and a half feet wide. You couldn't do much of anything in there, except what people normally have to do in a bathroom.

So, I put in the smallest microphone stand I could find, and Mary had to literally straddle the toilet bowl to get to it, and she did her master vocal as they were cutting the track. While we were cutting her track, at one point at the end of the song, she reached back and flushed the toilet. It was so funny, and it really made the session come alive with her down-to-earth antics. Even though her vocal was almost perfect, she did have a couple of lines she had to redo, so she had to get back in the bathroom, in the same position, to maintain the integrity of the sound of her vocal.

Mary was one of Peter's background singers, and she wasn't that crazy about the song because she was married and felt like she was being unfaithful to her husband just by singing it. Of course, when those royalty checks started rolling in, they both felt a lot more moral about the record. But for some reason, she got caught up in the star thing and wouldn't do background singing any longer. She also wouldn't do any more commercials that she was famous for, and had been famous for before she was a background singer. She eventually destroyed her marriage and career because of her ego. Bless her heart. I know she didn't mean for it to happen that way, but like I told you before, "Success is the hardest thing in the world to handle." It can destroy you in a split second if you let it.

If you ever decide you're a big star, you must maintain the business of keeping hit records rolling out every so often. If you don't, your live concert dates start going down in important venues and less pay-off too. Eventually, you're back to singing in clubs for $250 a week just like everyone else. And I go back to the famous saying I mentioned earlier in the book when the Hombres were drying up, "ONE DAY YOU'RE NOTHING, THE NEXT DAY YOU'RE A STAR, AND THE DAY AFTER THAT NOBODY KNOWS WHO YOU ARE." To become an established recording artist, you must continue to pump, not just records, out there to the public, but HIT records, and that's why having a good producer is so very important. That was our mistake as the Hombres, and it was Mary's mistake also.

Other artists we recorded during that time were Wendy Waldman and Donnie Fritts, who was Kris Kristofferson's organ player and a dear friend of all the people from our area. Fritt's record was called "Prone to Lean," because he was always just hanging around and leaning up against something. He was produced by Kristofferson and Jerry Wexler, Vice-President of Atlantic Records.

One night Kris and Donnie and I were alone in the studio doing vocals, and Kris pulled out a joint that someone in Nashville had given him only moments before he came down to Muscle Shoals. He thought that might be a good time to light up, while the place was relatively empty. We had a draft beer machine downstairs in the lounge, and Kris and I were sitting in the control room drinking draft beer out of champagne glasses when he lit it up. After about fifteen minutes, we had finished the joint and were absolutely stoned out of our heads. All of a sudden, I started getting this strange feeling coming all over me, and then I realized I couldn't move. My entire body was paralyzed. I looked over at Kris and he was the same way. So was Donnie. He was out in the studio and was lying down on the floor and wasn't moving. I thought we were going to die.

Someone finally walked in the door and realized something was wrong. We couldn't talk, couldn't move, and our bodies were just buzzing all over. They took the three of us to the emergency room, and we found out that someone had laced that joint with PCP, an animal tranquilizer, a lot of it. And it almost did us in. We were real careful after that as to whom we got our drugs from. But this was only a single joint, or cigarette. So we learned another valuable lesson. Never take a single rolled-up joint from anyone you don't know real well. There has to be a reason for someone to hand you just one joint and not a bag or a few. Never just one. Someone was trying to do Kris in, big time.

We also did an album on a songwriter friend of ours from Los Angeles whose name was Barry Goldberg. It was a fun album, but the best part was that it was produced by Jerry Wexler and Bob Dylan.

Dylan was late getting to Muscle Shoals, and we started without him at first, but we just could not get a single track cut for some reason. Bob and his wife, Sara, and family had driven all the way from California in a Volkswagen station wagon—you know, one of those hippie Volkswagens with no air-conditioning, and they were really wrung out when they arrived. This was in the middle of the summer, and they had picked a terrible time to drive in a bug with no air for over two thousand miles. But that's why he was Bob Dylan, I guess.

We had been trying this particular song for two days and couldn't even get a track worth listening back to. When Bob walked into the studio and sat down next to me in the control room, we cut the track in one cut. He had an aura about him, and I would almost be inclined to say he had an anointing about him, and everything we did had a special magic to it. It was the most supernatural, magical album we ever did, but it didn't sell a copy when it was released. However, just working with him made me realize why he was such an icon in the music business and in music in general. Sometimes he just had to be there. That's all it took, just for him to be there.

He went out on the back porch once, and was sitting there playing his acoustic guitar, and Pete Carr got his acoustic and started playing along. I went in and got the upright bass, took it out and started playing along; and Roger had some drumsticks and was playing rhythm on the wooden porch banister—all outside on the small back porch, and we just had us a little folk jam session for about an hour. It was so much fun and quite historic for me at the time.

We also did some of Barry's vocals outside in the vacant lot beside the studio. I used about five or six mic cables and strung them all the way out to the middle of the field along with headphones, and used the ambiance of the outside, the traffic, the birds, etc., as background. It was an unusual sound. It wasn't anything exceptional, but it was different. We even had David Hood driving up in his Porsche 911 while we were recording. It was cool.

We also had the privilege of recording Willie Nelson, an album called "Phases and Stages." What a fun record that was to make. He had some excellent players come down from Nashville to play with him on the record. He brought along John Hughey on steel guitar, Johnny Gimble on fiddle, and Fred Carter on guitar, along with David, Roger and Barry. The entire album was a concept album about the breakup of a marriage, with the first five songs being the woman's side of the parting, and the last six songs as the man's side of the dissolution of their marriage. It always takes a man an extra song to cop out for misbehavior (smile).

If I'm not mistaken, this also coincided with Willie's breakup with his wife at that time. He even told us a hilarious story about his coming home one morning, drunk out of his skull, as usual, and while he was asleep, his wife sewed him up in his bed sheet. When he woke up, he said it was like he was inside a huge marshmallow or something and couldn't get out. It was hilarious afterwards, but he said it scared the hell out of him at first, because he couldn't figure out what was going on. Needless to say, she was sick and tired of his hanging out in bars every night, like most musicians, and coming home drunk with lipstick all over him and a cheap perfume smell. So he surely wasn't trying to hide anything, or at least it appeared that way. It was a very fun session, and Willie says even to this day that it's the best album he's ever done, and I tend to agree with him. One song on there was a big hit, "Bloody Mary Morning," and it stayed on the charts for a long time.

We also cut one of the most talented groups of musicians I've ever been in the studio with, besides the Swampers of course, but the group was called "Orleans." They were led by now Congressman John Hall (D-NY), who represents the 19th District of NY. They were outstanding musicians. Just to give you an example of how good they were, they were just getting set up when I had to leave for a few minutes. When I came back, they were all playing, and man, they were cookin'! That's the only way to describe how good they were and how great they sounded.

I usually left the studio set up so a band could literally come in and plug in and start playing. In a lot of studios they tear the entire studio down, and when a band comes in they start from scratch in microphones, locales, etc. But the way I had it, you could just come in and sit down, plug in and start playing, because we were usually in the same configuration as far as instruments, mics, and direct boxes at all times. The piano was always mic'd, the guitars were always mic'd, the drums were always mic'd, and if a visiting band came in, they would usually only bring their instruments, and the drummer would bring maybe his own snare drum and sticks, and that was about it. We were so famous for our sound, they usually didn't want to upset the Muscle Shoals Sound applecart mystic, or "sound," literally. They were just wailing away on some song when I walked in, and finally I said, "OK guys, let's get our sound levels and hit it." They then all got up and went to their regular instrument, which was totally different than what they played on record or when they played live. I couldn't believe it. They were playing each other's instruments and were just as proficient on each other's instruments as they were on their own. They were just an amazing group and equally nice and gentlemanly. They were just regular guys. They were pros, we were pros, and we just got after it. The album ended up really nice with a big hit called "Still the One." Orleans was a fantastic group and a fantastic bunch of guys, to boot.

We also did a couple of what we called hard rock bands back then in '74 to '76. We did a group of wonderful guys with the weirdest name I have ever heard of. The name of the group was Lynyrd Skynyrd. Some of the nicest guys you would ever want to meet. We had more fun cutting their record than just about anyone that recorded at our studio. They were so loud, the girls in the offices up front and even downstairs had to literally turn their phones off when they were playing because they couldn't hear who was on the phone. Ronnie Van Zant was the leader of the group, and it was real interesting where they got their name.

They were from Jacksonville, Florida, where they also all went to high school together. There was a gym coach that was always getting on their cases about their long hair. Most everyone else was used to long hair by then, but this one coach, whose name was Leonard Skinner, just wouldn't stop harassing them. He was on their cases all the way up until they graduated, and they promised him that some day they would get even with him. Well they did. They murdered his name with spelling, and that's how they ended up with their name.

They were all great and fun guys. I loved each and every one of them, and I could write an entire book about their history. I do want to mention that Ronnie Van Zant and Steve and Cassie Gaines, along with their road manager and their two pilots, were killed in a plane crash in southern Mississippi in 1977. The rest of the band members were all injured, some of them quite seriously. The bass player, Leon Wilkerson, started coming to our church in Florence in 1982, and had a very serious encounter with the Lord Jesus. So I know that after his death of liver disease and emphysema, he's with the Lord now for sure, along with Billy Powell, the keyboardist who just died in January of 2009. God bless you all; I miss you very much, still.

Chapter

17

Something quite interesting happened to me one night when I was at the studio alone that I must tell you about. The building was a simple shotgun building with a basement, and at one time it was a casket company, which was a perfect place, since there was a cemetery just across the street from the studio. There were rumors that the place was haunted, and I know two facts that will prove that it could have been true, if you believe in that kind of stuff. First, we had a room in the back of the studio that we used to store tapes and also our lead guitar player's amps when they were cutting live with the rhythm section. Every single guitar player that used that room has either died or had something very traumatic happen to them in their lives.

Eddie Hinton was simply not all there for the last few years of his life. I loved Eddie, so I don't want to say anything derogatory about him, but mentally he did have some problems that he had been afflicted with most of his life. Tippy Armstrong, another lead guitar player, committed suicide, and Pete Carr, my dear friend, at one time in his life had a bout with depression and had to have shock therapy. They actually erased part of his life from his memory bank, to blot out certain low points of his life that were making him so depressed. Every guitar player has had some kind of bad ending, or part of their lives taken from them. Rod Stewart, who I put in that room ONE time only to do his scratch vocals (just enough vocal to lead the band through the song), wrote on the top of the door (much to my surprise when I found it months later), "Rod Stewart went f...ing mad in this room," and then signed it and put the date right beside it. It's still there.

One other thing. I was downstairs in the lounge where the draft beer machine, TV, and bar were, and I was waiting for the Lynyrd Skynyrd guys to show up to unload their equipment for a session the next day. Since I couldn't see Kathy at night, and I didn't want to go home because Mandy had school the next day and had to go to bed early, I volunteered to stay and let them in when they arrived. They were supposed to arrive at about 8 p.m. The door to the studio was locked, so I figured when they arrived I would hear the trucks pull up in the parking lot, and would go up and let them in. There was no one upstairs in the studio at all, and I had it locked tight.

All of a sudden, I heard what sounded like an entire band with their cases and amps and equipment loading in upstairs. They were bumping and making all kinds of racket. I was hung up on a TV show, so I figured someone had shown up, unlocked the door, and let them in. I planned on going up in a few minutes to say hello to all the guys and make sure they got everything in the studio so they could then go to their motel rooms. After about fifteen or twenty minutes of all that, things got real quiet, and I was afraid they might have gotten off without me saying hello, and I didn't want that to be the case. I also wanted to know who had opened the door for them to unload all of that equipment.

It had sounded like they were unloading enough equipment for two bands, but they carried a lot of sound equipment with them, so I figured they might have just put everything in there for safety's sake. I went upstairs, and the door was still locked. There were no cars or trucks in the parking lot, and when I opened the door and walked into the studio, it was like absolutely no one had been there. It was just like I had left it a few hours earlier. There was no sign that anyone had been there, at all. I'll just leave that alone for you to figure out. I don't want to even think about it any longer. I also know that there were times when I would be there by myself mixing, and I would swear I saw someone walking around out in the darkened studio. I just never felt like I was alone. Was it haunted? I don't know, but....

I know that I've possibly left some good times and wonderful artists out of this part of my life, but I've tried to give you a fairly good idea of what it was like to actually make music history the way we did in the few short years that I was working at MSS. Much more wonderful things happened in Muscle Shoals before I arrived, and even more after I left, but my years there were not over by a long shot. I was just burned out, and besides that, there was another season of my life to be lived at the time. I would be back here in a few years, much to many people's surprise, but not quite the same person as when I left.

My good friend, Jimmy Johnson, noticed I was headed downhill mentally, physically, and was just getting burned out on music all together, and he tried to encourage me. One day he loaded me in his big old Cadillac, took me down to the Tennessee River in Sheffield, and pulled up in front of a huge building. (It was huge to say the least.) It was the former US Naval Reserve building, with a very large crane right in the middle of the building. When a boat needed repairing, they would back the boat up a ramp, right to the edge of the front of the building, and with cable attached to the crane, literally lift the boat up and swing it into the building, fix it, and then send it back for more duty.

The original MSS building, where I did all of my work, was at the famous 3614 Jackson Highway in Sheffield. Jimmy showed me their plans, which I hadn't been aware of, about what they intended to do with the building within the next year, but I just could not get into it one bit. I did love these guys like they were my blood brothers, and that hasn't changed one bit, and they remain my friends to this day. Unfortunately, Barry Beckett had several strokes and heart attacks and passed away on June 10th, 2009. He was three years younger than I, and what a talented man he was. At one time, a couple of years after I left, he took the city of Nashville by storm as a producer and session player. He was even president of a major record company at one time, but that was for a short season, too. I sat right beside him for many years and loved him very much, and I will miss him terribly. As far as the new studio, though, no matter what Jimmy said in the way of encouragement, I just did not care. In my heart, my life in music was over, for a season anyway.

The session that, ironically, was my favorite of all time, and at the same time my last session for MSS, was on a group called the Sanford Townsend Band. They were without a doubt the very best of the best as far as players and writers. They had all rented a house out in Los Angeles and had been rehearsing for this album for over a year. They were going to be produced by Jerry Wexler and Barry Beckett, and already had a record and publishing deal with Chappell Music while they were in LA rehearsing. They were also given weekly salaries in order to live while they prepared for this record, and, man, were they prepared.

We must have cut the tracks in four days at the most. We got most of the tracks cut and most overdubs done and were just getting started on the vocals. We had completed about four or five of the vocals, backgrounds included, and I was starting to lose it. Jerry sat on one side of me, and Barry on the other. One of them would say, "Start the tape," and the other would say, "Stop the tape." One would say, "Go ahead and punch in," and the other would say, "Don't punch in yet." I finally got up and just walked out of the control room. I got in my car, went home and got my bikes and all my equipment, and told Frankie, "I'll see you later," and I drove up to Bruton Branch and stayed blasted out of my mind for a solid week. No one knew where I had gone, yet everyone knew where I was. One by one, all my riding buddies started to show up, and they stayed with me all the way through.

By the time the weekend arrived, we must have had fifteen people up there with me, and not one soul said a single word to me. And another big surprise, Frankie, herself, drove up there. I didn't even know she knew where it was, but she brought Mandy with her, and they stayed all day Saturday. Mandy went out riding with me, and not one single thing we did scared her. She loved every second of it. Frankie wouldn't do anything close to getting on a bike, just like she would never do *anything* that I did. She wouldn't have anything to do with anything I did, whether legal or illegal. She just wasn't interested in my life. But coming up there the way she did meant a lot to me, and I'll never forget it.

I mentioned this earlier, but before she left for West Memphis and right before we signed the divorce papers, she only said one thing, "I don't want to do this." But that was the extent of her fighting for our marriage. She was a good woman, a good wife, and a very good mother. We just didn't fit together for some reason. But we did keep it together, some way, for thirteen years, which were important years for our daughter. I'll always be grateful to her for that.

I had been at Bruton Branch for a week, and by Sunday, I figured it was time to go back and face the music. I had been taking so much junk, drinking too much, smoking too much, and I felt like doo doo from head to foot. I very silently walked back into the studio Monday morning and sat down behind the console. After a short wait,

Wexler and Barry walked in and very calmly said, "Let's work on ...," and they gave me a title of a song. I walked over to the tape machine, loaded the tape on the machine, sat down, and we started working. To this very day, not a single person has yet to say ONE SINGLE WORD to me about me walking out on the session for a week. They acted as if I had just left at the end of the day before.

Later on that afternoon, Steve told me he wanted to talk to me and asked if I would take a ride with him in his car. When he started talking to me, he was weeping as he talked. He said in a quivering, tearful voice, "Jimmy wants you to know that I am now the Chief Engineer, and I am now in complete charge of the recording at Muscle Shoals Sound." I felt so bad for him. First, because they didn't have the guts to tell me themselves. They made Steve do it, and it was sort of a tacky way to really put me in my place. I didn't blame anyone. I had made my bed, so I had to sleep in it.

I finished all the overdubs, all the vocals, and when it came time to do the final mix, I walked into Jimmy's office and turned in my resignation. It was the right thing to do, and it was what I needed to do. I wasn't doing anything but hurting the company now. With my attitude and my behavior, it wasn't good for me to represent such a wonderful bunch of guys who had included me in such a great season of history-making music. It was time to go.

As a postscript to that session, I knew Wexler and Barry would somehow not let what I did go by without some sort of repercussion. When the album came out and was a big hit, especially "Smoke From A Distant Fire," under the credits for engineers, they listed me last. Even though I had done all of the recording, they put me last as an engineer, but it didn't bother me. My ego didn't need pumping up anymore than it does today. I know who I am and what I've done, and that's enough for me. I don't regret anything I've done; I just wish I could start all over and do it over again, but it doesn't work that way. That's why it's so important to make good choices throughout our lives and think about what they're going to mean years down the road. And also, what we're going to say when we eventually have to stand before our Creator and give an accounting for our lives and the decisions we did make and try to justify them before Him.

Shortly after I had moved Frankie and the kids to West Memphis, I had a chance to sell Jimbo's chopper, which I had brought back to Muscle Shoals on my motorcycle trailer. It was a Triumph 650cc, and it was chopped at least thirty-six to forty-five inches. That meant the front wheel was way out in front of the bike, and it had no shocks whatsoever, which is why they call them "hard ass" bikes. They can get extremely rough on the derriere when not ridden on very smooth surfaces. A Bike like that was every street biker's dream (except the big thing now is Harley-Davidsons). I rode the chopper a few times, but being a dirt biker at heart, I just had to ride on dirt and grass and through mud and mountains. Since I only had my 185 trail bike, a wonderful guitar player and friend, Wayne Perkins, from Birmingham, Alabama, offered to buy Jimbo's chopper, and I had a chance to get a very slightly used, top of the line, Suzuki RM250 motocross bike.

So it ended up being the story of my life. It seemed like things always worked out for me as long as they were right and good. So while I was waiting for the delivery of my RM, I also realized that I couldn't live the lifestyle I wanted to pursue driving a Mercury Cougar. Even though it was a cool car, I couldn't put two bikes on the bumper like I had been putting the 185. So I went down to my favorite Chevy dealer in town, and sat down with my very, very, exceptionally wonderful friend, Jerry McGee.

Jerry was nice enough to come bail Wyker and myself out of the Sheffield jail one morning about 1 a.m. for what the little guys with doughnut sugar all over their uniforms called "crossing the center line" of Montgomery Avenue in downtown Sheffield. I mean, we should have made the Ten Most Wanted for that violation. We had simply stopped by the Dairy Queen after returning from Bruton Branch late on a Sunday night, We had been drinking all day, but I had taken a couple of valiums right before we got into town, in order to start coming down from all the speed I had taken that day. With a couple of chili burgers on top of that, by the time they did a breathalyzer test on us, we both came up as sober as a judge (not by today's standards, though). They decided to keep us in jail anyway for noticing the sugar on their uniforms, so Jerry McGee gladly got out of bed and came down, paid our bail of $100 each, and got us released. He was a treasure of a friend.

So, I went down to the Chevy dealer where Jerry McGee was working at that time, and I ordered a brand spanking new Chevy Silverado pick-em-up with as many bells and whistles as I could possibly get in 1977. It had power windows, a big V-8 engine, a posi-traction rear end, as opposed to 4-wheel drive, and I ended up putting in my own killer sound system. It had leather seats, cruise control, tilt and telescopic steering wheel, and a sliding glass back window. It had about as much extra stuff as you could possibly get on a pickup truck, and it drove like a dream. I also drilled four holes in the bed of the truck and put in eye-bolts for tying down my bikes. It was ready to go, and so was I.

My only regret was the color I picked. I chose a two-tone blue, light blue with dark blue panels. I wish now I had gotten red. And since my Cougar was already paid for, they gave me enough for it that my truck payments weren't much more than my phone bill each month. It was a sweetheart deal. Of course, with Jerry McGee handling the financing with the bank where my friend Dutch McCall was manager, the financing took about as long as it took me to go to the little boy's room and get rid of some used coffee. I really, really enjoyed that truck. And I was able to go out in the deep, deep boonies on several occasions. Once I even rescued a couple of stranded bikers who should never have even left home that day.

Chapter 18

Pat and Brenda Pepper were friends that worked up on the Tennessee line at the Club 13, which was owned by my friend Mike O'Rear, a local songwriter and entrepreneur. They had been living out on Wilson Lake just above the dam for several years and decided to move up to the line to be closer to the club. So they asked me if I would like to take over their house on the lake, and I jumped on it. The night I came back to Muscle Shoals after moving Frankie and the kids to West Memphis, I came back to that empty house. All I had was a mattress, a coffee table, a lamp, and few assorted knives and forks, and that was pretty much it. All of that was lying out in the middle of the family room, which was the largest room in the house. I came home that night and just lay down on the mattress and cried myself to sleep. God, it was so empty in there. And Kathy was at home in bed with her husband.

After I moved out on the lake, Kathy came out almost every day. The drive was a bit longer for her, but it was much more secluded. She even came out and spent an entire Saturday with me once. We laid out in the sun in the back yard, and kept going back inside about every hour and a half, making love, then grabbing a snack and heading back out in the sun. We took a short ride in my fishing boat over to David Hood's house, but no one was at home, so we came back, and about four that afternoon she left. It was sort of a strange feeling being together all day for the first time, and even though I felt so secure having her all to myself that day, there was something starting to go wrong, but I couldn't put my finger on it.

I was beginning to go to different motocross courses and enter races in various towns around the Shoals area. The idea was to pay a certain amount to enter a race, and after all the entries were in, the track owner would count up the entrance fees and match what we had contributed to pay first, second, and third place finishers. Most of the riders started to get sponsors to pay for their bikes and repairs and oil, etc. I had no financial help whatsoever, so at that time I was riding well, but not making any money. But I was having the time of my life being able to escape to another completely different world on Sundays, and it was exhilarating to say the least. I did make enough to pay the rent for a few months and buy some groceries, and I was also getting unemployment from the state. Jimmy was nice enough to tell them he "fired" me so I could draw unemployment for a year.

There was one race I must tell you about, because it involves a very good friend of mine, Dick Cooper, and it shows you not only the fun, but the competition and determination of winning motorcycle races, no matter what kind. There was a place called LaGrange Mountain, which was just a couple of miles south of Muscle Shoals and was someplace to go occasionally for a quick ride, but wasn't anywhere near as much fun as Bruton. One particular weekend they had what they called an Enduro Race. It was a race for sixty miles through mountains, valleys, creeks, any kind of terrain you could possibly imagine. Classes were determined by engine size, so they would let each rider in their class leave in two-minute increments and then time you according to when you left against your finish time.

I used my 185 in the Enduro because it was better for climbing mountains and steep hills and had more low-end torque than my motocross bike. My motocross bike was made for speed, but the Enduros were about maneuvering and climbing. Obviously, they were called Enduros because it was all about endurance, which is what begat my fate in this particular race. There were checkpoints all along the way about every ten miles where they would check you off and give you a drink of water if you needed it. They also had emergency equipment just in case, which in my case really saved me.

When I was into my first leg, my front tire went flat. I would usually carry a flat tire kit, which was a canister that would not only repair the leak, but fill the tire back up with air temporarily so you could finish what you were doing. When I got to the first checkpoint, I was praying they would have a flat tire kit, and they did, thank God. We inflated my flat tire, and I was off to the races once more. I was really doing well, and when I came to the next-to-last checkpoint, they told me I was in first place. My good friend and fellow "Out-To-Lunch-Bunch" rider "Chainsaw" was quick on my tail. It was Dick Cooper, one of my dearest friends, even today. I was so close to the finish line, I could see the people down there waving me on.

All of a sudden, I came to a deep mud hole. I was so excited that, instead of taking the few extra seconds to go around it, I decided to go though it, and I got stuck. My bike was buried in mud up to the seat. I tried and tried to pull the bike out of the mud hole, but I was so exhausted, I couldn't muster up the strength to pull it out. Several riders who were an entire lap behind me came by, but NO ONE would stop and help me out. Not one single soul had any compassion for me, not ONE. Then, here comes the guy in second place, Dick Cooper. I said, "Thank God, Dick, you came along. Please help me out of here." He looked at me and laughed and said, "You've got to be kidding. I'm going down here and get my first place trophy," and he rode right past me. You talking about pissed off? I was totally pissed.

But I finally started laughing and realized what a foolish question that was of me to ask in the first place. I was finally able to get out after about ten minutes, but I was so tired I could hardly make it the 150 feet to the finish line where I got my second place trophy. Dick and I laughed about that for at least a year. As a matter of fact, we laugh about it every time we talk. He got me good, and he knew it. He simply beat me. That's the way the old ball bounces, and I wouldn't trade those times for anything in the world. It was my childhood that I finally got at thirty-seven years of age, and it was long overdue, that's for sure.

When Frankie and I got our divorce finalized, I sold the house within ninety days. It wasn't but about two weeks after my family left that I moved out to the lake. We made a huge profit on the sale of the house, but I used my part to pay off her car loan. We had two dogs that I loved very much. Patches was a beautiful, sleek black Doberman with red patches on her neck, and as loyal as a dog could possibly be. I also had a Heinz 57 doggie named Taffy. Taffy was just a mutt, and so funny. Whenever it would rain, Taffy would go out in the rain, just look straight up into the rain and let it hit him right in the face. I laughed every time he did it, it was so funny. The house on the lake was an old house with only one bedroom and one floor furnace, with a fenced-in back yard for the dogs. It was on the major part of the lake, but just a few feet away on an inlet on Lake Wilson just east of Florence. It was cozy, but we were about to experience two of the coldest winters of our lives in '76 and '78.

Now that I was unemployed, I was collecting unemployment, hoping to start making just a little bit of cash racing. But that was going to take some time, and I needed a sponsor of some sort, so I needed some income to keep me going. I did some free lance mixing out at Wishbone Studio for Terry Woodford, which helped a lot, and some at Al Cartee's studio, too, but the sound at Cartee's studio was atrocious, so it was quite difficult to mix there. One thing I really appreciated about Terry Woodford at Wishbone was the fact that he had told me earlier that on any business I sent his way, he would give me 10% of the studio costs. When I agreed to do the mixing for another client, the client paid me to mix the album, but about a week after the session had finished, I got a check from Terry for over $600 for my 10% of the studio time we had used. I didn't expect that.

Terry was a man of integrity, and I always appreciated that about him. We had a mutual admiration for each other's honesty and integrity from some things that went down between him and the MSS guys when I first came to work for them that I had completely forgotten about, but Terry hadn't. He told me later how much he appreciated the fact that, when he was called on the carpet for something in particular, and they asked me to witness the conversation he had with someone else, even though I just started to work for the guys at MSS, I still told the truth, even if it was not in their best interest, but was in favor of Terry. Honesty always pays off in the long run; believe me, it does. When you tell one untruth, you end up having to tell many more untruths to cover the first, and you end up a total liar with absolutely NO integrity whatsoever.

So, back to my financial situation at the time: I was hitting the trails every chance I got, mostly on Sundays. One of my first races was out near Cherokee, Alabama, less than a mile from the attorney general's home that Jerry McGee and I had visited. It was one of the first motocross courses I ever got on, and it almost ended up being my last race, coming close to being my last *everything*. I had sort of a mentor for motocross racing that I learned quite a bit from. I learned very quickly that riding on a closed course against other riders was not nearly the same as trail riding with climbing hills and power lines.

My mentor and I ended up riding against each other in the first race I entered at Cherokee. He was on a Kawasaki and, of course, had on the Kawasaki green outfit with matching shirt and racing pants, with motocross boots along with his green Kawasaki bike. I was on my yellow Suzuki RM with the number 4 on the front, and I was wearing a "Memphis Horns" and "Doobie Brothers" T-shirt for protection. Man, was I a beginner, and I didn't even have motocross boots yet. One of the first things I learned about riding dirt bikes is that there are two things you must protect at all times: your eyes and your feet and ankles. With the frame of mind I was in, I probably would have raced without a helmet if they had let me.

The whole concept of motocross racing is that we would encircle the course—about a three-quarter mile course—for exactly twenty minutes. They would then give us a white flag, beginning with the rider that was in first place, which meant two more revolutions of the course to the checkered flag. The course gave you all kinds of obstacles to have to deal with. At least three, sometimes four, complete 180-degree turns using what we called berms, where the dirt eventually builds up and sort of makes a wall of dirt for you to turn on.

Then there were minor jumps, major jumps, and whoop-de-doo's, where there are about twelve to fourteen ditches about three feet apart that would rattle your teeth out of your mouth if you didn't treat them correctly. The idea was to jump them about four or five at a time, if possible. That's why it was important to know the course before you got out there and made a fool out of yourself. Some-of the 180 degree turns would be just a few short feet from where you would land after going over a jump. It could be difficult at times, because you would be going very fast after you completed the jump, but you would have to come to almost a complete stop in order to make the turn and use the berm to quickly take off again. That's why it was so important to be able to go from 0 to 60 in less than two seconds. Sometimes you would really need to go from 0 to 60 in less than ONE second.

There was a young guy that was really, really experienced that ran away from us all, but my mentor and I were in for the third place money. He was ahead of me by just a few feet, and I had one chance to pass him, or he had me beat. The only place I could pass him was going over a very high jump, which was the biggest jump on the course. We both hit the jump at the same time, but somehow we met in mid-air and got our handlebars tangled up right at the peak of the jump. Eventually we came down and went tumbling end over end about five or six times and ended up in a cloud of dust.

When I got up, my bike was crooked, my neck was crooked, and my handlebars were twisted, but he was in just a little bit rougher shape than I, because he was a little dumpy in stature and a little slower at recovering. So that allowed me to get started before he did, and I finished ahead of him by about six feet and got third place. The only problem was my third and fourth cervical vertebrae were so out of place that my head was literally sitting to the side of where it should have been. Instead, it was sitting on my left shoulder. The left side of my entire body was real hot, and my right side was ice cold.

I got up, got my gear together, got my money, and headed for my chiropractor's house in Tuscumbia, which was the closest town to Cherokee, thankfully. His name was Dr. John Peacock, and he was a special friend as well as my chiropractor. When I knocked on his door on a Sunday afternoon, he was quite surprised to see me—until he really saw me and knew I was in big trouble physically. He led me back to his bedroom and laid me down on the bed. He said when he reached down to feel my neck it was like putting his hand in a paper sack and finding a den of rattlesnakes. He jerked his hand back and said, "Jerry, I think your neck might be broken." I told him I didn't care, just pull it back in place, and let's see what'll happen. I can't even tell you how much it hurt.

I literally had to carry my head around in my hands for about three months. I had no muscle tone in my neck muscles at all. When I would sit down and go to get up, I would have to literally reach back and pull my head with me when I sat up. That's how bad it was. Another thing you have to understand is, when I graduated from high school, I weighed a little over 150 lbs. At this point in my life, with all the stuff I'd been through, plus the incredible shape my body was in from riding in the second most enduring sport in the world (second only to rugby), I only weighed 119 lbs, soaking wet. There was not one ounce of fat on my body. Even though there wasn't much of me, it was solid muscle.

I went to the ER that night just to make sure my neck wasn't completely broken. They offered me something for the pain, but like an idiot I told them NO, and when they offered me a neck brace, I said NO. Man, was I in a rebellious state of mind or what? When I would get out of bed, I would have to roll out to the right, grab my head, pick it up, and then adjust the rest of my body under it. After about two months, I was back on the track, but that was just the beginning of the injuries I suffered. In addition, after going over a short hill and making a sharp turn at the same time, I twisted my left knee about 180 degrees. I couldn't walk on it for about five weeks, but I could ride just fine. I just took a cane everywhere I had to walk.

You've got to understand, here's a 37-year-old fart out there racing against 17 or 18 year-old kids that have been riding dirt bikes since they were old enough to walk, and I had been riding for just about a year, and that was mostly trail riding. But I was determined. And I had one advantage over them, I thought. A good supply of amphetamines and beer, lots of beer. And enough joints to keep an army high for a month. Those were things I was never without, yet the only thing I had to pay for was the beer. I had good friends and good connections as far as drugs.

Now you know why I was so fearless, painless, and just flat didn't care if I lived or died. My two favorite songs were the theme songs for my life at the time: "Take It to the Limit" by the Eagles, my favorite group of all time, and "Life in the Fast Lane" by the same fantastic group. That's the way I was living my life by then—foot loose and fancy free, yet miserable and trying to live for two people and so lonely I could hardly stand it. I was so lonely that, as much as I loved Kathy, I started cheating on her. I didn't pursue a single woman; they pursued me. They would just show up at my place, since I was finally single. They would get what they wanted, and what I wanted, and then leave with no strings attached. Some of them had been thinking about what it would be like for years, as had I. And I was simply using them to keep me company and for sex; that was all it was. Most of them were married.

I kept begging Kathy to do something about her situation, and she kept saying, "I will, I will." So I waited and I waited, but it was starting to hurt too much. I needed her to make some kind of effort after all I had given up, but she didn't seem to be too anxious to mess up a perfect situation. She had all the sex she needed from me, and all the security she needed at home. Why mess up a good thing, huh? I was her mistress, or whatever you call a male mistress. I guess "lover" is the best word for the moment. She really took me for a ride. It took twenty years to mend my broken heart, but time heals all wounds.

Chapter

19

I started hanging out with my good friends Mike O'Rear and Pat and Brenda Pepper up at the Club 13 as often as I felt like driving up there. Mike owned the place, and Pat was manager when Mike wasn't there, and was also the bartender. It was about fifteen miles up Highway 13, and needless to say, I enjoyed their company. I especially enjoyed being around Brenda. She was the most down-home Southern girl I had ever known, but she was pure Southern Alabama beautiful, and the attraction was mutual. Even though I loved Kathy, my relationship with her was slowing down considerably. She had started coming out less and less, and I knew there was something going on that was not right.

Mike then came up with the idea of making his club into a disco. He asked me if I would like to design it, help build it, and run it, if he paid for everything. So, we found carpenters and sound guys to do all the installation. Most of them would work just for the free beer. I told him to give me a couple of days to think about a design, and we would get started right away. I was excited. I also looked forward to spending more time being around Brenda. She was a very dear friend and remains so to this day. I had never designed or built a disco, but I knew sound. I came up with a very unique idea, and he loved it, so we began putting it together.

The dance floor was quite long and rounded on the ends. It was about 35 feet long and 16 to 17 feet wide. The rounded corners worked out in my favor, but were a "booger bear" for the carpenters. One thing about discos was that you couldn't sit at your table and talk, because the music was always too loud. So, I came up with the idea of putting a four-foot hood all the way around the ceiling of the dance floor, then putting Bose speakers, the very best top-of-the-line speakers, up on the inside of the hood all the way around, yet pointing down at the dance floor. You could hardly see the speakers, but when you walked onto the dance floor, you were surrounded by the very best sound money could buy.

I got some great JBL 750 watt amplifiers for every two speakers. I had eight speakers total under the hood, hooked up to four 750 watt amps. We had a sound booth that was open but separated from the dance floor, with two turntables and a fader between each turntable where you could fade from one turntable to the other either fast or slow depending on the key or the mood of the song or the genre' that was playing. This was before CDs, so everything was either on vinyl or cassette, but most preferred vinyl records.

I also went down to the record store in Florence and educated myself on the latest in disco music. I loaded myself up with about $900 worth of 45's and long-playing disco records and albums of every kind that was out there. Disco really changed the style of popular music at that time, and one of the biggest influences was a group I was destined to be working with eventually from across the big pond, the Bee Gees. And that scenario wasn't as far away as you might think.

We had us a hit in the disco. People started flooding into the place, and I'll swear it reminded me of the El Toro Lounge when the Hombres were such a hit. The place was packed almost every night, even during the week. The sound was exactly as I had hoped it would be. You could be sitting at a table right next to the dance floor and carry on a normal conversation without having to raise your voice, and yet when you walked onto the dance floor to dance, the music just enveloped you. It was a tremendous success.

So between the disco, the few bucks I would make racing, plus my unemployment income, I made it okay. I didn't have a lot of overhead. My friend Chuck Killen down at Universal Cycle helped me keep my bikes running, so I really didn't have a lot of overhead except rent. Somehow I always had everything I needed. I didn't eat very well, because I'm not a cook. All I could fix were eggs, bacon, hash browned potatoes, and toasted English muffins. I must admit, I did borrow two hundred dollars from Kathy one time, but now I realize that was just "sugar-momma money" (smile). I earned it.

I would drive up and run the disco for Mike every Thursday through Saturday, and he would pay me fifty dollars a night. I worked at the disco on Saturday nights until 2 a.m., then, I'd be up at 5 a.m. the next morning to get ready to go racing, depending on how far I had to drive. The first thing I would do when I awoke was take two black beauties with a cup of coffee. Then I'd feed and water the dogs and hit the road, sometimes as far as south Alabama and other times as far as west Alabama or eastern Georgia. I went all over the place. Of course, I would need to get there as early as possible in order to learn the course, or I would be in big trouble.

I went to south Tennessee a few times and also to southeast Mississippi once. I was always alone, yet I wasn't alone. At first, I imagined I had not only Jimbo with me, but Kathy too, but those hopes and dreams began to fade quite fast after the Christmas of '77. I was hurting so much inside, wanting to be a part of her life, that right before Christmas, I found an angel for her made out of pine needles. It was beautiful the way it was made. I put it in her mother's mailbox just a day before Christmas, with a note attached that said, even though she didn't know me, it would make me very happy if she would put it on her Christmas tree. I signed it simply, someone who loved her and her family.

Kathy told me later that she did put it on her tree, because they always went to her mother's house on Christmas morning. It was only a couple of weeks after Christmas when I realized that I had to leave. She admitted, not straight out, but suggested that she just couldn't leave her husband, and I realized she had just been playing me along the entire time. I was simply her lover, and she had used me strictly for sex. She had never had ANY intention of leaving her husband or getting a divorce, and she just wasn't sure what she wanted any more.

I deserved everything that came on me, because I believed in her. I had given up and sacrificed so much, and had hurt so many people that loved me, just for her, and it was all a big lie from the start. Yet she didn't have the courage to tell me the truth. She was a liar, and she simply used me for her own pleasures. My last couple of phone calls to her, she said she "didn't have time" to talk, and I could see the writing on the wall. It was over. I don't remember, but I'm pretty sure I never even said good-bye to her. I just left.

That was one of the hardest winters we had endured in north Alabama, and the day I decided to leave, I drove down to Brenda's mother's house in Haleyville, Alabama, just south of Russellville. They took Patches, my beautiful Doberman, for me and promised to take good care of her. They had two of their own, so I knew she would be in good company. I knew I would miss her. She was the best dog I had ever owned in my life. We got her when she was a pup from Harvey Thompson, the tenor saxophone player with the Muscle Shoals Horns. She was so special. I had named her "Patches" in honor of my first session and the first gold record I earned as a genuine member of the Muscle Shoals Music society, you might say.

When I would walk out of the house there on the lake, especially at night, I had about ten concrete steps to walk down to get to the yard. The house sat up on a hill and was built high in case of lake flooding. When I would open the door, Patches would meet me at the top step. She would be beside me about half-way down the steps, then, she would start circling the entire yard checking for anything out there that might harm me. By the time I reached the bottom step, she would be there beside me and would stay with me the entire time. Also, every night when I would pull up into the driveway, she and Taffy would meet me right at the fence by the driveway, without fail.

One weekend in particular when I was away racing, I came home quite late, and only Taffy met me at the fence. I knew immediately something was wrong for Patches not to be there. I went into the back yard and started calling her and calling her. Then I walked out in the front of the house and called her and called her. I got no response. And Taffy, bless his little heart, kept standing on the dock barking. I walked out to the end of the dock and looked around. All of a sudden, I heard something barely swishing around in the water. I then ran and very quickly grabbed a flashlight and came back. I pointed the flashlight down, and all I saw were these two little black nostrils sticking up out of the water. It was Patches, and there was no telling how long she had been out there treading water, just trying to stay alive. There was no place for her to climb out, because the banks were not only straight up, but were covered in brush and bushes.

I reached down quickly, grabbed her collar and pulled her out of the water. She was a big Doberman, very heavy, but I used every muscle in my body to get her up and at least leaning against the dock until I could work the rest of her torso up onto the dock. Once I got her completely up and out of the water, you could have witnessed the happiest, most blessed, completely exhausted and soaking wet dog you have ever seen in your life. There is no telling when she had fallen in and how long she had been in the lake treading water just trying to stay alive, waiting for her master to get home and pull her out. I'm telling you, there was nothing sticking out of the water but her two nostrils; that was it. It was a miracle from Heaven that she was alive, a Divine Miracle.

While I was down at Brenda's house in Haleyville, her mom asked if I was hungry. I said yes I could eat a little something. I was famished. I couldn't remember the last time I'd had a good meal. Then, I remembered I had visited one time before, and she had cooked dinner for us, just Pat and Brenda and I, and it was the best food I had ever put in my mouth. This time, it was only Brenda and I and her precious mother, and it was so good, and the food was so real, I swear, and the company was the "best of the best." I could have stayed there forever. That meal sustained me for three days. That's how filling it was and how good it was for my neglected body, vitamin wise, that is. I thought I was going to have a nutrition attack.

Brenda also used to come visit me out on the lake quite often, and it was always at the right time. She was about the best friend I'd ever known, because I knew she was sincere. It wasn't easy for her either, because she loved Pat, but in a different way than we loved each other. I loved her in our own special way. So Pat, if you read this book, it was my idea. I was the one that asked her to come keep me company. I know I'm giving you the impression that I was quite fickle in my behavior at that time, but things were different then. Besides, Kathy and I were gradually slipping away from each other. I could tell that things were changing fast.

It seemed like all Kathy came out for was sex, and then she was gone. I was starting to realize that Kathy wasn't interested in anything I did—only when I was going to be home. From the day I met her, she never asked me who we were working on in the studio. She didn't care if I won or lost my races; never talked about her family. She just wanted pure, unadulterated sex. Sound familiar? Things were all starting to come into the light. Attitudes were different. But Brenda was as real as real can be. She and Pat divorced not long after I left, and she came to visit me in Miami, also. She was and is one of the most special ladies I've ever known. She's now a physical therapist in Russellville, Alabama, and married to a doctor. I talked to her one time, and she had just given birth to her beautiful daughter, Jamie, who is the spitting image of Brenda. She looks exactly like her mother and has that same sweet, gentle, spirit that Brenda has. I'll bet you anything that her grandmother taught her how to cook, too.

I gave my dog Taffy to one of the bartenders at the Club 13 that I trusted would take good care of him, so I felt real good about who I left my pets with. I did find out about six or seven years later that three kids, about ten or eleven years old, went to the movie "The Doberman Gang" and ended up shooting and killing Patches with a pellet gun when she was innocently and harmlessly walking down the road only a few feet from her home.

So, all of a sudden, I realized it was time to get the hell out of there. I got a trailer, hooked it up to the trailer hitch on my pickup, loaded both bikes in the truck, and put everything I owned in the trailer. When I pulled out of the parking lot of Muscle Shoals Sound on January 3, 1978, after saying goodbye to all the guys there, especially Steve, Greg, David, and Jimmy, there were two inches of solid ice on the ground with about seven inches of snow on top of that, and the snow was still falling like crazy. I pulled out onto Highway 72 west, called the highway patrol, and asked them the quickest way to Memphis without using Highway 72, and I went to see my little girl before I headed south.

Where was I going? I didn't have the slightest idea. I was just going. It normally takes two and a half hours to drive to Memphis. I drove it, in those conditions, in three hours and fifteen minutes. I spent the night with Mandy and Frankie, got up the next morning, and simply headed south, destination Florida (period). Pat Pepper's sister, Theresa, lived in West Palm Beach, Florida, and was a close friend of Brenda's, and she told Brenda that I could stay with them—her and her roomy. They had an extra bed I could crash on until I could decide what to do, or I could just use it as a pit stop on the way to where I thought I would be going. My first inclination was to go down in the Keys and get a job on a fishing boat or something. I wanted to get out in the ocean, get some sun and warm weather, and do something I'd never done before. I just needed room and board to start with, so I wasn't that particular.

I drove all day and all night and got there about 7:30 the next morning. Theresa met me at the Sunshine State Parkway exit and took me to their place in West Palm Beach. I got introduced to Florida—the wrong way, that morning. I had been there about thirty minutes and was getting ready to crash when there came a knock at the door. It seems it was the apartment manager, and I was told to take that "awful looking truck" and trailer, and go park them around back where they wouldn't be visible to any passing motorists or tenants. "Uh, excuse me, 'awful looking truck'?" I was saying to myself. "My relatively new Silverado, that had more bells and whistles than most of the cars in that awful looking parking lot? You're joking, of course." They were not joking. So I moved it just to keep peace and not get Theresa in trouble.

I slept off and on for about two days and then decided to unhook my trailer and drive down to Miami and see some old friends at Criteria Studios, Tommy Dowd for one. I also wanted to call some friends, namely Steve Alaimo, owner of TK Records, and the Albert Brothers, Ronnie and Howie, who had their own production company. When I walked into Criteria, I knew no one at first. When I asked if the owner, Mack Emmerman, was in, they said he was out for the week. When I asked for Tom Dowd, they said he would be out in just a few minutes. I waited for a while, and after about twenty minutes, Tommy walked out. When he saw me, he barely recognized me. I had lost a lot of weight, and my head was shaved, which was not the case the last time he had been in Muscle Shoals with Rod Stewart. We chatted for a few minutes, and that was about it.

I then decided to go back to West Palm Beach, store all my things in a rental space, turn the trailer in, and free myself with some time off to decide what I wanted to do. I would wake up in the mornings, have a little coffee, go out and get some breakfast, then smoke a joint and drive out to the beach. Something kind of ironic happened the first couple of days I was there that I decided to investigate. About ten years before, while I was still at Sound, I was introduced to this guy that was supposed to be the Top Guru at horoscopes in the country. I paid him to do a complete and total study of my life, make a chart on me, and give me a reading, which he recorded on a cassette tape. Most of it was about my coming future and how he, according to the alignment of the stars, saw my life working out.

So I sat there on the beach in Palm Beach and listened to it. It was about a one and a half hour long recording of predictions for the next ten years from when he started the "study" and it had been about that long since he had done it. I was very curious as to how close he was going to be in light of what had happened so far. What a freaking joke that turned out to be. I had paid that fraud $150 to hand me a cassette of absolutely nothing at all that I could relate to. Whoever this guy was talking about sure wasn't the Jerry Masters that I knew. I mean, he wasn't even close on anything that had happened to me.

I once heard a good description of horoscopes from a very smart man. Horriblescopes, as I call them, are sometimes right, but he said that even a clock, when it's totally broken and not running, is right twice a day. I also, later in life, found a Scripture in Isaiah 47:13 that says, "You are wearied with your many counsels; Let now the astrologers, those who prophesy by the stars, those who predict by the new moons, stand up and save you from what will come upon you. Behold, they have become like stubble, fire burns them; they cannot deliver themselves from the power of the flame."

Anytime we predict or prophesy by the Spirit, it must be subject to the burning fire of the Lord. Prophecies must be like precious stones, gold and silver, which will heat and can be shaped, but cannot be destroyed by any force except our Living God. But I'm getting way ahead of myself here, so let's go back to reality now that we've put astrology in its rightful place, which is on the comics' page of daily newspapers. Needless to say, I took my $150 cassette tape and threw it in the trash can at Palm Beach, Florida, in January of 1978, and decided to go get some coffee.

Chapter

20

A few days later, as Theresa and I and her roomy were watching something on TV, and I was sitting there wondering what Kathy was doing, I got a phone call from Jimmy Johnson in Muscle Shoals. I have no idea how he found out where I was. He said he had called Mack Emmerman, the owner of Criteria, and told him I was in town, and that he might want to talk to me. Mack was very familiar with my work, as he had heard from different artists and producers about how good an engineer I was. He had also personally worked on a lot of the tracks I had cut when artists came to Miami to do their string sessions with Mike Lewis, who did most all of the string arrangements at Criteria, including the Miami Symphony Orchestra.

I told Jimmy that I had visited down there just a few days back, and I figured that Tommy Dowd would inform Mack that I was in town, but he didn't. He never said a single word to anyone. Now, that was a huge surprise to me. Why in the world would Tom Dowd not want anyone to know that I was in town? That's where I stood on his list? Did he possibly think that my presence there might be a threat to him? Me, a threat? I got a good laugh out of that one. Then I got to thinking, I'd really been selling myself short. I carried just a little more weight than I thought. But there was just one problem. WHO SAID I WANTED TO STAY IN MUSIC??? Not I, says the author of this book!! But I went ahead and called Mack the next morning, and he invited me to come down and talk. He seemed excited that I was in town, and probably assumed I was just visiting. I'm not sure. I asked him how his staff was, and he said he was full as far as engineers, so I didn't put a lot of promise in my getting a job there, but I thought it would be nice to go down and visit and just see what was on the plate, so to speak.

Now, it's confession time on my part, everyone—about something that I've failed to mention ever since I realized that Kathy's and my dreams (or, now I must say, my dreams) had been blown completely out of the water and I made the decision to leave Alabama. When I started thinking about how much she had fooled me, lied to me, and used me, and never meant a single thing she had told me, it was a bit much to bear. It didn't really start sinking in until my drive down to West Palm. My heart had been totally broken to pieces. Yes, I had been unfaithful, even to Kathy, but it was out of loneliness and needing someone to care, or to just be there for me. I really had no excuse for my unfaithfulness. But I wondered what she had been saying to her husband? I wondered what she had been thinking when she was making love with him. She had "acted" like they didn't even have a physical relationship. But she had also "acted" like a lot of other things, too. Still, my heart was totally broken in half.

I started crying on the way down to Florida. Then, every morning I would wake up, and I would start crying again the moment I realized where I was. I would cry off and on most of the day. The pain in my heart was beginning to be unbearable. I had this giant lump in my throat and emptiness inside. I tried to pray, but I had no relationship with God. I didn't even know where to begin to ask the Creator of the Universe to bless my adulterous relationship and make everything come up roses, yellow roses, too. This started to get worse, instead of better. It was like the further away I was, the worse it was. I figured after a while I would run out of tears, but I drank enough beer to keep that from happening.

So, the morning after Jimmy called, I got in my truck and drove about 55 or 60 miles south to Miami, and met with Mack. As I walked in the door of Criteria, I met someone who ended up being a long-lasting friend, even today. A flaming, red-headed ball of fire named Margie Curry. She *ran* Criteria, just to be honest. A lot of companies have employees like that. Margie was someone that kept up with everything and everyone, even when she didn't need to, just because that's the kind of employee and person she was. We hit it off right from the start, but she didn't know it. She buzzed Mack and told him I was there, and he said for me to come right up.

I had never met Mack in person, but I had known of him for years. He was a very high-strung man, smart, knowledgeable, very nice to me, and expressed much admiration for the work he had heard that I had done over the past six or seven years. He explained, in detail, how all my instruments sounded, and asked me how I did that. After about thirty minutes of tech talk, he asked if I was looking for a job or just visiting. I told him my situation, and told him I wasn't even sure I wanted to stay in music. I then told him my outlandish plans, and he laughed and said, "You've got to go sailing with me as soon as possible." He had a 52-ft. Irwin, which was a $250,000 sailboat, before extras. It was a floating apartment, yet two people could sail it, because it had an automatic pilot, and that's what we ended up doing quite often.

He christened it "Danny's Dilemma," named after his wife. And after getting to know her better, it might have better been named, "Mack's Dilemma." Danny was a sweetheart, as far as I knew, but then again, I didn't have to live with her. But, I could tell that Mack could have possibly been a handful, as far as a wife is concerned. Mack, along with a guy named "Jeep" Harned, built the very first MCI Recording Machine in Jeep's garage in Ft. Lauderdale in the early 60s, I believe, and it was eventually what got MCI Recording machines, MCI gear, and Criteria off the ground in a big, big way. But all that comes later.

After Mack and I visited, he took me on a tour of the building. Criteria was a beautiful studio. It was located right off West Dixie Highway at NE 149th Street. It had four individual studios, all of them completely different from each other. In the main building, when you walk in the front door, immediately on your left, was Studio D, which was the newest of all four studios. The studio, itself, was very small, but the control room was huge. Even though the studio was tiny, I amazingly, somehow, did several string sessions in there, but it was very crowded. It had all pecky-cypress wood on the walls, which is a very absorbent wood. Therefore, it keeps sound from bouncing all over the room, and gives the engineer a totally flat response on playbacks through the speakers.

Down the first hallway on the left was Studio B, in which the console actually faced 90 degrees to the left, so you had to look to your right to look out into the studio. Down at the end of the hallway was a production room and a mastering room, with a lathe for cutting discs for vinyl. We have since gone to digital formats, so we no longer need lathes for cutting vinyl discs. Studio A, which was right in the center of the main building, had a small control room, but a huge recording studio. It also had movable walls, so you could make the room any size you wanted to simply by moving the huge, 30-foot walls, which are on casters, either in or out. The ceiling was at least 50 feet high and was very reflective, which made strings sections sound like they were in a symphony hall.

Studio C was at that time in another building, yet attached to the main building, so you had to go outside to access it, and it had more privacy for extensive sessions that could last for weeks when booked for that purpose. It had a medium-sized control room and studio, and it was good for artists who wanted to come and stay and take their time, as it had its own lounge, pinball machine, dressing rooms, parking, etc.

Right before I left Miami, they added a fifth studio, which is very unique in that it has two control rooms, one on top of the other, both with SSL consoles, and an L shaped studio. You can record in one studio while someone else is mixing in the other control room. They also have something else that is quite unique. It's a set of huge speakers, with two 18" Tad speakers as woofers and tweeters and horns, driven by Bryston amps that can be accessed by either studio. They're on an elevator that can raise them or lower them depending on which studio books them first. A very unique idea, but I don't know if it was successful or not, because I was back in Alabama by the time they had Studio E up and running. But the theory was ingenious, as far as I was concerned. The only thing about big speakers like that is the fact that they can really fool you sometimes, simply by the volume. It's always good to use midsized or even smaller speakers, too, so you can keep the sound of the record in perspective.

When Mack and I came back to the lobby, I was immediately drawn to the business office, because I wanted to get to know Margie better, plus Danny Emmerman sat at a desk right next to her. I, loving women the way I do, wanted to go flirt with them for a second, even though I didn't feel very sexy, or romantic, or anything like that. I just wanted to meet them and see what they were like. All of a sudden, from behind me, came a loud yell, "Jerry Masters! Man, I've been hearing your name and your work for so long…it would give us great honor if you would come in here for a minute and give us an opinion on this mix we just finished." I turned around, and much to my surprise, it was none other than Barry Gibb, the Chief Bee Gee. Talking about surprised, I was stunned that my reputation had gotten this far south to anyone other than Tom Dowd and Mack Emmerman. I was amazed at how well-known my name was to everyone at Criteria, especially the producers and some of the older engineers.

So, I walked into the control room of Studio D, Barry handed me a set of headphones (they always mixed on headphones), and I listened to their final mix on "Tragedy." They had just mixed it minutes before Mack and I walked into the lobby. I had never in all my life heard a record that sounded that good, that clear, an almost perfectly-mixed performance. It would go down in history, along the group itself, as one of the most noted departures from what music had been like in a genre', and would turn the entire music industry upside down. The rhythm was just perfect. The incredible vocal performances by Barry Gibb, singing the lead vocals, practically in the range of female singers, and the stacked vocal backgrounds were just stunning. I don't know how else to say that it was the best sounding record I had ever heard in my life. I felt like all my years of making and mixing records were totally for naught.

After it was over, it was deathly quiet when I took my headphones off, and finally someone said, "Well?" I hesitated for a second, and then said, jokingly of course, "It's alright." It took a minute for them to realize that I was being sarcastic. So, when I smiled at them and started laughing, they finally realized it, and then everyone fell on the floor laughing. I told them what I just told you. It had double platinum written all over it. It was recorded and mixed by Karl Richardson and producers Barry Gibb and Albhy Galuten, who was from Memphis also. We had never met up until that day, but all of our reputations had preceded that moment, so it ended up being a gathering of a "mutual admiration society."

I was quite humbled by the entire reception on my first two visits to Criteria, with the exception of Tommy Dowd's "loss of memory" that I had stopped by. What an experience. Do you know what happened to me in that twenty minutes I was in there with the Bee Gees and Karl and Albhy? Believe it or not, I FELL BACK IN LOVE WITH MUSIC. I'll swear, I couldn't even be faithful to my first love, music, which had been my destiny since it had been firmly planted in my soul that night when I was five years old, at 2016 S. Cedar St. in Little Rock, Arkansas, my home town.

I was awakened the next morning by a phone call. Both the girls were gone to work, so I had to get up and answer it. It was Mack Emmerman. He wanted me to come down and talk about the possibility of going to work for him. I told him I would be down there in a couple of hours. When I arrived, I got a big smile from Margie, which made me feel good. Even though I had been crying, I think I was hiding it quite well. Mack said he wanted me on his staff, yet he had no place for me. I said, "Well that's nice." He asked me if I minded just hanging out and watching the second engineers, how they worked, where everything was located and just getting the idea about where and how things operated down there. He said he would pay me $5.50 an hour, which I believe at the time was just a little over minimum wage, which was no surprise at all.

Of course, I had no place to live in Miami, so I had to go apartment hunting. I drove all around the studio area, but for some reason, I couldn't find anything or anyplace that appealed to me or that looked like I could afford it on $5.50 an hour. I asked someone at the studio if they knew where there might be some apartments for rent, and they suggested I go down in southwest Miami where they had more affordable housing.

So, off I went to south Miami. I went down I-95, which I soon became quite familiar with, then went west on the Dolphin Expressway to 826, then south on 826 to SW 122nd. I drove about four or five more blocks and saw some small, one-bedroom apartments that were around $250 a month with only a $200 security deposit. I found an apartment, but it seemed like hardly anyone spoke English. But that was alright. It was small, compact, and would suit me fine until I could save up some money and find a nicer place nearer the studio.

That was another problem. I had no money to get the apartment. I had run out of mammon, and I had less than a hundred dollars in my pocket. I thought about asking Mack for a quick loan, but then I thought, "I don't want to start off by having to borrow money." So I called my dear friend Jimmy Johnson in Muscle Shoals, and I had a check in two days for $500. Then I had to go back up to West Palm and get all my stuff out of storage, which meant I had to rent another trailer. Somehow, I was able to pull it off, and by the end of the week, I was settled into my abode, yet I was twenty-five miles from Criteria. But that was alright for the moment because it was a start. That's all I needed, "a start." I knew things would start happening, because that's the way it had been my entire life, and it was almost like someone else was sitting upstairs directing my life with a baton. Things always seemed to turn out the way they were supposed to, for some reason.

They teamed me up with a young kid named Kevin Ryan, from Connecticut, whose dreams were as big as the Atlantic Ocean, and I was basically an assistant to an assistant. Kevin kept reminding me over and over that he felt that the first time a 1st engineer's position opened up, he would be the obvious choice. He sort of treated me like I had never been in a recording studio in my entire life. He explained things to me that I knew like the back of my hand, but I allowed him to "teach" me the ropes, and I said nothing of my past, my history, nor my accomplishments, at all. He showed me how to wrap up a microphone cable, how to put the mics back in their proper places, and various things like that.

The one thing about MSS was the fact that we never tore our set-up down. Everything always stayed in the same place. I could go from one session to another session without having to change hardly anything except the name of the tape box. Occasionally, when we would have a complete change of recording styles, we would move things out of the way and sometimes not even use the drum booth. We did that on the Traffic album and with Lynyrd Skynyrd and Blackfoot, where we used the drum booth for a guitar amp booth, because they would literally play their guitars so loud, no one in the entire building could hear to talk on the phone. So occasionally, the two ladies who assisted us all at Sound, Diane Butler, downstairs in the Publishing Company's office, and Carol Little, up in the receptionists'/secretary's front office, would just unplug the phones and lollygag until the guitar parts were finally finished.

So Criteria's way of making records was totally different from the studio I had come from in Northwest Alabama, and it was culture shock at first. Whenever I would go around and wrap up mic cables, Kevin would come along behind me and un-wrap them, then, rewrap them, each and everyone. I just sort of smiled. I wasn't about to toot my horn one bit. I realized I had a lot to learn in the big city, so I took the education seriously. Working in the big city like that was a whole different bag than what I was used to, and I had a lot to learn. But I did know how to wrap up a mic cable, AND mix records, just between you and me (smile).

Depending on the situation, when someone wanted to book a session at Criteria to cut three songs, they would book a three-hour session. The studio manager, Jack Smith, was a dear, dear man who had lost his ability to hear after many years in the business, and who was Criteria's version of the famous Mix Magazine's humorous character, "Smiling Deaf Eddie." He would book the musicians and put in the request for outboard gear, the microphones, etc. He was basically the "man in charge" of all sessions that came through there.

When we reached our peak at Criteria, business wise, we had all four studios going around the clock, Studios A, B, C, and D—24/7. The maintenance department was the best I had ever imagined in all my life in the business. They had eight maintenance engineers, all very accomplished techs, who knew each piece of gear inside and out. When someone would book a session, they would book not only outboard gear, which was usually done by the first engineer, but also the tape machines they would need for recording and mixing. In some cases, some engineers liked to keep a quarter-inch machine running all the time just to capture things that were said or played, just for safety's sake—but, back to the three-hour session.

When the 1st engineer would walk in, he had exactly three hours to set up, get sound checks, cut the tracks, do the extra overdubs, vocals, the backing vocals, and mix the project ready for vinyl—everything within that three hour period. While at MSS, when things were normal, and with everything the way it had been the day before, I could just walk in, listen to them run the song down one time, then the next time hit the record button and record. What a difference it was. It was almost culture shock for me. But I was always hoping and waiting for that call that never came from Kathy saying, "I'm on my way to Miami." I was crying my eyes out and getting that lump in my throat again whenever I had the privacy and time to think.

There was a sun roof on the very top of the building there at Criteria, and very seldom did anyone go up there. But when I started working there, I would make a habit of going up there in the mornings when I first arrived, and I would just meditate, try to stop crying, and I would pray. I would always wake up in the mornings crying. The moment I awoke and opened my eyes, Kathy would enter my mind, and I missed her so much I would start crying immediately. I would cry all the way to the studio, at times so hard my tears prevented me from seeing well enough to drive. But I just tried to give it to God. That was my only hope.

I actually just talked to God. I would tell Him how I felt, and ask Him why He wouldn't allow Kathy and me to be together. I would thank Him for taking care of me all these years and keeping me alive, and I would cry even more. Then I would talk to Him some more. I would just literally pour my heart out to Him. It's kind of ironic that a few years later I discovered, to my surprise, that that was the best way to pray—just simply talk to Him like you would be talking to your best friend. Thankfully, He eventually became my Best Friend. But unfortunately, later on, actually within just a few weeks, I discovered something that would make me stop crying. Cocaine.

I once asked God what addiction was, and He told me that the very first time you put any kind of drug or any other addictive substance in your body, you spend the rest of your life trying to get that first, initial feeling back. But it never comes, ever. In AA they call it "chasing the dragon." Therefore, before God could become my Best Friend, I had to do something I never thought I would have to do. I had to go to hell and back. I was getting ready to begin my trip.

I chased Kevin around from studio to studio, never really telling him who I was or where I even came from. All I did was listen to him tell me how great he was and how soon he would become a 1st Engineer, which was his major goal in life. There was a session going on in studio C, across the parking lot in its own separate part of the building, with the fantastic Joe Cocker and Allen Toussaint producing. I don't know how much you know about Allen Toussaint, but he's one of the premier producers, musicians, songwriters, and icons in the entire music business, and he had been for many, many years.

He was from New Orleans and was the catalyst behind the Neville Brothers, with Aaron Neville singing those beautiful, vibrato controlled vocals, and also Ernie K-Doe, Fats Domino, Lee Dorsey, and Dr. John. In addition to those, Mr. Toussaint was a fantastic piano player and writer. He has a string of hits and productions that not only brought him to the forefront as one of the most respected and admired producers and musicians in the world, but also got him inducted into the Rock and Roll Music Hall of Fame. And on top of all that, he was also a real gentleman, and a gentle man.

They were using one of Criteria's top senior engineers, Alex Sadkin, who all of a sudden, and to the surprise of a lot of people, suddenly took a job at Compass Point Studio over in Bimini, Bahamas. He picked up and left right in the middle of Joe and Allen's session. Compass Point Studios was owned by Chris Blackwell, who produced the Traffic album, "Shoot Out At The Fantasy Factory" that I did in Muscle Shoals, and he was also the owner of Island Records.

If you'll remember, earlier in my memoirs, I told you that it seemed like I was always in the right place at the right time, all throughout my life. So Alan goes into Mack's office and they try to decide what they're going to do now after losing their crack engineer. Who could possibly take his place? Well, Mack just happened to mention that he had just hired a guy with a ton of experience. When he mentioned my name, Alan said simply, "Tell him to come on, and let's get to work."

I had met Joe Cocker a couple of years before, so I walked into the control room, sat down, and we went to work as if nothing had ever happened. It was amazing at how easily it went. And Kevin, along with the rest of the staff, just stood there with their mouths open. They could not believe what had just happened. A stranger walks in off the street and picks up one of Criteria's most prized sessions in its history, and you would have never known I hadn't started the sessions from the very beginning. Needless to say, not many people around there had very much to say to me for quite some time. They were still in shock. And I was in there working. Allen and Joe Cocker and I were just having the times of our lives, and everyone to this day has no idea how quickly I became, according to Mack about six months later, the most productive and money-making engineer in the history of Criteria, up until then.

Another thing that was so rewarding about that session was that Mr. Toussaint, after we were through with the session, called me out into the studio where no one was and told me that in all his career, he had never had such an easy time switching engineers in the middle of such an important session and having it go so smoothly. He also mentioned my professionalism and the relaxed atmosphere I created when I was in there, and how he and Joe both had never experienced so smooth a transition as the one we had to make in the middle of Joe's vocals. Coming from Alan Toussaint, that was, without a doubt, the best compliment I have ever had in my life, and I treasured every moment I spent with them. My heart did about 40 flip-flops with pride and thankfulness after that conversation.

Chapter

2I

After I had been in Miami for about six or seven months, my mom came down in her new Chevy station wagon and brought my son, Mike, my daughter, Mandy, and one of Mandy's friends. They spent their days with all the Cuban kids in the complex that were their age, and they seemed to have a good time. I was having to hide my "coke" problem from them as best I could, but I would sometimes not come home until daylight, then I'd sleep for a few hours and get up and try to be half-way social while they were there. But they didn't notice, or if they did, they didn't say anything.

They came over to the studio a couple of times and watched us record. As a matter of fact, they came over one Saturday when I had been asked to record a group from TK Records, which was partly owned by Steve Alaimo, my old friend who was in business with a guy named Henry Stone. The group was Foxy. They had a big hit out at that time, but they didn't like the drum sound they were getting over at TK Records, so they had asked if they could come over to Criteria to record. I ended up not only engineering their second album, but I was also one of the producers by the time we finished it after about six months of on and off recording. We also made a little history which I'll tell you about later.

Foxy's first hit was a giant of a disco record called "Get Off." The album I did on them was called "Hot Numbers," which was also the title of their single, and it did quite well on the disco scene. It went to number 4 on the R & B charts and also made the top 20 on the pop charts. The leader of the group was a young Cuban guy named Ish Ledesma, and the drummer of the group, who really knew what he was doing in the studio, was a friend named Joe Galdo. Whenever I make a trip to Miami now, I always have to go over to Dennis Hetzendorfer's house, where we all, including Joe Galdo, play poker. We have a great time playing quarter-limit poker.

Dennis was also a very faithful Criteria engineer who did many of the Julio Iglesia's records. They would spend weeks in studio D whenever Julio was in town. Dennis was always the assistant engineer on all of Julio's sessions. He was also a good engineer in his own right and very faithful, nice, and cordial. He had absolutely NO ego problems, whatsoever, which was not always the case with engineers that reached that level of engineering.

After I had been in Miami for a short time, there was one thing I noticed that I hadn't thought of before until I saw this beautiful red sports car sitting in the parking lot with a For Sale sign on it. Not many people in Miami drove trucks. It so happened that Mack had this Datsun 240Z, one of the very first ones made, in 1969, even though the history says it wasn't released until 1970, and it was in excellent shape. It was fire truck red and was fast as fast could be. As a matter of fact, it would go from 0 to 60 in eight seconds.

So I sold my pick-up, very quickly I might add, by advertising in the auto-trader. It sold to a paramedic for exactly what I asked, so I paid my truck off and bought Mack's 240Z. Now I felt like a true Miami native. I had more fun driving that car. One weekend I drove over to Naples, which was directly west of Miami on highway 41, on the Gulf side of Florida. It went right across the very center of the Everglades. I spent the weekend over there with Charlie Chalmers and Sandy Rhodes Chalmers, his wife, and Donna Rhodes, her sister, whom I had a slight crush on, to no avail. Their father was the famous "Dusty" Rhodes on the Grand Ole Opry.

On the way back I started feeling my oats, so I decided I'd see what that 240Z would do on the open road, since there was hardly any traffic. It was 2 a.m., and the road was straight as an arrow, but only two lanes. My 240Z had 180 on the speedometer, so I decided to see how much of that I could get out of it. I got up to 110, and it started acting like it just wanted to go faster, so I moved it on up to 120, 130, and finally 140 mph. That little red jewel absolutely loved it. I was a bit stoned at the time, had been all day. I pretty much stayed that way all the time, and I started imagining a huge alligator out strolling across the highway and what it would do to me if I hit it going 140 mph. So I slowed down to 100, and it felt like I was going 25 mph. What a rush that was. That was the only time I really pushed it hard as far as speed, but it was a fun car, and it got a lot of attention too. Edie (my present wife) even mentioned that before we'd met, she had seen me around town a couple of times and remembered me quite distinctly. A slick-headed man driving a red 240Z back then could get a few quick looks, especially from women. Boy, I thought I was a hot dog.

At one point, I was working with an artist named Stephen Bishop from Los Angeles, who had an enormous hit titled "On and On." Because of his schedule, we were literally working almost twenty hours a day for about nine straight days. The only thing keeping me going physically was cocaine. My nostrils swelled up so badly that I couldn't even breathe, and working those kinds of hours really hurts you creatively. If I had been able to rest each day and only work for seven or eight hours, I think his album would have sounded much better.

And another thing, Stephen didn't have a producer, so it was kind of like a community production with only Stephen, me, and Kevin, who was my assistant engineer. We actually over-mixed several songs by not reaching a certain point where the song sounded really good, being willing to print it, and moving on. We just mixed each song till there was nothing else you could do to make it better, and the album ended up not sounding very good. I take all the blame for letting him put that kind of pressure on us. We could have taken more time, gotten more rest, and had a much better sounding record, but we just mixed ourselves into oblivion. I promised myself I would never do that again.

I'll put it to you this way. I made a rule for myself years ago. Anything you do after seven hours in the studio, you'll probably end up coming back the next day and redoing. Most people can only take so much trauma or pressure on the ears and body from the speakers being played constantly. I believe most people in the business have seven-hour ears, no matter what they say, especially if anyone on the session—artists, musicians, producers or engineers—are doing drugs or drinking alcohol. You have to be nice to yourself and plan ahead in order to have time to finish what you started, and finish it right. One of Jerry's laws!

If you wonder how I was making so much money for Criteria, just take $175 an hour (which was their rate) and multiply it by 20 hours a day, for nine days. The studio time alone was $31,500, plus the extra equipment rental I needed for the mixing. And they were paying me $6 an hour. I did that off and on for over a year. Can you imagine how much money I was making for them?

At one point, I happened to be working with the Albert Brothers, Ronnie and Howie, remixing some Crosby, Stills, Nash and Young tracks, and I got a call from Johnny Rivers in Los Angeles. He wanted to come all the way to Miami from Los Angeles just to work with me. Mack bumped the CSNY session right on the spot, and in comes Johnny. I'm telling you, the entire place was standing on their head wondering where this bald headed, shaved headed, slow talking, Southern redneck, scrawny engineer came from and what the hell was it about him that was turning the entire place upside down. I said scrawny because at the time I only weighed 119 lbs. That was from racing dirt bikes, and I looked very emaciated. But in spite of all of that, even the bookkeepers were in shock trying to keep up with all the revenue coming in. I loved it. I was having the time of my life.

After I had been there for quite some time, and right in the middle of a session, the receptionist sticks her head in the control room and says, "Jerry, there's a Kathy on the phone for you, can you take it?" I almost told her to tell her I couldn't talk to her, but I just had to see what she had to say. Well, she didn't say much of anything. All she did was make small talk, "How are you, are you doing alright, are you enjoying living down there, etc. Well, I gotta go. Take care of yourself now. Bye." If I could have reached through that phone line, I would have taken her by the throat and… (fill in the blank). But I do have to give her credit for one thing. I found out later that she had called every recording studio in south Florida until she found me. Wasn't that nice of her?

The history I mentioned earlier about the Foxy session was the fact that I was the first engineer in the state of Florida, if not in the United States, to use 48 tracks by locking up two 24-track machines on the entire album. MCI had built a lock-up device that would use SMPTE time code (which is like a very precise clock down to one thousandth of a second) on each tape, and it was the common denominator to keep both machines running right along with each other in order to have more tracks to record on. So you say, "Why?" When you have groups like Foxy, they liked to do what we called "stack" vocals. If you sing a harmony part to a song, then go back to the top and do the same thing again, but on a different track, you get what we call a "rub." In other words, two vocals singing the same thing on several tracks sound like a whole bunch of different people singing along, but perfectly together, and it sounds smoother, bigger, and better.

So every time we would do a harmony part, we would stack it three or even four times, then do another harmony part, stack it three or four times, then one more harmony track, for a three part harmony, yet each vocal was sung four times. I just can't tell you on paper how good that sounds. But you have to have a lot of tracks to do that. So, we would cut the basic track, bass, drums, guitar, keyboard of some kind, and piano or such. So there you've used eight tracks for drums, two for stereo guitar, bass, and piano, left and right, stereo. So that's as much as 14 tracks we used just to cut the basic track. We still had percussion, lead guitar, another rhythm guitar, horns, strings possibly, and lead vocals. That's already more than 20 tracks, and it doesn't even include background vocals which need each part stacked. Follow me?

When we first started making records in the early 60s, we had only one track to work with. We would do the entire performance at one time, including the fade and lead vocal—everything. If anyone made the slightest mistake, everyone had to stop and start all over again until everyone got it perfect all the way through, with not one single mistake. That was not easy to do. So having our 48 tracks made making a quality, great-sounding record so much easier. It didn't necessarily "sound" any better quality wise, but we were able to do things with vocals and stuff we had never done before.

Of course, using 48 tracks like that at Criteria was also quite costly, because we had to use two rolls of 2" tape for each four or five tunes, and we had to use an extra 24-track tape recorder. So, we would have a master tape and a slave tape. They had to pay for all of that tape, plus we had to pay rent on the MCI lock-up system they had created just a few weeks before our session. Criteria Studios was MCI's testing ground. Criteria was Jeep Harned's experimental studio where MCI tried all their new equipment before they put it on the market for sale. Even when they would invent new consoles, they would come install them in a particular studio and have us work on them for weeks before they would even consider putting them on the market for sale to their distributors all over the world.

As a matter of fact, we had a major part in the designing of the MCI 600 series console, simply by using it and making suggestions to improve it in certain areas...move this section over to that section, and so on. We were the ones that had to use these pieces of equipment for hour upon hour and year after year, so our input was invaluable to MCI. At that time, MCI was one of the top-of-the-line equipment manufacturers, and Mack and Jeep started the entire operation up in Ft. Lauderdale in Jeep's garage many years before.

When I was completely finished with the Foxy album, the Bee Gees came in right behind me, in the same studio, using the exact same equipment to record a new album. They were hotter than a firecracker at the time, and they had to keep the hits a coming. They were selling millions upon millions of records, and it's important to keep your momentum up, or you'll lose your audience and your market share, and theirs was HUGE. They went through the same processes we did, used the same SMPTE time code, cut all their tracks, mixed all their tracks over to their slave machine, and did all their stacking of vocals, which took weeks of hard work.

After about three months of long, hard labor and extremely long hours of work, when they got ready to mix, they hooked their master machine back up to their slave machine, which had all of their hard-earned back up vocals, but they could NEVER get the machines to lock up. They were so angry, disappointed, pissed, and just went totally ballistic with MCI to no avail. They lost every one of those vocals they did. They tried for weeks and weeks to figure out how I was able to do my entire project without ANY problems, not one, yet they were dead in the water. They lost their entire session and had to start all over again. They had every technical engineer at MCI down there trying to figure out why it no longer worked, but it NEVER worked for them.

Do you think perhaps someone was showing me favor? Would it make you stop and think for a minute why it worked for so long and so perfectly for me? Yet they come in right behind me with superior engineers, or at least someone might perceive that they were better or more proficient. It remains to be seen; just hold on. You'll find out why in just a few more pages.

I want to pay homage to a friend and peer I had while working at Criteria who meant so much to me. Not only while I was down there, but even afterwards he remained dear to me. He has gone to be with the Lord, at a very young age, too. His name was Steve Gursky, and I loved him more than any guy I've ever worked with, other than Steve and Gregg at Sound. We hit it off immediately.

The first time we ever went out to eat dinner together (which we ended up doing often) it was less than a week after I had been there, and we went to a Hungarian restaurant on Biscayne Blvd. at about 138th or 139th street. We were there for at least three hours. We had such a good time, and I have no idea what I ate there, but it really didn't matter. We bonded immediately, just like blood brothers, but it was musical blood at first. Much later we bonded again, because Steve had recently developed a relationship with the Lord, and his life was totally changed. I wasn't aware of his changed life until a few years after it happened, but it was very important to me.

Steve died at his mother's house in Ft. Lauderdale on November 20, 2005, of heart failure. He was only 55 years old. I learned so much from that guy, and the last time we talked on the phone, just a few weeks before he died, he was telling me how much he had learned from me. The day you stop learning from the people around you, you might as well just go on and check out. That's the whole meaning of life to me, learning, one from another, and changing and being willing to change.

Something else I learned from Steve Gursky was love, unconditional love, agape love, the God-kind of love. He was my brother with another mother. He was a special man, and I miss him. So, between Steve Gursky, Margie Curry, and of course Margaret, another dear friend who worked there and was a pal of Margie's, I made some very dear and lifelong friends while I was there in Miami.

My biggest problem, of course, was my mental condition because of my broken heart, plus the cocaine, and trying to get Kathy out of my craw, which caused me to drink very heavily. I almost died several times while alone in my apartment. I would go on binges, usually about three days. I wouldn't eat, sleep, brush my teeth, shower, or take care of myself in any way. All I would do was snort a gram of coke over a period of about two or three hours, then get so wired I'd have to drink at least a fifth of scotch to come down; then I would get so drunk I'd have to go back and get more coke to wake me back up; then back to the scotch, and back and forth, and back and forth.

Please don't think that this was a constant thing for me to do. It would just be every month or so, and sometimes I would go several weeks without going on one of these binges. Of course, the longer I was down there, the more often it would happen. There were times when I didn't know where I had been or what I had done. It was just total insanity.

One morning about 9 or 9:30, I awoke in a pool of blood on the steps of my apartment building, about two or three steps down from the front door of my apartment. Someone had stabbed me in the back. I had a severe stab wound in my back, but I was too blitzed to go to the ER or call anyone. I just went into my apartment, put a towel on the bed, took about seven or eight (10 mg.) valiums, and slept for about eighteen hours, at least.

The cut was only about two or three inches long, but deep and only in the muscle, and the pain was very intense when I came back to my senses, which was quite some time. I was alone in the apartment, and the only door was locked and bolted. I was lying on my right side, away from the door in the fetal position with my hands between my knees. Staying in that position, all of a sudden my bed just started jumping up and down like someone had their giant hands under the mattress and was picking it up and dropping it, over and over, but very fast. I was so frightened, I couldn't move. I couldn't roll over and see who it was; I couldn't move at all. I was literally paralyzed with fear. After approximately ten minutes of this, it stopped, and I simply went back to sleep. I knew that the devil himself had been in my apartment and had tried to take my life, but my Lord had other plans for me, and I believe that my guardian angel fought him off.

That act of total disregard for my life gave me a real wake-up call. I started realizing then that I was going to have to make some serious changes in my life, or I was going to run out of life in Miami. I had to start being careful who I hung out with, and I started playing racquetball more often, trying to sweat some of that poison out of my body and just trying and get my body back in shape physically. Like I mentioned earlier, I was down to about 119 lbs. when I arrived in Miami, and the only thing that was keeping me from wasting away was all of the Italian food I was eating, plus I was drinking a lot of red wine with it.

Chapter

22

I had so many interesting sessions during the time I worked at Criteria. A lot of our clients came up from South America, and one gentleman came in from Trinidad. When he walked into the control room, he handed me a paper sack, and in the paper sack was his tape he wanted me to mix. It seems he had it on a hub, instead of a reel, which means the wrap on the tape had no protection, and it all came apart. So I had to find the beginning of the tape and slowly, by hand, rewind it all back onto a reel, about seven or eight songs. Thank goodness it was only one-half inch tape. Any other size would have been much harder. When we finally got through rewinding the tape, I had to mix it, and he walked out of there in total disbelief that what he had on tape could sound so good. He had a grin on his face that probably took two weeks to wipe off. He had no idea how good his material sounded until I got hold of it.

I know I'm bragging now, but so many people talked about how good I was as an engineer and the fact that I had the Master's touch, but the reality was that I had been doing it for so long, it just came to me naturally. And it was also a gift that had been given to me by my Father, not my natural father, but my Heavenly Father. It was what I called a "been there, done that" type of situation. There was hardly a situation that could happen in the studio that I had not at one time or another faced or had to deal with. But in my heart, I knew I had a lot more to learn, and it was soon to come as the years rolled past. I was given a gift, and I used it the very best I could.

Another session that was probably one of the biggest and most complex sessions I had ever done in my life was with a gentleman from Puerto Rico that was South America's answer to Henry Mancini. He was a genius when it came to writing and arranging. We had worked together before on a couple of simple tracking sessions, but this time he put a session on me that I thought I would never be able to do.

You know I told you earlier about studio A, and how you could move the walls in and out and pretty much make the studio any size you wanted to. Would you believe I almost had to have the moving walls removed from the studio for this session? Now dig this, and you've got to understand something here, we did this session totally live, with no overdubs or anything. It was all live. We did the rhythm section, bass, drums, guitar, piano, guitar, and a full orchestra, a 16-piece live orchestra and a full string session. There were approximately sixteen to eighteen horns, reeds, brass, flutes, piccolos, French horns, a harp, and a 22-piece string or symphony orchestra, plus, background singers, and the lead vocal, all at the same time, LIVE!! And we somehow put it all on 23 tracks, saving one track for automation when we mixed, which we did as soon as we got through recording.

We did five songs and mixed, and we did it all, including sound checks, in three hours. I usually take at least an hour to do sound checks on just a rhythm section under normal circumstances. And let me tell you something, people were coming in there from all over the building. This guy's arranging was so beautiful, if you've ever heard Henry Mancini's songs and productions, it was just as good, but it was all in Spanish. God, it was so beautiful.

Once I got all the sound going, and we ran the first song down before recording, I thought I was in recording heaven. I can't even remember his name, either. And another thing, he spoke NO English and I spoke NO Spanish, yet we communicated perfectly. He would say something to me in Spanish and I knew exactly what he was trying to say, and he understood me the same way. It was just incredible. I guess it was because we were speaking in "music." It was supernatural. The entire thing was just plain supernatural the way it all went down. It was making music and recording it at its very best. It was the epitome of recording. Now that's a pretty big word for a high school graduate from Arkansas, isn't it?

Another fun session was trying to get Burt Reynolds to sing. Yeah, Burt Reynolds—a very real, fun and talented guy. He was doing the music for "Smokey and the Bandit 2," in which the entire movie plot is centered around a song he was trying to promote called "Let's Do Something Cheap and Superficial." Snuff Garrett from Los Angeles was the well-known producer. They had already done all the music, and they needed to put Burt's vocal on, so they chose Criteria and me.

Burt had a club right up the road in Jupiter, Florida, just a couple of miles north of West Palm Beach. Of course, Burt was all nervous and afraid he wasn't going to sound good, and said he was depending on me to make him sound like Frank Sinatra. I told him, "Burt, there is not one single button on this console that says TALENT." He got a big kick out of that. After I made some more jokes and just treated him like a regular guy, he started to relax.

Burt really is just another guy like you and me. He's what I call a "man's man." He just acts real. He has no "Holly-Weird Air" about him—he's just a regular guy. So after he got out there and heard himself in the headphones, with some nice sounding echo, we knocked it out in about an hour and a half, and he went away very pleased. All in all, it was a lot of fun, and he invited me up to his club in Jupiter and told me he would give me the VIP treatment, but I never got the chance to drive up there. I should have, but I don't like to be fussed over, and I'm sure he would have made a fuss over me being up there, because he was so relieved by the fact that it was so painless to get his vocal.

I also did a lot of recording with a group called "Dr. Hook" and their producer Ron Haffkine from Nashville, who was also in business with Shel Silverstein, who so happened to shave his head like I did. Everyone kept wondering who Dr. Hook was, but in reality, it was simply the name of the group, and there wasn't a person named Dr. Hook per se'. The guys that did most of the work and had those incredible voices were Ray Sawyer and Dennis Locorriere. Ray was the one with the worn-out old cowboy hat and the eye patch, which was caused by an auto accident in '67. Dennis sported nothing but a beard and a terrific voice, so the both of them, who were also famous for their antics on stage, were the main part of the group.

Their first big hit was "Sylvia's Mother," and the story that surrounds that record is quite interesting. It seems that Shel Silverstein, my slick-headed buddy and very talented poet and author, wrote all of the music for a movie titled "Who Is Harry Kellerman and Why Is He Saying All These Terrible Things About Me?" in which Ron Haffkine was the musical director. Ron had received a demo from Dr. Hook, and Shel liked what he heard, so he went up to New Jersey and heard them. He hired them to do the music for the entire movie, which included "Sylvia's Mother."

They also had a big hit called "On the Cover of Rolling Stone." We did an album, or should I say we finished an album, called "Pleasure and Pain" that was begun in MSS by my good friend engineer Steve Melton, so the sound was outstanding. We did mostly vocals and some guitar overdubs. Shel was also a poet, and I did a lot of editing of Shel's poems with Ron, and that's how we originally met. When the three of us, Shel, Ron, and I would go out to dinner, we got a lot of stares, because it was so unusual to see TWO people with their heads shaved back in those days. I had shaved mine in 1975 right after I met Kathy, because of the dust and mud that would get in what hair I had left, which was quite long, yet very thin, and always looked the best when it was dirty. When I washed it, like I said earlier, it stuck out and made me look like Bozo the clown. I kept my head shaved for many, many years, and eventually everyone started shaving theirs. I, being the rebel at heart that I was, had to finally give up and let my hair grow out, at least what little I had.

But back to Shel, who was a poet and author, and I might add, an author of many successful children's books as well. Haffkine released several albums on Shel, and I did the editing, which was quite easy, but very time consuming. I had to do all of the editing by razor blade, where as now we do it electronically, and it only takes seconds, but the poems Shel wrote were quite interesting.

I also did an LP on an artist by the name of Cheryl Lynn, who had a big hit in '77 called "To Be Real." She was produced by a gentleman from England named Barry Blue. Of course, like most of the producers I worked with, we became quite good friends. As a matter of fact, we went sailing together on the 4th of July on a 36' Islander. With Barry being from England, and our celebrating our freedom from Britain on the 4th of July, for the fun of it, while out in the middle of Biscayne Bay, we calmly and much to his surprise, threw him in the ocean. We forgot to ask him if he could swim, but he was able to dog paddle long enough for us to tack around and come get him back on board.

Mandy was with us then, also, as she was every summer I lived in Miami, and my new gal friend Becky, a very beautiful lady from North Carolina who I was extremely attracted to. (If you think I became celibate when I moved down there, you are very mistaken.) One summer when Mandy went home just in time to start school the next day, she walked right past her mother, and her own mother didn't even recognize her. We had bought her some new clothes; she had a new "Miami" hairdo and was so tanned she looked like an African-American. Her mother didn't recognize her when she got off the plane until she walked up and said, "Mother, it's me, your daughter Mandy," and her mother almost fainted.

But we always had a good time when we were down there. Mandy met a friend across the street from where we lived. There was a restaurant where most of Criteria's personnel, including Mack and Danny, would go for lunch every day. The owner had a daughter Mandy's age that lived up in Hollywood, Florida, and they became instant friends. I sometimes wouldn't see her for days, yet I knew she was in safe hands. Also, she had a good head on her shoulders, and I trusted her completely. She also started hanging out with some of the popular groups that came in there to record. She was traveling in pretty fast company, but there was always someone in the group of young people that kept an eye on her and made sure no one took advantage of her. Let's just say that three summers in Miami helped Mandy grow up pretty fast, but no drugs and no alcohol. Those were my rules, and she was faithful not to break them.

I think one of the most fun things I did while living in Miami was sailing for the first time, I mean REAL sailing. I already mentioned the 36' Islander, which was owned by one of our maintenance engineers, Henry Saskowski. Henry was a delightful guy. He actually lived on his boat up in Ft. Lauderdale. It would comfortably sleep at least six, and in all reality sleep up to ten, if necessary. It was just after Christmas, and we had a break in the action at Criteria, so Henry and I, Kevin and his sister, and a couple of other friends of Henry's decided we would take a couple of weeks off and go over to the Bahamas and spend New Year's with the Bahamians. They love to party and celebrate over there, especially during the holiday season, and you can always find something going on somewhere there. We also took CC with us on the trip. CC was Criteria Cat, a feline that just walked in the door of the studio one day, and we adopted him.

So we sent a couple of the old salts, who had made long trips like this before, to the store to stock up on provisions for the trip. We contributed $100 apiece, and they went and stocked up on everything they thought we would need. I had given my Ben Franklin to one of the guy's, and for some reason, he didn't report to Henry, our captain, exactly who paid what. We made sure that they bought plenty of beer, which was the most important provision, of course. Then six or seven of us made the maiden voyage over to Bimini on the 30th of December. We planned on docking in Bimini and spending New Year's Eve there.

We all wanted to watch the bowl games on TV, so Henry took his TV. He normally had it hooked up to cable when he was docked in Ft. Lauderdale, but when we reached Bimini, we needed to buy an antenna. When we finally docked in Bimini, after about a seven-hour motorized trip, I climbed up the mast and put the TV antenna at the very top. We then ran a coaxial cable from the antenna down to the TV so we could pick up the major network stations in Miami, which was only about 50 miles from there. We didn't sail over, because the seas were a little rough out in the Gulf Stream, and we didn't feel like tacking all the way over with no direct, steady winds. So we just motored over.

Most sailboats that size have a small engine to use until they get out on open water where they can pick up breezes and start sailing. I think the greatest thing about going out in a seagoing sailboat is when you actually cut the small motor off and then just depend on the wind and the seas. CC did not like the vibration of that engine at all, so he just found a hiding place and stayed there till we docked.

The Gulf Stream, which is like a huge deepwater river, runs north from the lower Caribbean all the way up to above Iceland, and it constantly runs about 5 to 6 knots per hour. That's what keeps Miami so warm in the wintertime. The warm water from the Gulf Stream and the south winds blowing across the top of the warm water from down south keeps south Florida sub-tropic most of the year. So the idea is that when you leave Miami and set your compass to go to a certain place east of Miami, you have to allow for the Gulf Stream when you set your compass. If you vary off your compass even a couple of degrees, you'll end up either north or south of your intended destination.

We left about midnight on the 30th of December and arrived in Bimini about 8:00 the next morning. It wasn't a fun trip because of having to use the motor, but it was the best way to get there, taking the weather into consideration. We sailed in shifts the entire trip, so each person could get some rest, and all we had to do was stay on course. By the time daylight came, up came the beautiful sun, and we could see Bimini. We spent all New Year's Eve Day cleaning the ship, going into the village, and just having fun being together.

About 11 p.m., as small a village as Bimini was, they had a parade down the main drag. You should have seen some of the costumes. They were beautiful in one way, but very voodoo inspired in another way. Voodoo is very popular in the Bahamas and seems to be the religion of the islands, but it's an evil force that is very spiritual and controls many lives there. So after the New Year's Eve parade down the main drag of Bimini, we sat around all the next day and watched some of the bowl games on TV. I think my team got creamed by Alabama in the Sugar Bowl, but you usually see the Arkansas Razorbacks on New Year's Day as much as any of the other teams that make bowl games a priority each year.

Also that afternoon, we did a phone patch on Henry's ham radio set, and I was able to talk to Mandy for a while. When I told her exactly where I was and what we were doing, she wasn't a bit surprised, because she knew me, she knew Henry, and she even knew the boat because she had been on it on the 4th of July when we threw Barry Blue into the ocean. We had contacted another ham radio operator in Nashville, Tennessee, who then had patched our transmission into his phone system, called Mandy collect, then patched us in together, and it was so cool. It thrilled me to talk to my favorite girl in the world on New Year's Day.

On January 2nd, we left Bimini and headed north for about 20 miles, then went east around the north side of the islands and across the Bahama Banks. The Bahama Banks was a large body of water between the northernmost island and Paradise Island, which is where Nassau is located. They called them banks because they were so shallow; the entire area never was any deeper than maybe 40 or 50 feet, but averaged about 20 feet in probably 75% of the area.

The trip across the Banks, which took us most of the evening and night, was where I realized we were right smack dab in the middle of the Bermuda Triangle. It was about 4 a.m., I was sailing the boat, and the only other creature awake was CC. We had the sails trimmed real tight, and we were really moving, almost 12 knots an hour. The depth of the water never got deeper than 20 feet. I had to constantly keep my eyes on the compass and the depth finder while sailing. If we ever got in water less than ten feet deep, we would be in serious trouble, because we were drawing nine feet in Henry's boat. That meant his keel was almost seven feet long.

Everyone else was asleep, and all of a sudden, the wind just stopped and the sails went limp. I looked down at the compass, and it was just spinning around and around. It was like someone had a giant magnet and was just winding it around the compass. I had no idea where we were or which way we were pointed. So I woke Henry up and told him what had happened, and he said, "Welcome to the Triangle."

There was some kind of strange feeling that we were sitting in infinity, but were frozen in place. Before we stopped, we had a 12 to 13 knot wind coming out of the southwest, then all of a sudden, the wind completely changed directions and started coming out of the northeast. It was the strangest thing I had experienced in my life on a sailboat. Finally Henry got us back on our heading, which had changed considerably, and we proceeded to the open water of the Atlantic Ocean.

As we left the Banks, the water went quickly from 20' to 800' deep. As we approached a small island on the Atlantic side, we went around to the other side of the island and docked in a small bay where there was hardly any wind. We found a good spot about 100 feet off shore and anchored. We had a master plan we intended to carry out. This small island was where cruise ships would anchor and send hordes of tourists onto shore to eat, drink, snorkel, and just frolic in the water and sand. They even put up volleyball nets, set up three bars, several booths where they had cooks come ashore early to cook hamburgers, hot dogs, etc., and lots of beverages, either soft or hard.

The island was less than 1500 feet wide and about three blocks long, and by anchoring in the bay, it gave us protection from the wind from the north, south, and west. So being settled in the bay, we just chilled for a few hours. We knew that about 2:00 o'clock that afternoon, a cruise ship was going to weigh anchor just the other side of the island and bring about 200 tourists onto the island for an afternoon of fun. About 1:45 p.m., we took our dinghy and rowed ashore and walked the short distance to where the guys were getting the food and drinks ready. We also had some time to challenge them to a couple of volleyball games before the people arrived from the ship.

Once the people got there, we just pretended to be in their group. We ate, drank, and made merry with them for about three hours.

Man, those hamburgers were so good, and the booze was just what it was supposed to be. But most of all, it was FREE. We stayed there for about three days and repeated our little intrusions every afternoon. It seems that that particular place was a scheduled stop for all the cruise ships on a particular cruise line, and they would come one right behind the other. What was really funny was when the people would start to get on their boats and start motoring back to their ship, we would be left there, just sitting on the beach and waving goodbye to them. At one point I was just sitting there thinking about how nice it would be to just stay there all the time and live off the afternoons of cruise ship frolicking for the rest of my life.

Before we left Bimini, a couple of our guys had to take a Chalk's seaplane back to Miami to go to work (but we also had a couple of charming friends join us a few days later). We anchored right off of Nassau, or Paradise Island. Henry took the dinghy to the main island and hitch-hiked in the back of an old pick-up full of hay to the airport. They made it to the airport and picked up Bruce Hensal, another engineer from Criteria, who flew over and landed at the major airport in Nassau along with his girl friend who was a flight attendant for Delta Airlines. We proceeded on from there for another ten days of looking around the Bahamas, just seeing if there were any other places we could get into trouble.

One other quick thing; when you're on an extended cruise on a sailboat like that, you have to really conserve your fresh water, because you can only carry so much. So, when we would wash dishes after a meal, we would take all the dirty dishes, and two of us would get in the dinghy and go out and wash them in the ocean water. Then, we would get back on the boat and rinse the salt water off of them with about two inches of fresh water in the sink, then dry them and put them away. That way we conserved our drinking water, and if you're wondering, we always used ecologically safe dish washing liquid in the ocean, so as not to pollute the Atlantic. Color us green.

During that entire time, and as a matter of fact the only time EVER in a sailboat, I got stuck only once by getting into shallow water. It was at a place in the Eastern Bahamas called Chub Cay. We tried backing out, but eventually we had to get a "smoke pot" (that's what we called motor boats) to finally pull us out of the sand. Like I said earlier, Henry's Islander only drew about 7 or 8 feet, which means that's how long his keel was, and we always kept our eyes on our depth finder. But, coming into Chub Cay, someone wasn't paying any attention, and "me thinks it were the captain." While we were at Chub Cay, they had a real swanky place to dine, so we put on our finest rags and went in and had ourselves a feast of steak, lobster, baked potatoes, salads, lots of wine, and made a real evening out of it. I almost died that night of "nutrition" (smile).

There was just one more major incident that I've got to tell you about as far as this trip was concerned. It was the "icing on the cake" of the entire trip. We were cutting across the middle of the islands on our way back to Miami. It was one of the most beautiful days we had on the entire trip: 85 degrees, the humidity about 70%, and just enough breeze for us to make about 9 knots an hour. All of a sudden we spotted these big things in the water that looked like bales of hay. They were about the size of small cows. As we pulled up alongside of one, we grabbed it and pulled it into the boat.

About the same time, we heard this noise behind us, and just in time, we saw the tail of a giant whale that had leaped out of the water and was headed back down. We got pictures of his tail and figured him to be about 180 feet long. A huge whale and what turned out to be a bale. It was a huge bale of Marijuana, and it was so wet it felt like it weighed a 1000 lbs. We took it, opened the cowling over the motor, and placed it on the motor to dry it out as much as possible before we got back to Miami. And you'd better believe we kept our eyes and ears open for any planes, choppers, or speed boats. We knew it was cartel drugs, but didn't know specifically whose.

When we left Miami we had had to report to the Coast Guard the name of the boat, the registration number, how many souls were on board, and their NAMES. We were supposed to check back with them and let them inspect the boat the moment we returned, but we didn't. We went straight to Felix Pappalardi's house where our cars were parked. I failed to mention that two of my dearest friends in Miami were Felix and his wife, Gail Collins. Felix was, without a doubt, one of the sweetest, most sincere and loving men I've ever known, and I miss him very, very much. Felix played bass with a group called "Mountain" and was also the producer of the much more famous super-group "Cream," with Jack Bruce, Eric Clapton and Ginger Baker.

Felix lost his life in 1983 when Gail shot him while he was in bed asleep because of her jealousy over Felix's alleged adulterous affairs. That was such a surprise to me, because Gail never seemed to be that kind of person to me, nor did Felix. They often had me over to their home for dinner and just fun. We all had mutual respect for each other's success, as Gail was a real artist in her own right. We had a wonderful relationship, and I'll never forget either one of them. The last I heard, Gail was living somewhere in Europe.

So we headed straight for Felix's house, docked the boat, put the bale of grass in MY trunk, and everyone split as fast as they could. We were all out of there in ten minutes, then Henry sailed back up to his home port in Ft. Lauderdale. Henry said that the Coast Guard called him a couple of days later and scolded him for not checking in when we came ashore. I took the bale to my apartment, went out and borrowed as many fans as I could find, and spread it all out on the floor of my living room on the top of bed sheets. And did it stink! It smelled like dead fish. It stunk to high heaven for at least a week. If my landlord had walked into my apartment while I wasn't there, or if he had even knocked on the door, I would probably still be in jail.

But to make a long story short, I eventually got it all dried out. We filled up nine large garbage bags, and we sold it for $9,000 with the exception of the six grocery sacks I filled for our own personal use. Split six ways, it was a very profitable trip, not to mention one of the most fun things I had done in a long, long time. Thank you for inviting me, Henry.

And one other thing—the entire trip, Henry had assumed that I had not contributed to the cost of the provisions until the very last day when I told him I had given $100 to his friend who had bought the supplies. He felt like a fool. That entire trip he had made himself miserable thinking about me trying to get a free ride and a free trip, and all he had to do was ask, and he would have had a much, much more peaceful trip, instead of one filled with anger towards me. There's a lesson to be learned in there, if you will just meditate on it for a while.

Chapter

23

I also was involved in the recording of a group called the "Henry Paul Band." Henry had formerly been with the Outlaws and had decided to go out on his own, so he came to Criteria and did an album called "Grey Ghost," which was dedicated to Ronnie Van Zant, lead singer with Lynyrd Skynyrd. Ronnie had died tragically in a plane crash a few years earlier in south Mississippi. Henry was a kindred soul, and we hit it off right from the start due to our mutual respect for the past accomplishments we both had made. So it was a very smooth recording, and I made some great friends because of it. They also did a concert out in the boonies of Ft. Lauderdale in a place called the "Sunrise Theater." All I can say is, if you've never been there and you go looking for it the first time, be careful of what you're smoking, and get explicit directions. I liked to never have found it.

They opened for the Allman Brothers Band, and it was a night full of Southern rock and roll like you wouldn't believe. There was a lot of Jack Daniels Black being consumed that night straight from the bottle, most of it right on stage, to the audience's delight, for some reason. But the music was kickin' and I barely remember the drive home. Boy was I a mess at that time in my life. It was only by God's grace that I survived things like that. It took a while, but He eventually yanked the slack out of my rope, and I will be eternally grateful. Believe me, I will.

There was another session that I did that I had almost forgotten, and that's strange, because it could have changed the course of my life at the time. There was a singer from Israel, who was also an actress, who had starred in the movies Casino Royale (a James Bond movie) and The Silencers, with Matt Helm played by Dean Martin. Her name was Daliah Lavi, and she was absolutely out of this world, movie star beautiful, but was just as nice and sweet as she could be. She was so far out of my league that I didn't even think about anything except making her voice sound half as good as she looked. She had done all of the music in Israel, and the tracks were awesome, to say the least, but they weren't very funky. But not everything has to be funky these days.

We took about a week to do all of her vocals, at which time I spoke with her quite a bit about Israel, specifically because I loved Israel so much and would have loved to spend the rest of my life over there. I had read the book of Exodus in the Bible while I was stationed in Okinawa, and I had immediately fallen in love with Israel. I have always been very concerned about their plight to simply live in peace, and even more so today.

As I talked to Daliah, I found out that one of her best friends in Israel was the wife of Moshe Dyan, who was the military commander in Israel at that time, I believe (if not then, at least shortly before). Daliah's friend had many close friends in the Israeli Army, or the IDF. So, as I told her how much I loved Israel and wanted to live there, we also ended up talking about what I had done when I was in the army. She found it extremely interesting and she said she would talk to her friend about the possibility of me using my abilities in the security section of the IDF. She did talk to her friend and said the possibility was quite high that they could use my training for their needs in communications intelligence.

I was so excited. The first thing I did was call Mandy to tell her. Mandy got real quiet and then started crying. I asked her what was wrong, and she said, "If you move to Israel, I will never get to see you again." I had never thought about that. So I pondered on it for a couple of days, and then I called Daliah at home and told her I wouldn't be able to follow up on this wonderful opportunity. She said she totally understood, but that the door would always be open. I wanted very strongly to be a part of Israel's struggle to live in peace, but I had to let it go.

Daliah and her husband did stop and take the time to buy me a beautiful black silk blouse, and not only that, they took me to The Forge the last night of the session. I had the time of my life eating the best filet mignon, The Forge's famous potato skins, and the best merlot wine I had consumed in a long, long time. We ended up with an album full of fantastic vocals, to boot. So not all was lost, and I made a great friend in Daliah Lavi and her husband. What was his name? I could never take my eyes off her long enough to find out.

It wasn't long after that that business was so slow at the studio, it was getting to where I didn't have the money to make a car payment any longer or keep the car up the way it needed to be. I knew someday, if it was well taken care of, it would be worth a fortune because of the good shape it was in and also being one of the first ones made. So I put an ad in the paper, and it didn't take long for me to get a buyer. As the ad was being run in the Miami Herald, I went up to the Honda shop and checked out their road bikes. Being a Suzuki man myself, because they always had the market on dirt bikes, I always felt like Honda had the market on road bikes, with the exception of Harley Davidson, of course. They had two slightly used 400cc bikes for sell at a very reasonable price. One of them had a small dent in the gas tank, so I went for the other one. It was maroon in color and only had about 450 miles on it, so I got them to hold it for me until my car sold, which was not a long time at all.

All of a sudden I was a road biker for the first time. And to be honest, it wasn't that bad. With a road bike, traffic suddenly takes on a whole new dimension. I could weave in and around cars that were in long lines and take short cuts that cars couldn't take. I was having fun with it. I couldn't carry a lot of things on it, but I could carry all I needed for one person. So I was now the proud owner of my first road bike. I might also mention that I ended up dating for a while the young lady that bought my car, but she tired of my drug use very quickly, and that started me to really thinking about my lifestyle.

Living in Miami and working at Criteria was probably one of the most memorable seasons of my life. Another thing I did on a pretty regular basis was go sailing with Mack. Mack had a 52' Irwin that I mentioned before, which is actually a yacht. It even had a huge king-size bed and bedroom below, along with a kitchen, bar, shower, you name it. It was a luxury yacht at its very best. It was a huge boat, and most importantly, it had an automatic pilot. That means that I could trim the sails while Mack was down below rolling us a joint.

Mack would always have our lunch catered. They would bring it to us just before we cast off, and we would store it until we got hungry, usually sandwiches or salads of some sort. We had more fun, just the two of us, on the open seas, sometimes listening to soft jazz, or just listening to the boat splitting the waves. I'm sure he will always keep those times deep in his heart, as do I. And every time we would start heading for home, there would be a school of dolphins on both sides of us. It was almost like they were our escorts back into Miami, protecting us, and welcoming us back after being out all day.

Living in Miami was very eye-opening. I enjoyed that city like none other at the time, but things were starting to change very quickly there, and I knew at a certain time that my days in Miami were beginning to be numbered. Then I met Edie. Before I go any further, let me introduce you to two other friends I met down there that were important in my life.

The first one is Mike Lewis. Mike was a string arranger who did 99% of the string arrangements that came through Criteria. I must have done at least 50 string sessions with Mike while I was at Criteria. He always requested me, because for some reason, he thought I got the best string sound of all the other engineers. And that was unusual, because up until I came to Miami, I had never done a string session in my life. And when given my first chance to do strings, I did it the best way I thought it should be done, which was totally unlike how any of the other engineers did them. Maybe that's why my way was the way Mike preferred. It was fresh and new as far as string sounds went.

I remember once I was doing a huge string recording, and I had Schoeps German-made stereo mics from Mack's personal stash in his office. I put them way up high in Studio A during a large string session, and before I actually turned the mics on, I looked at the peak meters of the console, and they we going crazy on the high frequency end. I wondered what could be causing that kind of reaction to the mics, yet it wasn't audible to me in the control room. This was about the time they were having riots in Liberty City, which was less than ten miles from where we were in northwest Miami. So, out of curiosity I walked outside into the parking lot only to see two huge Huey military helicopters hovering right above the studio. That satisfied my curiosity as to why the peak meters were going crazy. I couldn't start recording until they left, so I started waving at them to please move, covering my ears and pointing toward the recording studio. They finally got the picture and moved a couple of blocks.

When I would stand on my balcony across the street and look toward Liberty City during that awful time in Miami, it looked like what Atlanta must have looked like when it was burning during the Civil War. I never could understand why certain cultures choose to destroy their own neighborhoods and towns when they throw those fits of anger and frustration. You would think they would want to go destroy their enemies' neighborhoods. Oh well, just thinking out loud.

So back to Mike Lewis and my other friend Peter Graves. Mike Lewis, in addition to being a terrific friend (and he is to this day), was just a few months older than I. On my 40th birthday, in December of 1979, he gave me a Miami Dolphin's sweatshirt with the number 40 on it, which was a "hand me down" from his 40th birthday just a few months before. I might also mention that I became a huge fan of the Miami Dolphins football team while living there, and I remain so to this day. I went to many of their home games, and we had a ball.

Peter Graves was a producer and arranger, but mostly horns and record productions. At the time, he was producing a record for an artist named Edie Jelke, who was married to a very wealthy man. When her husband asked her what she wanted for her birthday, she said she wanted to go into a recording studio and make a record for the Lord. She had recently been converted to Christianity and was born-again after reading the book "The Late Great Planet Earth" by Hal Lindsay. So she was on fire for the Lord, but her husband couldn't care less. But he wanted to please her, so he gave her $20,000 to cut three sides in the studio. She asked Peter to produce her records, and Peter had requested me to be their engineer.

When Peter brought her over to the studio to see where she was going to be recording, we met for the first time, and I was immediately smitten by her beauty and her personality. She was so open, free, full of fire and energy, and just always made everyone around her feel good. I needed someone like that in my life at the time, so we became instant friends. She had a smile that would make the sunrise blush. Of course, as the project started and we spent a few days together, we became quite close. But other than being good friends, nothing ever happened between us.

Every evening when we would get through recording, her husband or Edie herself would take us all out to eat. It made no difference where we went, because money was not a problem. Edie was quite serious about being a Gospel singer. And with the advent of her records, she had dreams of forming a band to back her and going out on the road to evangelize, using the success of her record to draw people to her concerts. That was a very typical dream of most Christian artists and singers, and she had all the things she needed as far as finances and the willingness to get going with her new ministry. All she needed was a popular record, and she could be on her way. But it's not quite that simple.

You have to understand that over 1,000 records are released to the public every week. You must have already in place marketing, promotion, and publicity to get your record off the ground, plus, you have to sometimes deliver records personally to radio stations in order to hope for even a chance to get them played over the air. None of those requirements were in place, and her chance of having a hit record was slim to none. But I didn't want her to be discouraged, so I did all I could do in order to encourage her and make sure she got the best-sounding record she possibly could.

When we were finished with her record, we all went to THE place in town to eat, "The Forge," on 41st St., on Miami Beach. It was five-star dining at its best. As a matter of fact, that was the place I told you about that Daliah Lavi and her husband took me after her session where I wore my new black silk shirt. At our table was Edie, Edie's husband, Mickey Jelke, Peter Graves, his wife, Cathy Ellis, and Mike Guerra, my assistant engineer. I mean, we put the feedbag on big time. That bill should have been right around a thousand to eleven hundred dollars. That wasn't a lot of money to Mickey Jelke, so it really wasn't a problem. They were totally out of my league financially, but I appreciated their generosity by feeding us so lavishly during the session. Getting good meals was not in line with my income while working at Criteria, so anytime I had the chance to eat a healthy meal, I really went for it.

Mickey's family was from New England, and they started the very first butter company in the country. It was called Jelke's Lucky Oleo Margarine. But the company, in a hostile takeover in 1948, was bought out by Lever Brothers for $22 million. That was a lot of money back then, but that was not the future that Mickey and his brother had in mind. However, they wanted to stay alive, so they went along with the robbery, and when Mickey died a few years back, his estate was estimated at $11 million, which was Edie's to have when he died.

So they were sitting pretty, financially, and Edie could go out and buy anything in this world she wanted. But being the type person she was, she didn't take advantage of that. She needed a new car, and she could have bought any kind of car she wanted, and paid cash money, a BMW, a Jag, Rolls, anything her heart desired. But she went out and bought the car she liked the best, a Buick Electra Limited. And I'll tell you something. That was the best car I have ever driven in my life. It didn't last as long as it should have, but it was the smoothest riding, easiest, most comfortable car I have ever been in. It was what we called a "floater."

When Edie would go shopping for clothes, she would go to JC Penny, Sears, and your regular clothes stores, not the high priced Miami Beach shops where you would pay a fortune for a simple dress. She was level-headed, appreciated her lifestyle, and did not take advantage of her husband's wealth in any way at any time. To me, that showed integrity in a woman.

I came to find out eventually that she was a Navy brat, had lived all over the world, and her parents were of moderate to low middle income, and she was a twin with a sister named Carroll. She also grew up with two other sisters and a brother. She'd been up, and she'd been down, so she knew how to enjoy the finer things in life, yet she wasn't afraid of being a normal person like me, either. I liked that. And besides all that, she was extremely beautiful.

But she was a pistol when it came to her personality. She loved to party. She would get all dressed up and go out drinking wine and dancing all night while her husband played back-gammon. She said he once lost $90,000 in one game. I could not even relate.

About a month after Edie's session, she called me and asked me if I'd like to come over to her house to swim and have lunch with her and her husband. I figured, why not, so I got on my bike and rode over there. It was in the Sans Souci neighborhood just east of Biscayne Blvd at about 125th Street. It wasn't that far from where I lived, but the neighborhood itself was quite exclusive. Mickey was there, and I was glad he was; we had a cordial time. I liked him, and I think he liked me, for a short while, that is. He and I played some ping-pong, and he showed me that, for a man his age, he was pretty quick and agile.

I didn't stay too long, but I knew there was something going on between Edie and me, and as much as we tried to avoid it, we did talk on the phone a couple of times. I was just tired of adulterous relationships, and I was determined not to get involved in another one.

I knew it was wrong, so I did nothing to encourage it. We met for coffee a couple of times, too, but I just didn't want to get involved with a married woman again, especially one named Jelke. His family was extremely wealthy, and he did run with a pretty rough bunch of guys. I also found out he'd been in prison for a short period, a federal prison, but I never really found out what he'd been convicted of. All I know is that when he needed something fixed or taken care of, it was no problem. Get my gist?

Chapter

24

Business at Criteria was starting to slow down to a crawl. I was still going off on some of my binges, but it was a bit more difficult without a car. I remember getting all crazy one night and going down to the Grove, Coconut Grove that is, and going to a few clubs. For some reason, instead of drinking on top of a couple of grams of coke, I took a few Quaaludes, 714's they were called. I was floating, and I was about fifteen to twenty miles from my apartment. So after a few hours of mingling with some friends, I got on I-95 north on my bike, and all of a sudden I started getting that same feeling I had with my 240Z out in the Everglades. How fast will it go? I had my bike up to between 90 and 100 when I finally came to my senses and slowed down. I made it home, quite stoned, but not in as bad a shape as I was used to getting. I was sleepy, so I went to bed and went to sleep. I was sure proud of myself the next morning for not extending my binge. There was something deep inside working on me, but I couldn't figure out what it was at the time.

A couple of weeks later, things were REALLY getting tight, no work, no income, but always having what I needed, strangely enough. Edie called me at about midnight one night. She said she wanted to come over and visit me, right then. I knew this day would come eventually, but not at midnight. The feeling between us was just too strong for it to just lay there forever. It seemed that when Edie finally got her record cut, she wanted to start going to church on a regular basis and draw closer to the Lord. But Mickey wouldn't allow her to even keep a Bible in the house, much less go to church.

The straw that broke the camel's back was that an hour or so before she called, Mickey had told her he wanted her to go up on the stage at the Jockey Club, where they were long time members and where they went practically every night. He wanted her to go up on the stage before the band came back, take the microphone, and tell all of their friends that the whole thing about her "getting saved" and wanting to be a Gospel singer was a fluke. He wanted her to publicly denounce Jesus Christ and tell all of "their" friends that her Christianity was a lie, and meant absolutely nothing to her, or he was going to kick her out of the house and leave her penniless. She said, "Absolutely not." She then went into the ladies powder room, stayed for about forty-five minutes crying, praying, asking God what to do, and then she called me and wanted to know if she could come over for a while. There was even a telephone in the ladies room. I said alright, come on over if you really need to. She did, and she never left.

All of this went down in the later part of October of 1980. On November 25th she signed a quick deed on the house and property, asked for a very minimal amount of money, just enough to get out of town, $1,000 a month for only one year, and we were married in Good Shepherd Lutheran Church. Good Shepherd was a Spirit-filled church Edie had frequented many, many times. I even went with her a couple of times, and it was the most peaceful, anointed, Spirit-filled church I had ever attended in all my life. I can't even begin to explain to you the feeling I had when I was in there, but it was simply the presence of Almighty God, I was to discover later. The pastor's name was Robert Barber, and he had the Spirit of God all over him every time I saw him.

We got married on a Saturday afternoon, and they were doing construction on the church. As a matter of fact, they sold bricks for a dollar each, and every Sunday when people walked into the sanctuary, they paid their dollar, took a brick, and put it in a pile for the workers to put up on Monday morning. So, for our simple four-person marriage, plus the pastor, we had an engineer friend named Al who was my best man. He lived at the apartments along with Margie's friend Margaret, who was matron of honor for Edie. While the ceremony was going on, there was noise like you couldn't believe from the workers building the new sanctuary, but it didn't bother us. I just thought it was kind of pertinent as a reminder of what my life had been like (pandemonium), and we just went along with the program.

Edie and I had discussed getting married for several days before I agreed to go through with it. I told her I didn't think a piece of paper would mean that much at this point. I wanted to get to know her better before I made a lifetime commitment to her, but she insisted that we get married then. If I wouldn't do it, she said she would leave, and I didn't want to take that chance. So once again, I bit the bullet and went through with it. That was the third time I had gotten married when I wasn't ready or was unsure if I was doing the right thing for me, but in the end, guess what? You'll find out how it turned out as you read on.

We spent our honeymoon in our apartment watching Saturday Night Live, which was back when it was really good. I was also glad that Edie was in the same mode as I was, as far as alcohol. But I introduced her to smoking weed, and she acted like I did the first time I did it, decades ago. She would start giggling and laughing at anything or everything. After a couple of weeks, she started to really enjoy getting high on grass. We also put our share of vodka and grapefruit juice away every night, so I didn't feel guilty about that. Then I made a beer drinker out of her. She said she had never drunk beer before, but then she started enjoying the fizzy, bubbly taste of a good cold beer. So her joining in with me and my vices made us a lot more compatible. Even though she was a Christian, she was never given the chance to walk the walk, so about all she could do was talk the talk, if necessary.

A few days later, I came down with a terrible case of influenza. I was bed-ridden for at least ten days. But while I was bed-ridden, I got a phone call from a studio owner in Birmingham, Alabama, named Randy Matos, AKA Randy Richards. He also had eyes for being a producer/rock star some day. He was a spoiled little rich kid who had a great little studio in Birmingham called the Music Place, and he made me an offer which I told him I needed to think about.

Also, Mickey, Edie's ex, was making some pretty threatening phone calls when he heard of our marriage, and he wasn't real pleased with our behavior. To say I feared for my life would be an understatement, but he didn't really make a believer out of me completely. He was just hurt, confused, lonely, and had to get it off his chest. He told me that I had no idea what I was getting into by marrying Edie. I sure wasn't a prize myself, so whatever he meant, I think it all kind of evened out. And there was something much, much larger being planned in the heavenlies and eternity that neither of us was even remotely aware of and that we had no control over. It was already written in stone.

Randy's offer was too good to refuse. He offered me a nice weekly salary, plus he said he would pay for Edie to fly up to Birmingham and look for a place for us to live. He also offered me a year's signed contract, plus he said he would pay for me to bring in an assistant engineer who was good at repairing equipment. He got a good deal after all was said and done, and needless to say, so did I.

As we waited for my flu to subside, Edie started packing things away. She went through my closet trying to sort things out as to what we needed and what we didn't. Boy, was she in for a surprise. It was quite a humorous adventure for her to start going through all my stuff, because as she did, she started realizing who and what I was, and in addition, what I used to be. One of the first things she pulled out of the closet was a pair of motocross boots, still caked with Alabama mud. She laughed so hard I thought she was going to start crying.

I think I've mentioned it to you once before, but a biker needs to always protect two very important things, whether he is simply trail riding or racing. He must protect his eyes and his ankles and feet. One time my engineer protégé at MSS, Greg Hamm, bought a brand spanking new 400cc Yamaha dirt bike while we were working at Sound, and he just had to bring it over to the studio for all of us to see. There was a gravel lot on the west side of the MSS building, and that was the only place to park. But by the size, it was more than adequate for parking, even if you were going to record the 360-voice Mormon Tabernacle Choir. Right in the middle of the parking lot was one tree with one bush next to it.

I just had to test ride Greg's new bike, so I'm out there doing donuts and wheelies all over the place. All of a sudden I made a mad dash for the back porch, and guess what? I ran smack-dab into the middle of that ONE BUSH in the parking lot, and one of the branches swiped me right across my left eye. It left a very bad scratch on my left eyeball. The pain was almost unbearable. I have never had pain like that anywhere in or on my body. I went to an eye doctor immediately, and he put some medicine in the eye, covered it, and gave me a prescription for some eye drops to help the healing and hopefully diminish the pain as much as possible. Nothing worked very well at all. The only time it would stop hurting was when I would lie down flat on my back and not move my body, not one bit. I had to lie in bed at home for three solid days. All of this unnecessary pain was brought on because I didn't obey my own rules and because I didn't protect my eyes when I was out there showing off.

So Edie continued to pull things out of the back of the closet. She also pulled out my old motocross pants and some other miscellaneous biking gear, all still caked with mud from good old Alabama. That was one thing that I missed the most while living in Miami. Other than the seasons, I missed DIRT. All there is in south Florida is palm trees, sand, and concrete. Everything is green or white. So my old biker clothes, except for the boots caked with mud, went to the Miami city dump, along with some other stuff that I can't remember. I cleaned the boots up and polished them and sent them to my son. Naturally, I had to have an explanation for everything in the closet, and Edie ended up doing that to the entire apartment.

Before we leave my apartment for good, I'd like to describe it to you. It was a great place to live for me. As I said earlier, it was just across the street and about a third of a block down from the studio. It had a beautiful 25-meter, yet not standard, shaped pool. You could swim laps, but it had style too. We all did a lot of cooking out while I lived there. When I first moved into it, all I had was a coffee table, a dining room table with two chairs that I had bought from Sears, and a mattress. That was it. But after I realized I needed some furniture, I found out I could have my apartment furnished for only an extra hundred dollars a month. Wow.

I told them to go ahead and bring the furniture in while I was at work so I could walk in and hopefully feel just a little more at home than I was accustomed to. And did they surprise me! When I walked in, my mouth dropped open, and I could not believe my eyes. All of my furniture was white. My carpet was almost beige, but just a little lighter, so the colors worked magnificently. I had pictures on the walls; I had a sliding glass door with a southern exposure that opened up onto a balcony, which I had never even walked out onto until then. I had a couch and a matching chair, plus a coffee table made out of nothing but glass, and I had lamps in the corners.

In the bedroom, I had a king-size bed, a chest of drawers, a dresser with a huge mirror, plus a full-length mirror on the wall and pictures on the walls that made you want to go out and jump into the ocean they were so tropical. The walls were already white, the furniture was white, and my sliding glass doors and balcony faced south, which in Miami is ideal, because you always have light coming from the sun, even when it's at its lowest phase of the winter season. It made the entire place come to life. It was just beautiful, and for the first time in a very, very long time, I enjoyed where I lived and was proud of it. And after all this time with this nice apartment, I had to leave it. Just the thought of getting out of Miami was a challenge, but I also knew I was heading back to MY part of the country, where they had dirt, seasons, trees other than palm trees, and nice, friendly people, another thing that was becoming rare in Miami.

When I first got there, it seemed like everyone was friendly, but after a couple of years, things started to change, and I mean change rapidly. When I first got there, you could go to the grocery store, and most people would speak and smile and were very cordial. Not any longer. Everyone seemed like they were mad at everyone else. They wouldn't even acknowledge your presence. And another thing, you couldn't even find a job any longer if you weren't bi-lingual. You had to speak English *and* Spanish. It was time to go. And I was taking my new-found treasure and gift from God with me—Edith Anne Masters.

So Edie hopped an airplane and flew to Birmingham to find us a place to live, and I finished most of the packing, although I still had the flu. Randy met her at the airport and gave her a car to drive while she was there, and also a room at a nice hotel. She started looking south of Birmingham in the Hoover, Vestavia Hills area and eventually came up with the perfect place for us to live. Once you get south of downtown Birmingham, you start getting into very hilly and almost mountainous terrain. She found an apartment at the very top of a hill, overlooking some beautiful woods and a tennis court, which we played quite a bit. The complex was called Green Tree Apartments.

The entrance to the apartment building was a carpeted hallway. It was a one-bedroom apartment with a balcony that over-looked the entire complex. It was breathtakingly beautiful in the hills of Alabama. We had a fireplace, something I hadn't experienced in a few years. When she left to go up there, I told her, "I don't care what it looks like as long as it's nice and has a fireplace." It was like being in a whole new world up there. I didn't realize how much I had missed the real South until I had the opportunity to move back. You can only enjoy so much sun, sand, and palm trees and people who all talk funny. I had just enough of south Florida to know what it was like to "be a native," as one of the advertising brochures said. But I had had my fill of south Florida, period. After three complete years, practically to the day, it was time to go.

There was something else that hastened us to go ahead and leave Miami, and that was that, unfortunately, Mickey was starting to hassle us just a bit. He even called me a creep. I've been called a lot of different things in my lifetime, but never a creep. I liked Mickey because I believed he was a man of integrity and a gentleman, so I couldn't blame him for being hurt over the fact that he had lost his wife of eleven years.

Edie and I would occasionally go over to Sans Souci to play tennis on their public courts there, and you had to drive past the courts to get to Edie's former house. They were really nice courts, and that was something we both enjoyed doing. She was a good tennis player, whereas I was just average, but I could usually beat her just on strength more than anything else. Every time we would go over that way to play tennis (which we actually only did a couple of times), I would call it "enemy territory." I knew Mickey had the money and the connections that with one quick phone call, I could very easily end up with some concrete boots in the Atlantic Ocean or the Miami River, and I was constantly aware of that.

In addition, it was time that I started looking at my life and realizing that I had a major problem. More than one, actually, but one still hounds me even today. There was something deep down inside of me that made me seem to not have much respect for the institution of marriage. I didn't like that part of me at all. As a matter of fact, there were a lot of things about me that I didn't like, and still don't, but I knew I couldn't change my own heart after all those years. It was going to take some kind of supernatural experience to bring this reality into the light and have it exposed for what it really was. It was sin. It was sin of the worst kind.

I remembered that David in the Bible, after he became king, not only had an affair with Bathsheba, but went so far as to have Bathsheba's husband sent to war and put on the front lines where he would certainly be killed. At least I hadn't reached that point, but I could very well end up like that. One of the fruits of David and Bathsheba's relationship was that their first child was born dead, or died right after it was born. I learned all of that in Sunday school when I was very young, and it always stuck with me. I'm pretty sure, now, that I know what caused me to have that attitude, but I don't want to pursue it any further for fear of hurting someone I loved.

We left Miami in a big U-Haul truck and Edie's car with Mike Guerra driving. I wasn't fully recovered from being sick, so it wasn't a fun trip for me. Eventually I had to hand the truck over to Mike and ride in the car myself. We got on the Sunshine State Parkway, which was a toll road, right where it started at I-95 and 167th Street. The entrance to the Parkway was only a few blocks from where we lived. I'll never forget as we started boogying up the road that there were three to four times as many vehicles going north as there were coming south. In addition, I spotted an RV just ahead of me with a bumper sticker that said, "WOULD THE LAST ONE OUT OF MIAMI PLEASE BRING THE FLAG." I felt exactly the same way. Our destination was Pensacola, where Edie's parents lived. I wasn't looking forward to that at all. I knew they were going to be extremely disappointed in Edie because of her leaving Mickey, so I figured my head would be on the chopping block.

We left Miami about 7 a.m. and made it to Pensacola by 9 p.m. We also picked up an hour by going from the Eastern Time Zone to the Central Time Zone, so we made it in thirteen hours. That's pretty good with a truck that had a governor on it where you couldn't go any faster than 64 mph. Mike did a good job driving the truck; he was young, strong, very smart, and a really nice person. I was really fortunate to have him with us and to help us get a good start in Birmingham in a studio neither one of us had ever been in.

We arrived at Edie's parents' house at about 9:30 p.m., and I met her parents for the very first time. I later found out that her dad, Floyd, who was retired from the Navy, had been in communications intelligence also. In the army it was called the ASA (Army Security Agency), but in the Navy it was called the NSG (Naval Security Group). All of the communication security outfits were controlled by the National Security Agency. In order to work for the NSA, we had to have a Top Secret Crypto security clearance, which was three clearances above Top Secret, and also very costly to the government. The NSA had sent FBI agents to Little Rock, and they had talked to some of my ex-girl friends as well as their parents, also my teachers in high school, the kids I ran around with, and my neighbors. They had left no stone unturned in their investigations of me.

Floyd was either an interceptor or worked in crypto analysis, one. We never got into detail, because he had been on a ship during WW2, and at one time, his ship was blown in half. I can't even imagine what that felt like. Of course, the equipment and the mode of operation had changed quite a bit from the time he was in and the time I was in.

Edie's mother, Esther, was absolutely beautiful. It was then that I saw where Edie got her beauty. Her mother was Swedish/Norwegian. She had beautiful, pure white-like, ivory skin, and a personality to match. She still had that northern accent in her voice. Her parents were from North Dakota, where she grew up. Her first husband was killed, actually burned alive, in a house fire that almost took her life also. Edie's father, Floyd, was a hardhead, yet deep down he really cared for his kids and their spouses. He would just never admit it. He was also a know-it-all, and that trait rubbed off on several of his kids, including Edie and Carroll. Of course, I have no problems in my personality whatsoever (big smile). I was taken aback by how wrong I had been about Edie's parents. They were fantastic, and you could tell they loved her very much; therefore, they loved me, too, and it showed.

So we all spent the night there in Edie's parents' home, and the next morning, after a hearty breakfast, were off to Birmingham, which wasn't that far from Pensacola, maybe five hours at the most. Living in Birmingham was simply wonderful. What a great city to live in. One of the first things I noticed was that during rush hour, with traffic being bumper to bumper, it was like deadly silent. People didn't seem to be in that much of a hurry and no one honked their horns or lost their cool, but just silently waited in line and drove home. Had that same scenario been in Miami, all you would have heard would be horns honking and people cursing each other. It had always been utter chaos just trying to get home after work. In Birmingham it was almost like my ears went totally turned off. They were silent, no sound, no hassles, just peace and calm and tranquility. I was back home in the South, and it showed everywhere I went. Yee Haw!

Chapter

25

One of my first assignments at the Music Place was to mix an album on one of the original Temptations, Eddie Kendricks. The album was called "Love Keys" and was produced by Johnny Sandlin and Randy Richards, Randy's professional name. It was a very good album, and I think it was Eddie's last album for Atlantic, but it didn't do a whole lot at the time. As to why, I don't know. Eddie was a very nice man, and I truly valued his friendship. Unfortunately, he died in October of 1992 of lung cancer. It was a great loss for music and especially our loss personally.

The sessions at the Music Place were few and far between, even though it was a great-sounding room with fantastic equipment. Randy had a Studer A-80 24-track tape recorder and a very nice Neve 32 Output console, which had cajones like no other console had at that season of recording, plus all the outboard gear that we needed and an excellent selection of mics. When you marry a tape recorder with a console, there is no better marriage than the one Randy had in his studio. It was like having a Bentley and a Benz in your garage. In addition, with the exception of the studio at the original Muscle Shoals Sound in Sheffield, Alabama, the Music Place was the best-sounding room I had ever worked in and also one of the best-kept secrets in the South.

One of the main reasons for the Music Place not being successful was the fact that there were no really good, experienced, professional studio musicians in Birmingham. We had to import players from either Muscle Shoals or Nashville whenever we did a real session. Now, I'm not saying there weren't any good musicians in Birmingham. There just weren't any that had the studio experience that we needed in order the cut the records we were trying to cut. And it was expensive when you had to pay the picker's way down and back from Muscle Shoals or Nashville, plus their room and board for the entire time they were there. That really added up, plus put a lot of pressure on the engineer to get the songs cut fast and get the boys home ASAP.

We did a two-song session on Marilyn McCoo and did some local groups that had promise. Other than that, I spent more time on the tennis courts than I did behind the console. Randy did an album, which he had been putting together on and off for a couple of years, but when it came time to mix, for some unknown reason, I woke up one morning totally unable to hear anything through either ear distinctly. I went to the ENT specialist, and he gave me some medication to try to get some blood circulation up to my inner ear. When I told him I was a musician and engineer, he almost started crying. He gave me the impression that my ears were done for. He said that I would never be able to hear normally again. That wasn't very encouraging.

So Mike mixed Randy's album, which I was glad of anyway. I just wasn't in the mood at the time to mix Randy's album for some reason that I can't put my finger on. So it became a very restful and profitable year for me. Plus, Edie went to real estate school, then about ninety miles south to Montgomery, the capital of Alabama, and she passed her real estate test the first time she took it, and got her license. She then went to work for Chamber's Real Estate and immediately sold three houses the first month she was there. She had the perfect personality for selling things. She pretty much sold herself, first, and would eventually have people eating out of her hand. She started out like a flash, but started cooling off after a few months. I personally think she had her priorities out of order and spent too much time doing unnecessary things, but it was her job, so I let her either make it or break it.

After about fourteen months, Randy called me into his office and gave me the news that wasn't really unexpected. He had to let me go for lack of business. I had no idea in the world what to do at the time, but for some reason I wasn't worried.

One interesting thing that caught us by surprise while we were living in Birmingham was a snowstorm that came through and literally paralyzed the town. We were up high on a hill, so we weren't able to get down from our apartment to get food or anything. Then the power went off for five days. We moved our mattress in front of our fireplace and stayed there to try and keep warm, but it was still very cold. We were literally trapped in our apartment for five days. Edie got out on the balcony and used charcoal to cook our meals.

One thing that did work was our telephone, so I started making some phone calls up to Muscle Shoals to see what was going on up there work wise. I called Rick Hall, Jimmy Johnson, and Roger Hawkins, but there wasn't a whole lot going on up there either. Some of the snow started melting, so we decided to venture out and see where we could make it to. There was a Super K-Mart way down on the main road that led to the entrance of Green Tree, so we wandered down there. I bought a small portable radio so I could at least listen to some ball games and talk radio. We finally thawed out and tried our best to get back to as normal as possible. This all happened before Randy had given me notice, so it was not a real important time of our life.

When I finished my last day at the Music Place, I drove up to Muscle Shoals, about 125 miles northwest of Birmingham, and talked to Rick Hall about an opportunity of some sort. I had created a good reputation for myself since leaving Fame, and Rick knew I was pretty good at what I did, but his ego was about the size of the city of Birmingham, Montgomery, and a few other large towns put together. My agreement with him was that on any session of any importance that came in, he would give me the chance to engineer it, and other than that, I was not paid anything else. Rick owned an apartment out on his ranch just a couple of miles south of the Shoals, and he offered it to me to live in, free of charge, while I tried to establish myself back in Muscle Shoals.

We had a session coming in on the Osmond Brothers, who were old friends since "One Bad Apple" and "Sweet and Innocent," except that they had all grown up to be men. Donnie, who was only seven or eight when we did "Sweet and Innocent," was now a husband and father with his own family, as well as the other brothers Alan, Wayne, Merrill, and Jay. They were all very gentle and loving young men, as well as their wonderful father, George, who was a good friend. George and I spent a lot of time together just talking and sharing our lives while I wasn't behind the console, and I got to know about the family and what they all had going on back in Utah. They were all Mormons, of course, but we never discussed that. George passed from this world in 2007 at the age of 90. He was one of the sweetest, most gentle men, yet had his hand on his boys their entire lives and raised them to be the very best they could be. And he was successful.

So, Rick let me engineer the album, but he got some licks in on me right in front of everyone to let them all know that he was still the Main Man. I used some unusual microphone techniques when I recorded the tracks. When it came time to punch some guitar parts, he looked down at the mic's I had and noticed how unusual it was from what he was accustomed to. He looked over at me and said, "Why do you have this many mic's on the guitars?" I said, "I was trying to get a big guitar sound." He wanted the guitar to be on only one mic, so he didn't like that. Having to move more than one fader at a time wigged him out, even though you could group all the mics to one fader. However, instead of trying it my way, he looked at me, thought for a second, and then said, very sarcastically, "I don't want a big guitar sound; I want a little bitty guitar sound!"

The entire control room fell on their faces laughing, including me. I knew he would get me eventually. He wanted to make sure that I knew that I wasn't the hot dog engineer from MSS and Miami that I thought I was, and it was HIS studio, and he was going to have it HIS way. That little verbal exchange between Rick and me was so funny that the story is still being told in the annals of Muscle Shoals history.

Now one thing you must understand. Since I was only paid for sessions that Rick allowed me to engineer, it was strictly up to him whether I made any money or not. He had this idea that I would be bringing in all kinds of outside business from the other studios, which was not the case at all. They wanted me sitting there all day making phone calls trying to book sessions in the studio, and they would give me a certain percentage of what I booked. Other than that, I made nothing. And I tried for weeks to bring some work into the place, but Rick's reputation had a lot to do with some people shying away from the possibility. And there was a lot of plain old simple jealousy of Rick's success that made some stay away—their problem, not his or mine.

Of course, Edie was still back in Birmingham working for the real estate company, so I would always go home on the weekends and drive back up to Muscle Shoals on Monday mornings. They gave me an office to work out of, but Linda seemed to always be checking on me, making sure that I was on the phone trying to bring in business. I wasn't getting paid for that, but she made me feel like I was getting $500 an hour. One afternoon, Lenny LeBlanc and I were going to go play tennis. As I was leaving, about 2 p.m., Linda stopped me and said, "Where do you think you're going?" I told her where I was going, and she about blew a head gasket. It just made her furious that I was going to go play tennis. She wanted me there working for nothing trying to make them money. That started eating at me, big time.

Not only that, Rick had a guy working for him who was a superior musician, fantastic song writer, and a good engineer as well. His name was Walt Aldridge. He was an exceptional guitar player and pretty much did most of the engineering for Rick before I arrived. He also was responsible for overseeing the publishing company, which was full of a lot of extremely good songs. After that one Osmond Brothers album, I started to notice that Walt was doing most of the engineering. I asked Rick why he wasn't giving me anymore business, that I was starving to make some kind of income so I could move my wife up here.

Rick said, "I think you should go back to Birmingham. I don't think you should move back here." I told him, "I want to live back here, Rick. I don't want to live in Birmingham." So he said (and you're going to love this one), "Well, why should I pay you to do sessions when I've got a man here on staff that I pay every week to do the same thing?" I said, "If you will recall the conversation we had a few weeks ago, you said you would pay ME to do the outside sessions." He had nothing to say, so I went back to the apartment.

When I first moved into the apartment with the few things I had brought with me for the week, the first thing I noticed when I walked into the apartment was a Bible lying open on the coffee table. I hadn't paid any attention to it, and just went about my business. I woke up the morning after my talk with Rick, and on my way to the studio, I was determined to stay it out, but I started crying for some reason. I don't know why. I wasn't scared or sad or worried; I just started crying, and I kept crying. At times I would have to go outside or go hide back in the back of the studio. It seemed like no matter how hard I tried, I could not stop crying. I cried for three days, and finally I called

Edie and told her what was going on. She suggested I call a friend, Ronnie Eades, who I had heard just got "religion" and was serving the Lord now.

So I called him and simply asked him to please pray for me because I couldn't stop crying. Before I walked out the door, as I walked past the coffee table on the way out, I glanced down at the Bible for the first time since I had been there. When I picked it up, the first verse I saw just leaped out of the page at me. It said, "When a man takes a new wife, he shall not go out with the army, nor be charged with any duty; he shall be free at home one year and shall give happiness to his wife whom he has taken" (Deuteronomy 24:5). That was exactly what had happened to me in Birmingham. I had had a guaranteed salary for a period of one year, I had had hardly any sessions, and I had spent twice as much time with Edie and playing tennis than I had spent making records. I think God Himself had just spoken to me.

When I got to the studio, I went upstairs because I didn't want anyone to see me crying. My eyes were so red and swollen from crying for so long that I couldn't hide it. When I walked into a vacant office (it had actually been my old office from back in 1970, oddly enough), Ronnie Eades was sitting there waiting on me. I didn't even know he would be there. All I had asked was for him to pray for me. I didn't ask him to come down to the studio. He just knew what he was supposed to do, for some reason. This was the day, or hour, or moment in time that the Jerry Masters that you have known and been reading about throughout this entire book was getting ready to die.

As Ronnie proceeded to tell me what had happened to him and how his life had so drastically changed in the last year, I just cried that much harder; I was practically sobbing. The more he told me, the harder I cried. And inside, in the deepest depths of my inner being, I was crying out to God, "I want You in my life, Lord, I want what Ronnie has. I can't keep living my life with me as boss. I want to turn my life completely over to You." Yet I wasn't talking; I was just yelling in my heart. Then all of a sudden this incredible, supernatural, unexplainable "feeling" came over me, and whatever was making me cry turned into joy. Not happiness, but total JOY, like I had never known in my life. It was an amazing experience like nothing I had ever been through or even imagined in my entire life. It was better than any drug I had ever taken in my life, and I had tried them all at one point or another. All of a sudden, I felt like a brand new person. I felt clean, free, happy, almost as if I had died and been brought back to life, all within a ten-minute period. I had no worries, no concerns, no anticipation or anything whatsoever inside me, period. I literally felt like a new person. I actually got my driver's license out to see if I was still me.

Ronny never prayed with me or anything. He just sat there and smiled. He knew what had happened. After a while of just sitting there, I boldly got up, walked straight into Rick's office and told him, not asked him, but told him I was going to move back up here, and I needed to borrow $500 to go out and put a deposit down on an apartment. He just sat there and looked at me for a long time without saying a word. He then buzzed downstairs to Linda and told her to write me a check for $500. I could tell she was questioning him about why and for what reason, but he said, "Linda, just write the damn check," and hung up the phone. He still didn't say anything.

I was so full of joy, and he knew it, but he didn't know why or what to say. I turned around and walked out the door. I was a new creation in Christ Jesus and so filled with joy and peace, I must have been walking at least three feet off the ground. God not only gave me a new life, He filled me with His Holy Spirit. And it was almost more than I could handle.

That was on Thursday morning, April 29, 1982, at exactly 10:25 a.m., and even though it was only Thursday, I decided to go ahead and drive back to Birmingham. On my drive back to Birmingham all I could do was thank Him, thank the Lord for giving me new life. It was all I could do. When I walked into our apartment, Edie was just sitting there reading something. She hardly even looked up when I walked in. I immediately said to her, "Are you going to church Sunday morning?" She answered in the affirmative, and I said, "Good, 'cause I'm going with you." She just said okay, still never looking up from what she was reading. That's all that was said, but she knew something very strange was going on. And I could tell that inside she was screaming with joy and thankfulness.

I was up at 6 o'clock on Sunday morning. I was dressed and ready to go by 7:30, and the service didn't even start until 10:00 a.m. The Pastor of the church Edie had been attending was named Truitt Murphy. I had been to a couple of socials with Edie and had met some of the other church members. Plus, Truitt, being a musician, had been over to the studio a couple of times, so we had become pretty good friends. Yet he had never mentioned the Gospel to me one single time, or even invited me to church. Maybe he knew, maybe he didn't, but he was about to find out that the "hounds of heaven" had finally run me down and caught me.

When I walked in the door, everyone looked very surprised. No one could have wiped the smile off Edie's face—it was like a permanent fixture. I even think Truitt knew something was going on, because he usually preached for about forty-five minutes, and then sometimes he would give an altar call and other times he wouldn't (from what I understood later). That day he only preached about fifteen minutes, and you could tell his heart wasn't in his sermon. Then he said, and he barely got it out of his mouth, "If there's anyone here today that..." and that was it. I was standing at the altar by the time he finished his partial invitation. All the men of the church, along with Truitt, gathered around me, placed their hands on me, and I prayed the sinner's prayer. Truitt read Romans 10:9-10 that says, "...that if you confess with your mouth Jesus as Lord, and believe in your heart that God raised Him from the dead, you shall be saved; for with the heart man believes, resulting in righteousness and with the mouth he confesses, resulting in salvation."

When I got home, I got that scripture back out, using Edie's Bible, and I kept reading it. He should have kept reading through verse 11, because it says, "For it says in the following verse, WHOEVER BELIEVES IN HIM WILL NOT BE DISAPPOINTED!" And, man, was that scripture right. I can tell you for sure it's true, even today. You will not be disappointed. Now, if you think for one second that all your problems are going to go away, you might as well just forget the entire thing. Because not only do your problems not go away, they can even get worse. The only difference is, before my salvation all of my problems were MY problems, but now, they are HIS problems. And believe you me, He knows how to handle your problems. I'm a living witness to that.

One thing I left out about that Thursday night...I normally smoked a joint on the way home from the studio, but I had no desire to smoke anything that night. And when I always walked in the door, I would immediately grab a beer, or fix a drink. But I did neither. Just didn't want to. Then when we had dinner, I would always drink a glass of wine, and I passed on that too. And usually before I headed for bed, and after I had consumed quite a bit of alcoholic beverages, practically to the point of staggering, which was a normal evening, I'd pop a couple of valium. For some unknown reason, I passed on all of that this particular night. And Edie wasn't too crazy about me not drinking, because it was a habit of hers, too. But we were in this together, and she knew it.

I kept wondering how I was going to go to sleep. I was accustomed to drinking myself to sleep every night, and had been for many years. I always had to drug and drink myself to sleep as a matter of habit and addiction. I had thought several times about going to a place where I could dry out, but I just never seemed to get around to it. So when bedtime came rolling around, and I'll admit I was a bit restless, and had been just a little all night, I simply said to the Lord, in my heart, "Lord, how am I going to be able to go to sleep?" And this still, small, voice inside me simply said, "Just go in and lie down on your back, and let Me take care of the rest." So I did exactly what He said. All I remember is waking up the next morning feeling like a million dollars. I finally found out that the meaning of the word "salvation" also means deliverance, regeneration, and redemption. It's not just a fire escape, so to speak.

When I surrendered my life to the Lord, I was not only saved, I was delivered, redeemed, and there was a regeneration going on in my heart that was supernatural. All the Ten Commandments can do is show you where you are wrong. They can't save you; only reveal your sin. But salvation is a supernatural act of God that sets you free from sin and death and gives you new life. The old Jerry Masters died with Jesus on the Cross, and the new Jerry Masters had his spirit replaced by Jesus' Spirit, the Holy Spirit. So my spirit now is IN Jesus, who is sitting at the right hand of the Father, and my new spirit, His Spirit, the Holy Spirit, guides me now.

Will I make mistakes and sin again? Of course I will. It's my body's nature to sin, but my Spirit will start getting stronger and stronger as I learn about who I am and what I am now until I'm more like Him. There will be a constant battle going on between my flesh and my Spirit. It's up to me to make the right choices and grow in Him, but it's a long process that will continue until I'm with Him for eternity. And as far as judgment, I've already been judged and found innocent because of what He did on the Cross for me. So it's no longer what I do or don't do, from now on it's about what He DID on the Cross.

Chapter

26

The next morning Edie and I had mixed feelings about it, but we poured every drop of alcohol down our kitchen drain. We probably had the happiest drain in Alabama, but it was finally all gone. There must have been more than $150 worth of booze dumped that morning; then off I went back to the Shoals to find us an apartment.

I had another experience on the trip back that morning. I was listening to a Christian radio station, which was a first for me. There was a lady teacher on the station named Marilyn Hickey. She was talking about one of the fruits of the Spirit called the Baptism of the Holy Spirit, with the evidence of speaking in tongues. I'd never heard of that before, and I was afraid it was some sort of Holy Roller stuff, which I wasn't interested in. She said that it was a language that you develop over time and is a way for you and the Lord to converse, in which you really don't know what you're saying or praying, but God does, and by it not being a certain dialect, the enemy, or the devil, can't tell what you are saying. And she said that it gave you encouragement and edification and strengthened you spiritually, as well as talking to the Lord in your prayer language, which was yours only—it was your personal, direct line to the throne of God.

As I was listening to her describe the Baptism of the Holy Spirit, I simply said out loud, "Lord, I sure would like to have that." By the time I reached Muscle Shoals, I was speaking in tongues. I had a brand new life, and I was beside myself. The lack of finances didn't even bother me; the thought of moving back up to the Shoals didn't bother me. Even being back in the same town with Kathy didn't bother me. I didn't even give it a second thought. I just wanted her and everyone else I knew to experience what I had experienced, a brand new life in Christ. (I think having a personal, direct line to God is very, very cool. If you ever don't know what to pray, pray in the Spirit, or in tongues. That's the main reason it was a gift to us—not to show off in church or in front of others, but just between you and Him.)

But I found out I had to be careful. There were more Church of Christ churches in the Florence area than there were service stations. It even had a Church of Christ school called Mars Hill Bible School. It was a very religious town, and a relationship with the Lord has nothing to do with religion. One thing about the denomination of the Church of Christ was the fact that they are staunchly against musical instruments in the church. I've yet to figure out how they explain Psalm 150 that says, "Praise Him with trumpet sound; Praise Him with harp and lyre. Praise Him with timbrel and dancing (uh-oh); Praise Him with STRINGED INSTRUMENTS and pipe. Praise Him with loud cymbals (our current drummer loves that verse); Praise Him with resounding cymbals, Let everything that has breath praise the Lord" (Psalm 150: 3-5). But I don't want to get off and start preaching here, I just want you to know what we were up against in the area for one reason.

It seems that the Lord, all of a sudden, was making a giant sweep through the music people of the Shoals area. There were singers, background singers, musicians, engineers, studio owners, writers, and anyone connected with the music business that were all of a sudden being exposed to the Gospel of Jesus Christ. It was like a revival of sorts, and it was very fruitful for the Kingdom of God.

Edie and I found a cute two-bedroom apartment in Florence called Quail Run. No, I have yet to see a quail. There were probably eighty-five to a hundred apartments in the complex. In addition, across the street, the same real estate company that owned Quail Run had several two-story duplexes for rent. But the rent on the duplexes was just a little more than we could handle at the moment, so we got an apartment just up the sidewalk from the swimming pool and tennis court. The apartment was very, very small from what we were accustomed to, but it didn't matter as long as we had a roof over our heads.

Edie's real estate business in Birmingham was drying up like the Sahara Desert, so it seemed like we were divinely in line for a move to the Shoals. I tried to hang on at Rick's for a few more weeks, but it just wasn't working out, especially when Linda found out about my experience with the Lord. She was a member of a Church of Christ, and I saw sparks getting ready to fly, so I got out before the battle had a chance to get started.

I called Ronny Eades and asked him where he went to church. I figured he probably went to the best kind I would need at that particular time, so he took me over and introduced me to his pastor. I knew I wanted to go to a church that taught the entire Bible, including the gifts of the Spirit. The church was called Christ's Chapel, and the pastor's name was E. M. "Doc" Shell. I could see and feel the love of Christ all over him when I first met him. He said he thought it might be a good idea for us to chat before we started attending there, so we set up a time for the next day.

We met the next afternoon after lunch, and when I went into his office, I literally fell apart. I started out great, but as I explained what had happened to me in the last few days, I started realizing what an incredible Miracle had been done on my behalf. I started thinking back to all the years that He had His protective hand on me, and it just all started piling up on me at that time. What a time to fall apart. Right in front of my future pastor, and I thought I was cool when I first walked in. Once again I couldn't stop crying and sobbing.

All those years I was breaking God's laws as if they never existed and not one ounce of repentance on my part until now. I couldn't stop saying to the Lord. "I'm so sorry, I'm so sorry," and then it finally hit me. I finally realized what the word GRACE meant. It means "unmerited favor." Even though I didn't deserve my Salvation, when Jesus suffered at the hands of the Romans and even the people of Jerusalem that didn't know Him, He was doing it for me—so I could have this moment—so I could eventually know why it all happened in the first place. It all started making sense.

It was so simple. The Gospel of Jesus Christ is the simplest thing in the world to figure out once you've experienced it. I finally knew what I wanted to do with the rest of my life. I wanted to tell all the people I knew, or that knew about me, how they could experience the same thing and have life eternal with Him. But there's one word you have to put in your vocabulary that you can't ever forget, and that's SURRENDER.

You know, when a thief or robber sticks a gun in your back, you automatically raise your hands, and when the police arrest you for breaking man's law, the first thing you do is raise your hands. Now you know why, when you go into a church that really preaches the true Gospel of Jesus Christ, you'll see all the people with their hands in the air. The reason? They surrender! I love the old Gospel song that I've sung since I was a child, "I Surrender All." Listen to the words sometime and you'll understand the true meaning of giving your life and surrendering your life to Him for eternity.

So, once I had used up all the Kleenex in "Doc's" office, we were finally able to talk. I gave him a brief history of what I was about, and I told him about Edie and how we had met and all that. It ended up being a very good meeting for both of us, and he said, "I'll see you Sunday." And he did. Edie hadn't arrived yet, and I was still sneaking in and out of Rick's apartment, but I was keeping a very low profile.

I had one thing quite humorous happen just a couple of days after I came back from Birmingham and my visit to Truitt's church. I had returned to Rick's apartment and was awakened about 4:30 one morning by some racket coming from the barnyard, so I got up to see what was going on. I saw Rick and a couple of his sons out in the barnyard. There was a cow apparently trying to give birth to a calf, so I went out there to check it out. I had been to Truitt's church and also had heard Edie tell me of some of the things that Christians do these days, so I wasn't completely naïve about the gifts of the Holy Spirit. I knew that once we were born again, we had a gift of healing given to us. I figured it was pretty simple.

As I approached the crew, they had already gotten the calf out, and it was doing alright, but the mother wasn't in good shape. I asked Rick what were her chances of making it through the birth. He said, "She'll probably die." It seems the calf was turned in such a way that it was too hard on the mother, so she wasn't expected to make it, but they looked at it like, "Well, at least we got one to live."

After they had all left, about 5:45 a.m., I sneaked back out to the barnyard by myself. The cow was lying on its side and barely breathing. I simply laid my hands on her and prayed and asked the Lord to save her. I had no doubt that God would save her life, because I had prayed for her. So, when I got back to the studio later on that morning, I happened to run into Rick in the hallway, and I asked him how the cow was doing. He said, very nonchalantly, "Oh, she died about ten o'clock." It killed me. What faith I had, had already failed with my very first prayer for healing. I thought about it for a long time, but I didn't tell a soul. I later discovered, simply by listening and reading the Scriptures that it doesn't quite work that way. There's a lot more than just saying, "Be healed in Jesus Name," to making the gifts of the Spirit real in your life. So it was an eye-opening experience for me and very educational at the same time.

So that was my conversion in a nutshell. I went to Christ's Chapel on Sunday, and I must say, it was the most joy-filled church I had ever attended in my entire life. It seemed as though every person in there had just been given a million dollars or something. They were having their worship service, and they were singing a song called "Good Morning Jesus," and you couldn't have wiped the smile off their faces for anything in the world. I had never seen such joy in all my life. I met a lot of wonderful people during the service. And I wasn't Jerry Masters, world's greatest engineer or anything like that; I was simply Jerry, a baby Christian.

There was a particular couple at the church, Norman and Carol Jacobs, that were to eventually give us the groundwork and help us grow roots that would sustain us throughout our entire walk with the Lord, but that is part of growing up as a real, born-again, Spirit-filled Christian. I wasn't a CEO (Christmas and Easter Only) Christian anymore; I was a genuine Child of God. My new life was about to get on a big, new, unfamiliar roller coaster, yet I wasn't the driver any longer. And God wasn't my "co-pilot" either. He was my Pilot.

We finally got everything moved up from Birmingham, and when the moving truck arrived, there were so many helpers and unloaders there, I couldn't even get into my own apartment—and the pastor, Doc Shell, was right in the middle of it. When Edie started her real estate job, we went down and got her a new Mazda 626, so that left me driving the Buick (yeah! I loved that car). She drove the Mazda, and I put my Honda bike (yes, I still have it) down behind the apartment in an attached storeroom. The apartments were set on a slope so that each apartment had a huge storeroom beneath it.

Our patio overlooked the pool and tennis courts with about 50 feet of woods in between. That way we had a lot of wildlife playing and frolicking in the rear of the apartment between our place and the pool. There were quite a few college kids living there, and they weren't used to my shaved head, so they got a kick out of calling me various names, like "Kojak," "Ghandi," etc. I paid no attention to them until one day I caught some of them throwing rocks at the squirrels. When I yelled at them, "Whatever you do to that squirrel, I'm going to do to you!" the old rebel dirt biker came out of me momentarily. I was ready to do some butt kicking, but after a few minutes, I settled down. I'm just glad one of them didn't go down and French kiss one of the squirrels (smile).

So living there had its ups and downs. The construction of the units was done as inexpensively as possible, and the apartment above us had a floor about one-half inch thick—at least it sounded that way. We could hear everything that went on above us 24/7. It reminded me of one of Paul Simon's songs on "There Goes Rhymin' Simon" called "One Man's Ceiling is Another Man's Floor." When they would have parties, it would be almost unbearable because of the noise coming through the floor. Actually, if they had a party anywhere in our building, it affected all the other tenants. So they had to come up with a rule that any parties had to be shut down by 10 p.m. So those were basically our living conditions at that time.

Now, income was a problem. We had very little in the bank, and I tried to think of ways to generate some sort of income for each of us. I started letting everyone in the music business know that I was back in town and working freelance and at a reasonable rate. Edie did something that was probably the hardest thing she had ever done in her life, and I've got to salute her here and now for doing what a real wife, best friend, and soul mate does when the going gets tough. This is going to really bless your heart when I tell you, and it will show you why I always thanked God for putting Edie into my life when He did.

She started pounding the pavement for another real estate job, but to no avail. There just weren't that many possibilities for her at that time in a small town like the Shoals. Most of the real estate people in the area had been at it for years and years, and were firmly planted in the community and had been for years. That's when I finally realized what a closed town the Shoals area was to people who had not grown up there. We were considered "outsiders." And it seemed like everyone in town was related to someone else close by or at least knew someone related who knew someone that they were related to. If all that doesn't make sense, look up the word nepotism and see what it means. That's the story of the entire community of Florence, Sheffield, Tuscumbia and Muscle Shoals City, Alabama.

Now if you remember from my earlier description of Edie, she had been married to a very wealthy man. She could have had anything in the world she wanted, and paid cash in addition. Even when she finally went to work selling real estate in Birmingham, she had tremendous success up until it was time to move, and her commissions were quite good. Plus, she had been receiving $1,000 a month from her ex-husband for the past year, but that had run out in January.

So she had no income, and I had no income. She couldn't get her foot in the door of any company in the area, because no one knew who she was. So what did she do? She went down to Shoney's. Before she walked in, she sat out in her car and cried for an hour and a half because her days of being the Princess of Miami and Mrs. Mickey Jelke, the multi-millionaire's wife, were over. She was back to square one. Just like graduating from high school and starting all over again. When she was in high school, one day she stood out on the beach in Pensacola, Florida, in the cold of winter with no human being in sight, and in a loud voice, said, "I'm going to marry me a rich man and never, ever have any children." She literally spoke her life into existence, just like God spoke the world into existence. He said, "Let there be..." and it was. That just shows how our words are so very important and powerful that we have to realize that we can actually speak things into existence.

Sometimes you might say, I'm never going to do "so and so," and I'll guarantee you that eventually one day you will end up doing "so and so." I used to say I would never ever live in the state of Mississippi. "If they were going to give the USA an enema, they would insert it in the state of Mississippi. I would NEVER live in Mississippi." I've now lived in Mississippi for 21 years.

After Edie's hour and a half crying spell and prayer and realization that her life had taken a very strange turn, she faced reality, walked into Shoney's, and asked for an application to be a waitress working for nickels, dimes, and quarters. If you think for one second that that doesn't take guts, then you haven't lived. That took more courage and intestinal fortitude than anything she had ever done in her life. And she did it for one reason. She did it for us. And more than that, she did it for me. She could have very easily sat down and said, "You're the man of the house, you go out and find a job, any kind of job, and support me like you're supposed to." But she knew what I was supposed to be doing—making music and making records. She loved me enough to have the courage to go out and wait tables and carry heavy trays and wait on people that weren't very nice and that leave messes behind that, if it were in your house, you would never let them back in again, ever.

I'm sure she could write her own book on the experiences that she had while doing that job. She told me of one occasion that made me so angry. She was waiting on a table of about twelve people on a Sunday after church; they literally ran her legs off for almost two hours. They were rude, demanding, messy, and just not very nice. The gentleman that was to pay the bill, as he got up to leave, left a ten and a five dollar bill under his plate as a tip for Edie. Waitresses only made $2.01 an hour, and the rest had to be made up in tips. So their tips were the bulk of their income. As the gentleman was paying the bill up at the cash register, his wife casually walked back to the table and took Edie's fifteen dollar tip and stuck it in her purse, with Edie standing there watching her.

That's just one example of how people treat waitresses. They usually say, "Well, they pay her to work, why should I have to pay her, too?" It is a very humbling, dirty, long-hours and tiring job for anyone, especially a lady. And one more interesting fact you should know before I move on. The worst tippers in the world, and this is going to surprise you, are Christians.

Once we got established in our surroundings and Edie started working her job waiting on tables, she realized she wasn't going to be able to make very much money at Shoney's, mostly because of location, so she started looking around for other job possibilities doing the same thing. It appeared that Shoals tradition wasn't going to allow her a decent job, so to speak, so she settled into the waitress mode. And as long as that was going to be what she had been placed in, she was going to make sure that she did it to the very best of her abilities, no matter what it was.

I started putting the word out for any engineering gig at any studio I could find. The first thing they did when we began attending Christ Chapel was to stick a bass in my hands and put me up on the stage with the worship team, in which Doc's daughter, Donna, played the piano, and Ronny Eades played sax. They had a drummer and a whole room full of singers, so having a bass was something they weren't used to. I didn't have an amp, and I had to borrow a bass. I had forgotten that I didn't even own a bass any longer. So I borrowed a Fender Precision bass from Johnny Sandlin, who had produced Eddie Kendricks' album with Randy down in Birmingham. Someone else found me an amp that someone wasn't using; so in two weeks, I went from being a brand new believer to a "minstrel" or a worship bass player.

Donna played amazingly good piano for a young lady her age, and she was very beautiful and loved God like no one I had ever known. Of course, being a PK (Preacher's Kid) had a lot to do with that, but it was important that she had grown up in the right atmosphere and didn't have to go through all the junk that Edie and I put ourselves through before we came face to face with the Truth. Obviously, my musical knowledge and past helped improve the quality of the music a little; plus, I got to help the other musicians grow musically by sharing my experience with them and teaching them what I knew about bands, but coming from a different direction.

When I was on stage all those years as an artist, the emphasis was on us, the "stars," and our songs. But when you're playing in a real, true worship band in Church, the emphasis is on the King. The entire reason we were all there was to worship the Lord. I had to really make some adjustments in my attitude while in the "limelight" now. My thinking had to make the 180 degree turn that my Spirit had. That's the problem with being a Christian. It's a constant battle between the flesh and the Spirit. We were so used to living by the flesh, and we had to learn how to live all over again, by the Spirit.

I found out one thing that is not only true, but it was one of the most revealing lessons I learned after I became a Christian. IT TAKES MORE OF A MAN (OR WOMAN) TO SERVE GOD THAN ANYTHING ELSE YOU WILL EVER DO IN YOUR LIFE. As I write these memoirs now, in the present, I can verify that after walking this life out for twenty-seven years now, that statement never ceases to be true.

Chapter

27

We had what we called a sister church right up the street from us called Calvary Fellowship. It was called a sister church because it was not only a non-denominational church, but had the same beliefs and agendas that we did as Evangelical Christians. There was an incredible guitar player going to church there who had been born-again about two years before me. He was from Los Angeles, and had no idea why or how he ended up in Alabama. His name was Will McFarlane, and his biggest claim to fame was that he was Bonnie Raitt's lead guitar player for years. And a guitar player he was. He was married to a very godly woman, Janet, and had two children, boy-girl twins, Jamie and Nellie, and they were very sharp kids for their age. Not long after Edie and I moved there, Janet gave birth to a new baby boy, and they named him Robbie after Will's brother who was murdered on the streets of New York City several years before.

I think I've mentioned it before, but guitars are my least favorite instrument, mostly because there just aren't that many good players around—at least not studio-type guitar players. There's a huge difference. The difference is taste and not over-playing. Studio guitar players have to know when to play, and more important, when NOT to play; and when they play acoustic guitar, they can't make a lot of string noise on the strings when going from one chord to the other.

Will was the cream of the crop, a very godly man, but in addition, he was a tremendous songwriter, singer, and also an elder in his church. His voice reminded me a lot of Michael McDonald, who started out with the Doobie Brothers and Steely Dan. Will was the complete package. He could have been a big star in his own right, but he chose to go the route he was created for. His wife was saved long before he was, and when they arrived in Alabama, Will got tired of always being referred to as "Janet's unsaved husband." Besides, he really felt the call of God on his life.

One day he decided to take a walk out into the woods, and all of a sudden he just looked up and loudly proclaimed at the top of his voice, "God, if you're real, reveal yourself to me right now." And God did. Will said that, at the moment he yelled that, within seconds he knew without a doubt that God was real and that Will was ready to be birthed into the Kingdom right there in the woods, with no witnesses. When he went into the woods, he was Will, the great guitar player, but when he came out of the woods, he was simply Will, God's servant and a child of the King, who just happened to also sing and play guitar.

Will had a vision of putting together a band and going out on the road doing concerts in churches, playing in high schools and junior high schools, and even doing prison ministry. At the time, Calvary had two pastors, Steve Fatow and Neil Silverbert, both Jews from Miami, via Philadelphia. Not too long after I moved into town, Steve and his wife, Sandy, who ended up being dear friends of ours, decided to move their ministry to Knoxville, Tennessee, but while they were in Florence, Sandy and I became good friends. She had a very well-put-together prison ministry—not just women, either. She would go into men's prisons just as easily as women's prisons.

She was from Miami, too. Since Edie and I had met and married in Miami, we all connected very well, even though Edie and I were going to Christ Chapel. So many musicians had gotten saved (or born-again) when God made His sweep through the Shoals over a period of about five years. There was a lot of talent in the Church in the Shoals, which involved all born-again believers in the area.

We had a gathering one night where all the churches were involved. It was a pro-life, anti-abortion rally, and the worship teams from our two churches played the same night at the same place. Will and I had never formally met or talked, and he had never heard me play, but we knew of each other. Our reputations had preceded us, so there was a mutual respect already in place when we ran into each other that particular night.

He walked up to me and asked straight out if I would be interested in playing in his band. I was flabbergasted that he thought me good enough to play bass out of all the musicians in town, but it just so happened that, out of all the Christian bass players in town, which you could count on about three fingers, I was, I suppose, the best of the three. But more than that, I was willing to travel. The other two had regular jobs that kept them from being selected, so I was the only one that qualified, being unemployed and all.

Will also had a keyboard player and song writer who was the worship leader at Calvary named Joey Holder, who could flat play keyboards. He also wrote a standard worship song that is a classic in contemporary circles now by the title of "Unto the King." So, with Will, Ronny Eades on sax, Joey, and me, all we needed was a drummer. That was the one missing ingredient that prevented us from really becoming what we visualized happening with us as a band. We eventually ended up using about five or six different drummers, some of them not even saved, but we did end up with a very, very good band.

I would say that I was the weakest player in the bunch, not because I'm trying to be humble, but because it was simply the truth. I was NOT a good steward of the gifts that were given me from the very beginning. I always seemed to just get by using only my natural talent. I wasn't willing to PAY THE PRICE to be the very, very best at what I did. I was just lazy, and I let other things get in the way—mostly wine, women and song, and not necessarily in that order.

When we are given gifts, we are expected to use them to the very best of our abilities. And that means practice, practice, practice. That was something I never did. I was just lazy and content with getting by on my natural abilities. I could have been ten times the bass player I am now if I had only taken the time to pull myself away from the TV or golf or tennis, and simply practice. Then again, bass is one of the hardest instruments to practice on, because about all you can do is sit there and play scales, which I could do blindfolded.

Meanwhile, "back at the ranch" at Quail Run, I happened to befriend the General Manager of all the property in that area of town. He knew we were struggling a bit financially, so he asked me if I would like to be Resident Manager of Quail Run, only as far as keeping peace at night when he wasn't there, and just keeping an eye out for trouble or reporting violations of different sorts. So I gladly took the job, and he took $150 a month off our rent, which was a great help.

Then, after working at Shoney's for about three months, Edie was told she could make more money working at a Quincy's Steak House about a mile down the road from Shoney's. After interviewing, they offered her a job. It had a few more perks, not quite such long hours, and she didn't have to deliver such heavy trays of food. Plus, the tips were better because of its location. So she set her goal to be the very best waitress in Quincy's history, and she eventually made that goal. I'd never been so proud of my wife in the entire time I had known her. When I first met her, she wouldn't even go into a place like Shoney's or Quincy's. She would only frequent dining places that had valet parking and a maître d. That is a fact. That's the kind of lifestyle she gave up for me and to live her life for the Lord.

With Will, we started practicing together as a band once we found a drummer, and even though the drummer wasn't born-again, he at least said he was. He was living in Memphis at the time, and he never really made us feel like he was on the same page as we were, as far as the reason we were preparing to do what Will had the vision for.

We rehearsed every day during the day for two weeks. At the time, Will had an album out, and it was doing pretty well as far as contemporary Christian music goes. The single off the album was a song called "You Call Me a Dreamer." Just about every song on the album was good, and we learned them right down to the note. He told us that, while he was recording and mixing his album there in Muscle Shoals before I had arrived, the engineer he used was also the studio owner. This engineer and studio owner had a serious case of drinking too much, usually starting out in the mornings and going all day and half the night. Will said that, at one point while they were mixing, Will left to go run an errand, and when he returned about an hour later, the engineer was passed out drunk on the console, with the tape still running. I thought that was sad and funny at the same time. He said he would get so belligerent with Will that at times he would have to just go outside and pray.

I was thinking to myself, how valuable would a non-drinking, non-smoking engineer with more experience and success than all the engineers in town put together be to someone who needed an engineer available to work without all the baggage, too. So I started imagining the possibilities of me eventually making some money in the studios whenever I was available. I made a commitment to Will as far as the band, but I knew we wouldn't be working that many days on the road.

Once we got all of our songs together and felt like we were as close as we could possibly be, we got called for our first gig. It was in Cincinnati, Ohio. So, as a send-off the night before our first trip, we had a combined service of both churches, Christ Chapel and Calvary Fellowship, and we put on a concert and played all the songs we had learned. We gave everyone a little touch of what we were taking out as missionaries and evangelists of the Lord, and they sent us out with a covering, prayer and the laying on of hands as representatives of the Body of Christ.

There was even one wealthy man from a Baptist church in town that gave us a credit card, with no limit, to be used in case of emergencies. I thought that was an extremely generous thing for him to do, since he really didn't know any of us very well personally, but trusted us to do what we felt like we had been called to do at that time of our lives. I also noticed one thing that was a total surprise to me at first: we always had enough money in the bank to pay every bill and the rent and still have a little left over. It was like money would come from so many different places.

I even went out and helped a cotton farmer during harvest time for cotton once, and talking about getting in shape, that really put me in shape, especially my legs. My job was to stand in the big wagon that the combines would dump the cotton into and then stomp it down and pack it as much as I could until they brought another load, then stomp that down and continue to do that until they got as much cotton in the wagon as possible. They would then haul it off with a tractor to the cotton gins, which were just up the road. How many of you can say you were a cotton stomper?

The gentleman that gave me that job paid me twenty dollars a day to stomp cotton, and I learned so much from him, not only as far as raising cotton, but about being a man of God. He had been a Christian for almost sixty years, and you could tell he was a very wise man. His name was H. L. Rice, and he was one of the biggest farmers in that part of the country. In addition, he was a member of Christ's Chapel. His oldest son, Tommy, was a crop duster. H. L.'s wife, Eleanor, was one of the sweetest, most gentle, loving ladies we had ever known. She would always bring us lunch at exactly 12 noon, no matter where on the farm we were working.

H. L. was also the man who made Genesis 1:26 come to life for me, as he used it on his farm every day, and it worked. That particular scripture says that, as God's people, "we have dominion and rule over the fish of the sea, and over the birds of the sky and over the cattle and over all the earth and over every creeping thing that creeps on the earth." Now, I'm not preaching to you here; well, yes I am, but H. L. used this scripture to literally move his cattle from one pen to the other every day. He wouldn't drive them over there, he would simply TELL them to move, and they moved.

There are Ten Commandments given by God to Moses, but only one of them has a promise attached to it. It's "Honor Your Mother and Your Father that your days may be prolonged in the land which the Lord God gives you." There are so many people in this world that do not show their parents the respect they deserve, or they avoid them or neglect them because of things that might have happened to them when they were young, or it's too much trouble and inconvenient. You're still supposed to show them respect and honor them every chance you get.

I just want to mention one incident I had with my mother a few years before she passed on that really brought that commandment to life for me. I told you earlier how hard my mother worked to raise four boys and give us everything she possibly could, but in the end she almost worked herself to death by all the hours of overtime she worked in the freezing cold meat locker. Constantly, year after year, she would work anywhere from twelve to fourteen hours a day in order to pay the bills, clothe us, feed us, and give us a half-way decent place to live.

She even refused to get married again, because she didn't want us to have to submit to another man that wasn't our father. As much as she worked, there were slim pickin's as far as honorable men who were willing to take us all on at the same time. My mother was extremely attractive and remained that way far beyond the season when she should have started showing her age. We had a gene of some sort that allowed us to remain younger-looking than our age. Then one day she started visibly aging, and it was fast. My mom took so many medications for all the infirmities in her body as a result of working so hard, she just couldn't remain looking thirty years old forever. The lifestyle started catching up with her.

Right after I became a follower of Christ, I thought I was so much more spiritual than those that hadn't had the experience I'd had, so I considered them oblivious to the miraculous moves of God that I was being taught about. I started telling Mom how she needed to get filled with the Holy Spirit and be baptized into the Spirit and start talking in tongues like I did. I don't know what it is, but all young people reach a stage in their lives where they begin to think that they are so much smarter than their parents. It seems to happen in every family, at least for a while.

I kept hounding Mother about going to a non-denominational church and getting filled with the Holy Spirit, and she could then throw all of her meds down the toilet. She finally, after I continued proselytizing her for so long, put me in my place. She said, "Listen, Honey, I grew up in the Southern Baptist Church. My father was a charter member of South Highland Baptist Church, plus being a deacon for fifty years." She was crying by now. "You can't expect me to just stop doing what I've been doing all my life and jump into something that I know absolutely nothing about. I'm just trying to stay alive, so just leave me alone about all the tongue-talking Holy Roller stuff, and let me be what I am!" Then she hung up on me. She flat put it on me, and she crushed my pride like no one had ever done in my life. I was furious that she wouldn't accept this newfound life I had, and it about destroyed me when she rejected me like that.

We didn't talk again for almost a year. Then one night I was sitting outside by myself and this still, quiet, gentle voice came to me in my spirit and my mind at the same time. I knew it was God talking to me. He said, "My Son, you need to stop being a PREACHER to your mother and simply start being a SON." I had just been called on the carpet by my Heavenly Father.

I called her immediately and deeply apologized to her, and from that day forward I called her every single day. It didn't matter where I was, I would just check on her and spend a few minutes with her every day until the day she died. She died in 1998, and I still have a tendency to pick up the phone to call her. I finally catch myself, then I think back to when she was still alive and cherish all those days we talked and how much I loved her and appreciated her.

If your parents are still here, enjoy them as much as you're able. They're always going to be the people who brought you into this world and tried to help you through life, but they won't be around forever. In her last couple of years, she kept reminding me, "If there are any questions you want to ask me about your childhood or anything else, you'd better ask me now, 'cause I'm not going to be around forever, you know." And I did, and I'm glad. But I missed some, so I'll ask her in Heaven.

Our band finally booked a tour to be the opening act for a group out of Oregon called "Servant." It was time to go to work. They sent us plane tickets to fly out to Medford, Oregon, and join up with them. They were all on a bus, designed especially for each member of the band, so we rented a van and just followed them all over the country. It was a lot of fun, even though it was tiring, but we were younger then, so we were able to hang in there with one exception. About a week into the tour, I came down with a case of the 24-hour influenza somewhere in New Mexico. I had a fever; I couldn't eat; all I wanted to do was rest. I barely remember a couple of services we played because I was feeling so bad, but I survived.

Servant was a large commune of Jesus People, leftover hippies from the 60s and 70s. They were totally committed to the Lord, with their own farm out in Medford. There were probably twenty-five to thirty families, with kids everywhere, and they had cows and chickens, too. It was basically a rural place with all of their needs taken care of right there where they were. They grew their own food and weren't heavy meat-eaters, if they ate meat at all. The first morning, I had some real cream to put in my coffee for the first time I could remember. It was about twenty minutes old from what I could figure out. When I say they were Jesus People, they were just a bunch that loved the Lord and wanted to go out and make very loud music, with their own light show and smoke and all kinds of things to get kids' attention. They even had one song, the big finale, where they had two combustion bombs (harmless bombs of course) go off that literally shook the building or wherever we were performing.

Our bands were as different as night and day. They were much louder and used the effects, whereas we pretty much did a praise and worship set and prepared the crowd for their hard rock, heavy metal band. We played our first night there in the town of Medford, then headed north up to Portland, where we played the most anointed service we had ever played. Then we went south to several towns in California, then east into Arizona and New Mexico, then north to Wyoming, Utah, and Kansas, and we ended the tour in Memphis, of all places. It was the most interesting tour I had ever been on and my first as a Christian.

I also want to mention that our drummer, as soon as we were through playing, would always call a cab and go back to his room. It was a real challenge for us to accept, but we just kept doing what we were supposed to do. These saints, Servant, loved God more than any group I had ever been associated with; they knew their purpose and calling, and they did it with everything within them. They truly lived up to their name.

We did have one incident that happened at the very beginning of the tour that was quite humorous. I got my first taste of "religion." It seems Will had a distant uncle right outside of Portland who happened to be the pastor of a fairly large Methodist church. He invited Will to come to their Sunday morning service and speak to the congregation briefly about what the Lord had done in his life. I knew we were in the middle of it when the pastor introduced us from the audience and actually apologized for the way we were dressed, saying "we were dressed for travel." I actually had my best stuff on, and I thought we all looked pretty nice, but obviously not good enough for a Methodist church on a Sunday morning.

The service started at 10:30 a.m., and the pastor finally asked Will to bring his guitar and talk about his life at ten minutes till 12:00. Not good timing at all. At exactly twelve noon, you could hear car keys rattling all over the building. It was twelve noon and time to go. Will tried to rush his half a song and his brief testimony, and he finally finished at ten minutes after twelve. By that time, over two-thirds of the church had already left. It was then that I discovered the difference between religion and the real Kingdom of God. They weren't CEOs (Christmas and Easter Only), but they were pretty darn close.

As a postscript to that story, Servant played again up in Nashville a few months later, so I grabbed the church bus and took all the kids in the church, plus Edie and several more adults from the church, up to Nashville to see them in concert. Nashville was only about ninety miles north of Florence, so it wasn't a real long ride. Edie and I were standing right behind the sound board, out in the audience, and I knew when the bombs were going to go off, but no one else did and I didn't tell her anything about what was coming. When they did go off, I'll swear Edie jumped at least three feet straight up in the air. I laughed till I cried. We had about thirty kids with us and had a ball on the trip. It was really an experience they wouldn't have had if I hadn't volunteered to take them up there.

I drove that big yellow bus quite often. We had a school in our church called Chapel Christian School, from Kindergarten through the 12th grade, and once a week I would load the entire school and haul them down to the YMCA for an hour and a half of exercise and fun. Our church sat at the top of a steep hill in Florence, and one time I forgot to lock the brake down real tight. The pastor got a call about three o'clock in the morning because our bus had slowly crept, one gear at a time, about three quarters of a block down to the bottom of the hill until it rested right in the middle of a busy intersection. That was embarrassing, to say the least, and I learned my lesson about driving those big yellow buses.

We had a few down times when the band wasn't working and there was no session work. Doc was aware that both Ronny and I had no income at all, so he asked us if we wanted to start working on our PHD's while we weren't doing anything else. Of course we said yes, so he proceeded to give us a couple of shovels and a post hole digger, or PHD, and we started digging out the west side of our church building which was being overrun by a huge wall of dirt. The dirt had slowly shifted onto our property from the yard next door and was beginning to cover all the windows and pipes on that side of the building so that we couldn't get to them at all. It had crept up almost to the roof so that a person could hardly even walk around the building. We moved the dirt around to the north side of the parking lot where erosion had almost caused our parking lot to start sliding onto the road we were located on.

Now, I thought I was in pretty good shape because of the tennis I played at least three or four times a week and the full-court basketball I played a lot at the YMCA when I would took the school there once a week. I had stayed in fairly good shape in spite of all the drugs and alcohol I had consumed over the years. But Ronny wasn't in that good a' shape. He wasn't athletic at all, but he was solid physically, so he wasn't a pushover when it came to physical makeup.

We dug, and dug, and dug until we had blisters where we didn't think you could get blisters. We would dig down with the post hole digger and then scrape the dirt and put it in wheelbarrows, then move it to the parking lot, which was about thirty-five or forty feet away. It was hard, very hard physical work for us being in our early forties, but it was good for us. It also made a statement to a lot of other people in that town that couldn't believe that two of the most successful music people in the town's history would stoop so low as to actually dig dirt for a living. Doc was paying us minimum wage, and we would work from 8 a.m. to 5 p.m. every day. It was very, very tiring for us old former druggies and alcoholics, but it was sending a message that we weren't aware of at the time, but it was where God wanted us, and we didn't mind it a bit.

At one point, they were having a revival of sorts where they had a guest speaker come in to speak to the church all week. He would speak in the mornings for a couple of hours and then at night for a couple of hours. When they would start the service in the mornings, Ronny and I would slip in with sweaty, dirty clothes on and play in the worship band. After the worship was over, we would sneak back out and start digging and hauling dirt again, and I don't think anyone knew the difference, because we kind of kept away from the congregation as much as possible to keep our sweaty aromas from offending anyone, if possible. It was funny whenever someone would happen to catch us doing that. They would stick their heads around the side of the building and ask what we were doing, and we simply told them we were working on our PHD's. They just said, "Oh," and moved on. They didn't get it for a long time (smile).

When we first started, the amount of space between the church and the wall of dirt was about 12 to 14 inches, and that's all. When we finished the best we could, there was about four to six feet of space to move on that side of the building, which was a major accomplishment for two old farts that were used to playing or recording music for a living. But it taught us a lot about egos, submission, and obedience to the Lord and where HE wanted us at that time.

Chapter

28

Another interesting trip with Will McFarlane was to a Navajo Indian reservation in Farmington, New Mexico. This time we had to take all of our equipment with us including our sound system and instruments, so we rented a U-Haul truck, which I was elected to drive, of course. And it had a governor on it that would only allow me to go 64 miles an hour for the entire trip. Ronny was my navigator, and we had a wonderful send-off by the entire church on Sunday after the service was over. People were handing us money and credit cards like crazy just to make sure that we had all we needed.

Will would give us $20 a day for food and other necessaries, and I would always send in my tithe every three or four days. Even though it was only $2 a day, it was very important to me. So, I would get a money order every three or four days and mail it to the church. I learned about tithing from the very start, and I've been tithing, no matter what our financial situation, for the entire time I've been walking with the Lord. It was somehow pounded into my spirit from the start that every penny I earned belonged to God, but all He asked for was 10% to put in His storehouse for the poor and needy.

I've never one time since April 29, 1982, failed to give Him His 10%, and also given offerings, sometimes sacrificially, above and beyond the 10% to show my appreciation to Him for taking care of us the way He always has. And I've also wanted to help spread the Gospel throughout the world so that every person on this planet would have the chance to not only hear the Good News, but have a chance to be saved and have eternal life through Jesus Christ, which is the only way a person can make it to Heaven. Some of my offerings also helped in other countries with food and clothing for children that would sometimes go days without eating. God doesn't need our money, but He does need us to be faithful and obedient.

So we drove on all day up to about midnight that night and made it as far as Albuquerque, New Mexico. Once we left Amarillo, Texas, I started getting this funny feeling, and I couldn't put my finger on it. Ronny was feeling the same thing, but we simply thought it was the Holy Spirit ministering to us, because we knew all the saints back in Florence were praying for us. We spent the night in Albuquerque, then got up the next morning and headed for the hills and the northwest corner of New Mexico, the beginning of Navajo territory in Farmington, New Mexico.

About half way to Farmington, that feeling started really getting intense, almost to the point where I was getting giddy, almost like I was high on something. As we pulled into Farmington about 3:00 that afternoon, I saw a sign at the entrance to the city that read Welcome to Farmington, Elevation 5300 ft. That was when I realized what that strange feeling was. We had been climbing from the plains of Texas, which are about sea level, to over 5,000 feet in the air. We were getting high on the thin air. Our bodies had become sensitive because of the lack of drugs and alcohol in them for so long, and we weren't accustomed to that feeling. We had discovered a new drug, and it was free: 5,000 feet worth of high. Man, musicians will do anything to get high. Isn't it a shame (smile)?

We wondered where they were going to put us up, and they stuck us in a closed orphanage building. It was a pretty funky place, and when we tried to go to sleep that night, we discovered that all of the mattresses were urine soaked, and no matter what we tried to do, we couldn't escape it. They also had no blankets or pillows or sheets. God sure does have a way to bring you back to earth by giving you a small dose of what less-fortunate people go through. This was a valuable lesson to all of us.

The next day they took us out on the Navajo Reservation, which also included a stop at Four Corners. Four Corners is a small gathering place where the four states of New Mexico, Utah, Arizona, and Colorado all come together at one spot. There's a big circle with a diameter of about ten feet, and you can stand in Utah and Arizona and put your hands down into New Mexico and Colorado, or any combination of those four states. They had several stands where they sold homemade jewelry with a lot of turquoise that was very inexpensive. I purchased a necklace and matching earrings made of solid turquoise for Edie, and if sold retail probably would have cost at least $350 to $400. I paid $12.50 for them. She still wears them often, even now. We saw some of the most beautiful country I have ever seen in my life. I had flown over it many times, but this was my first trip on the ground, and it was breathtaking.

We were told a lot about the Navajo tribe and some of the things about the culture that made it stand out as one of the most interesting Native American tribes in the land. Having quite a bit of Native American in my blood drew me even closer to the tribal customs. I could relate to so much of the things that were destroyed by the white man, but other things you could never take away from them, ever. It's kind of like my life. I know the things I've done in my life as far as the music business. No matter what happens to me, I will always know who I am, what I am, and what I've done for the music culture in this country; and no one can ever take that away from me.

One thing incredibly unique about the Navajo is their language. It's different and more complex than any other language in the world. During World War 2, the Japanese were cracking every code that the military tried to come up with. The United States discovered that not only was the Navajo language unique, it was not understood by any other of the Indian tribes. So they put together a unit of Navajo soldiers that started their own communication network for the armed forces. And to this day, no one has been able to crack their unique language barrier. It put us up a notch on the Japanese and had a major part in our victory over them in the Pacific. They simply let the Navajo do all the commands using their language from one to the other. Every unit had a Navajo interpreter to copy the orders down in English and hand it to the commanders of the units. It was that simple.

We also learned that there is no word in the Navajo language for "tomorrow" or anything in the future. It's always either now or something in the past. So if you try and talk to them about eternal life, they can't relate at all. That makes the Gospel very hard to get across to them. But they do understand LOVE, which is the foundation of Christianity.

As we drove around the reservation, we noticed all of the junk people would have out in front of their houses, and that was how you could tell how wealthy they were. The wrecked cars, refrigerators and dryers and old appliances that wouldn't work were out in the yard as a display of their wealth. You've heard that "the one with the most toys wins"? Well, in their case, the "ones with the most junk were the wealthiest."

They are a very unique Native American tribe. I always grieve when reminded of the way they were treated by the white men who ended up taking everything that was theirs and forcing them to live on reservations, which were sections of land that the white men didn't want to live on at the time. It was one of the saddest and most abominable acts of the United States government in our history, up until now, of course.

Looking back at the way our government treated people then, and seeing how we are being treated now, shows me there is something inherently wrong with this people. It's greed and lack of love; it's groups of people that have a lot of money and want this entire world strictly for themselves and have no respect or care for the rest of society. Like the Bilderberg Group, the Trilateral Commission, the Council on Foreign Relations. They want to rid this world of 80% of the population, eventually. And they started over a hundred years ago. The holocaust was part of it, abortion, aids; it's all a plan put together by the wealthiest people in the world to rid the planet so they can have it all to themselves. Naturally, that's just my opinion. But these people are going to have to stand before their Creator someday and give an accounting for what they've done with their lives. They have no clue whatsoever what being in hell is like, but that's where they will end up, and my heart goes out to them because being in hell is being totally separated from God, and I don't wish that on anyone.

Just one more little fact about the Navajo Tribe—they did like our music. We left the Reservation about three days later and headed for Denver, Colorado. It was a gorgeous drive through the mountains, but it was even more beautiful as we approached Denver and ski country. We played a concert in Denver, then on to Cheyenne, Wyoming, for one night, then down the Rockies to the flatlands of Nebraska, the bread basket of the nation and nothing but fields, tractors, small towns, and brisk winds. Then we went on to Kansas City, Kansas, then completely across Kansas to St. Louis, Missouri. We then took I-55 South to Memphis, and then Highway 72 out of

Memphis back to Florence, Alabama, where it was a genuine pleasure to not have to sleep on a different bed every night.

You know, I was on the road with the Hombres and with Ace Cannon, Bill Black Combo, Charlie Rich, and Jerry Lee Lewis for many, many years. I think in my lifetime I most certainly have driven well over a million miles and have never even bumped into anyone's fender or had a flat tire or run out of gas. All those years with absolutely no problems whatsoever really got me to thinking about the fact that someone much, much larger than I had His hand on me all those years and all those miles. I lived through it all without a scratch, other than just wearing my body out drinking too much coffee and taking too many hits of speed before my conversion; after that it was just the coffee.

Can you imagine how many different rest rooms I've gone into and not caught any kind of disease? I was looking back on my life like that when I came to realize that God had had his hand on me my entire life and I hadn't even recognized it. It was then that I made up my mind to dedicate the rest of my life to serving Him and doing my best to do His will in my life.

I remember when my daughter, Mandy, told me she was pregnant and was getting ready to give birth to Cori, my precious granddaughter. Mandy said to me, "Daddy, I've spent my entire life doing what Mandy wanted to do and having fun being the life of the party. I'm known throughout Memphis as the party girl who is always out there on the dance floor with a smile on my face, but now, as I feel this life inside of me, and I'm getting ready to bring her into this world, I've decided I'm going to spend the rest of my life taking care of my children and making sure that they are loved, and never alone, and taught to read and write and love. That's what I've decided to do with the rest of my life."

I've never been so proud of anyone in all my life as I am of my wonderful daughter, because she has lived up to that commitment she made to me and herself; she did exactly what she said she was going to do. I'm still very proud of her decision, and she remains faithful to it to this very day.

I remember a time when Edie and I, Mandy, and Cori, drove up to Russellville, Arkansas, to see my son, Mike, who I am also extremely proud of, being a graduate from Arkansas Tech University, cum laude, as a music major. The night of the graduation we all had dinner together in Mike's honor at the Holiday Inn where we were staying. Afterwards, we all headed back to our rooms, and all of a sudden this violent thunderstorm drove us inside. Once we were safely in our rooms, we figured eventually it would slack up, but it just continued to pour down rain for at least two to three hours. Mandy and Cori had left all of Cori's books in the car, and Cori simply loved to read. I couldn't get to the car because of the driving wind and rain, and it was parked quite a distance from the rooms, out in the open. So, instead, Mandy and Cori were up till almost midnight reading the Russellville phone book yellow pages. Cori loved to read, and Mandy was able to teach her how to read even before she began kindergarten. That's how dedicated she was to her children. And she hasn't let up one bit even since my marvelous grandson, Jeffrey Blake Sappington, was born. Guess what he likes to do best? Yeah, you got it. Read.

I'm also so very proud of my son, Mike. He is the music teacher in a small town just outside Hot Springs, Arkansas, called Mt. Pine. He has students from the sixth grade through the twelfth. When he first arrived there and went for his first interview for the job, he was to meet his future employer, the principal of the school. He told me later, "Daddy, I knew it was the place for me when the principal drove up on a Harley."

Due to the determination of my son, at their first football game, to the entire town's utter surprise, out on the field to start the game came Mt. Pine's first ever High School Marching Band, complete with new uniforms and the whole bit, a first in the history of Mt. Pine. The town went absolutely crazy when they saw them. My mother (Me-Maw to Mike) and his mother, Jeanne, were there to witness this historic event. I could feel the pride two states away. Since then, he's also put together a concert band, a jazz band, and a choir, just for starters. And he's also helped several students get music scholarships to various colleges. I'm extremely proud of my son, James Michael Masters—obviously, a chip off the old block. I love you, son.

Another thing that we did with Will was one of my favorite ministries. I got to see what it's like to be on the other side of the law (because of all the things I should have gotten caught doing and somehow I never got busted for). We played at least fifty to sixty prisons, high school assemblies, and junior high assemblies during our tours. I enjoyed the prisons the most, because by all rights I should have been in one of them, and I told them that whenever I would get up to speak. We would be allowed to enter the prisons under heavy guard each time. We played hard-core prisons, not ranches where the rich guys go and play tennis every afternoon, but real prisons where the real criminals go and sometimes spend their entire lives.

One particular incident I will never forget was, believe it or not, in Raleigh, North Carolina, just a few blocks from the State Fair Grounds and the NC State football stadium. But it was maximum security. The entire length of the prison was about three blocks, and three or four blocks deep, with the main entrance about a block from the visitor's gate and the north end of the entire place. Between the visitor's entrance and the main assembly hall, where we were to play, were three guard stations, and the length was about a block and a half, total. We could have very easily unloaded all of our equipment right in front of the assembly hall where there was a gate which could have easily been opened for just about four or five minutes. All we needed was enough security to unload our equipment and leave it sitting there till we could walk from the visitor's gate and then move the equipment inside and set it up. It would have been so simple, practical, and easy on everyone's back, but they wouldn't allow it. To this day we don't know why.

So we each had to make at least three trips from the van, through three guard stations, then to the assembly hall, then back through the guard stations to the parking lot and back again. We had our instruments, our amplifiers, plus our sound equipment with a mixing board, speakers, microphones and stands. And to top it all off, it was pouring down rain, not drizzle. It was a torrential, monsoon rain. We prayed for help, yet not one single person offered to help us, even though we were coming to entertain not only the prisoners, but also the guards and staff.

The thing they didn't realize, though, is that we didn't come to "entertain" the prisoners and guards, but to tell them the Good News of Jesus Christ. But the devil knew what we were up to, and he did everything he possibly could to stop us. But it didn't work. So it was pouring down rain, and we took our first load through the first gate. The guard stopped each one of us and made us open our cases, whether they were guitars, or keyboards, it didn't matter. We had to open them in the pouring down rain.

I might mention that we ran down to the nearest grocery and bought a carton of those large trash bags. We poked holes in the bottoms so we could get our heads through, and we used those to keep as much rain as possible off our clothes so we wouldn't stay soaked all night long. When we got to the second gate, we had to do the exact same thing over again—open up the cases wide in the pouring down rain, and then a third guard station, until we got to the assembly hall. All of the equipment was soaked. Joey's DX-7 keyboard was so full of water that when he turned it upside down, water just poured out of the inside where all the electronics were that made the sounds for the keyboard. Same with the mixing console, my bass, Will's guitar, etc.

We each had to make three trips in order to get all the equipment into the assembly hall. I doubted that any of the equipment would work at all. We prayed over it all and just had faith that God would do a miracle and make at least some of it work. Would you believe that every single instrument worked perfectly, even the mixing console and Joey's keyboard? And here's the final blow to the enemy. There were 250 inmates in there when we started to tune up. They knew what we had been through, and they were as pissed as we were, but we plugged in and started to get sound. Every time we would plug something in and it worked, they would applaud.

We put on one of the best concerts that night that we had ever done, and at the end, when we asked how many of them would like to stand and accept Jesus as their Lord and Savior, surrender to the Lord, and invite the Holy Spirit into their lives, 235 out of 250 of them stood. I couldn't hold back the tears. I think the fifteen that didn't stand were already saved.

We, individually, started moving out in the midst of them. These were the hardest criminals in the state of North Carolina, except the ones on death row. We started praying for them in groups and individually, and they would come up and pray for us. It was just flat out a genuine church service right there in the middle of the prison. It was one of the most exciting nights of our five-year ministry, and I'll never forget about 200 of those faces that will spend most of their lives behind bars, but with the Lord Jesus taking care of their every need and causing them to eventually be just like Him.

One of the other Muscle Shoals artists who also had God miraculously butt into his life was an extremely talented guy named Lenny LeBlanc. Lenny was a fantastic song writer, artist, guitar and bass player, and a very good-looking guy. He had it all. He played with several bands around town and was the biggest star up at the state line clubs, 'cause all the girls just loved him, and they lined up for his attention. But the Lord got hold of him and changed his entire life just like the rest of us. He was getting ready to sign a recording contract with a guy from Orlando, Florida, named Jon Phelps. Jon not only had a record company, he was the sole owner of a school in Winter Haven, Florida, called Full Sail Center for the Recording Arts. It was one of the first schools in the country that taught strictly recording engineering, which included all the other things that go hand in hand to make you a total participant in the record business.

In its one-year comprehensive course, they taught maintenance, music law, sound reinforcement (live sound), video production, and other areas that were important to prepare young people to step into the music business with a full package of knowledge, including mixing and recording. They had the basic recording engineering class, which lasted about six weeks. Then, they had advanced recording engineering, which lasted eight weeks, where they would take you just a little further than the simple stuff taught in the basic engineering class. Then, the comprehensive course taught the whole nine yards, including the last four or five months of internship in an active, legitimate studio somewhere in the world where they were able to get their foot in the door.

It was expensive, but they gave their students an awful lot of information and hands-on experience in a very short time. It prepared them for just about anything that might pass their way if they chose that particular career for a lifetime. When I was coming up, nothing like Full Sail existed anywhere. You had to be self-taught like I was or have someone close to you walk you through all those knobs. Or you simply spent hour after hour just sitting or standing and writing down everything you observed, just like Steve Melton and Gregg Ham did. And they are the very best of the best now, much better than I will ever be.

So, when Jon Phelps came to Muscle Shoals to record Lenny's album for his label, we met and talked. He found out that I was basically unemployed and needed steady income. He became quite familiar with my past and was impressed enough to offer me a job with Full Sail. They offered me a chance to pick up some steady money, but believe me, I earned it, every nickel and dime. They would fly me down to Orlando and put me up in someone's house or an inexpensive motel. They sometimes had me rent a car, which was seldom, but mostly they had gofers (low paid employees that would "go for this" or "go for that") pick me up where I was staying and take me to the necessary place at the right time. They paid me the whopping salary of $10 an hour to teach, lecture, and oversee when the students would do "hands on" in the two places we had to work, which included a mobile studio called the "Dream Machine" and a studio out at Stark Lake, about twenty-five miles from headquarters in Orlando. It was a beautiful studio that sat right on the edge of Stark Lake. And the lake had gators in it.

When I first started going down there, all I did was lecture, but eventually they used me full time as an instructor. Jon had an assistant, a beautiful redhead named Esther. We eventually got to know each other quite well, and I got a chance to minister the Lord to her quite often. We became very good friends, and she had a lot of trust in me. She would pick me up at the airport and either take me where I needed to go or arrange for someone else to take me. Also, Jon was going through personal tragedy in his family at the same time, and I spent a lot of time with him, just praying with him and encouraging him.

The one big problem we ended up having was too many students and not enough time and places to work. And that was what eventually, after two years of steady work, did me in. At one time, we had so many students we were working 24/7. Each student was allowed so many hours alone in the studio for hands on mixing. Jon would recruit various bands in the Orlando area to come to a specific location, where they would take the Dream Machine and record them live, or else they would go out to Stark Lake and record studio-style. When they were working in groups it wasn't so bad, but once they got their recordings finished, each student of the group would get his or her individual time alone for mixing purposes.

In the first basic engineering course, they would get four four-hour personal mixing times. But in the advanced class, which lasted eight weeks, they would get six eight-hour personal mixing times. They would switch back and forth from the Dream Machine to Stark Lake Studio. I eventually ended up working 20-hour days for six days, getting one day off and then back for six more 20-hour days. I had quit smoking in 1982, when I was starting to get really involved in the Kingdom, and I was very proud of that. Smoking cigarettes is the hardest habit in the world to stop, because it's not only a habit, it's also an addiction. Stopping heroin is easier than cigarettes.

At one point, I was sitting back in the lounge, and one of the students left a cigarette burning in the ash tray, and I figured I would take just one hit off the cigarette to see if it would wake me up. It did, big time. And taking just one drag off a cigarette, when you were addicted before, is the dagger in the heart. Then, I had to have two drags, then three. Then, I started picking up cigarette butts off the ground outside after the students had smoked and gone back inside.

I was like a drug addict looking for cigarette butts large enough to light and get at least two or three hits off of. I remember when I was addicted to cocaine I accidentally dropped a big chunk of 'coke' in a urinal once at Criteria. I locked the door and got down on my hands and knees with a straw and snorted the urine-soaked 'coke' up my nose. That's how bad addiction is, even to cigarettes. But I was afraid that if I actually went into the store and bought a pack of cigarettes, it would be an admission that I was a smoker again. I was avoiding the obvious, but I wasn't fooling anyone, especially the Lord.

So, after two years of these incredible hours and no sleep, not being able to eat right, and being stuck somewhere with no car to drive, I just had to bail out. To be perfectly honest, I wasn't technically hip or educated enough to be a good teacher when it came to equipment and explaining why certain electronics did or did not do what they were supposed to do. I just wasn't a good all-around instructor. I've always felt that half of being a good engineer was technical and the other half relational. You had to be able to relate to the people you worked with, and for. You had to know how to handle people that weren't happy with what they were getting; and know how to deal with their egos— musicians', artists', and producers'. You have to be "in charge" of the entire thing. That's why the room we work in is called a "control room." At least that's the way I've always pictured what it takes to be successful.

Besides, I had trouble keeping my mouth shut about different individuals' spiritual condition. Were they going to heaven or hell? I had to care. Therefore, I had to talk about it. I did lead several of my students to the Lord, for which I was very thankful. I must say that the two years I worked at Full Sail were just as educational for me as they were for the students. I would hear things come out of my mouth that I didn't know that I knew. And I knew it was the Lord that was speaking through me and using me like a saint is supposed to be used. When I first met Jon Phelps, he was going through a very rough time, and he was so miserable. I prayed for him and with him every day I was down there. I cherish the friendship I made with both Jon and Esther, his assistant. By the way, they married and had a child not too long after I left.

Another thing, most of the time I spent down there was in the winter. One time in particular, when I got on the plane to go down to

Orlando, it was minus 11 degrees in Alabama. It was one of the coldest winters we had ever had. It always felt so good to get off that plane in Orlando after leaving Alabama in the freezing cold.

Chapter

29

I started getting some calls from Malaco/Savoy Records. The president of Savoy Records, Milton Biggham, in New York, wanted to come down to Muscle Shoals and mix some gospel choirs that he had recorded live, and he wanted to mix with me. The first one was a gospel artist named Clay Evans and the Fellowship Missionary Baptist Church. Now, I had never mixed a choir before, nor a black gospel album, but I had worked on several contemporary Christian albums like Lenny LeBlanc and J. W. Wallace when I first came back to the Shoals. I had also cut the tracks and mixed one of Will's albums, but not this black gospel thing with these enormous choirs, all done live, not in the studio—but live with a lot of ambiance. The mics weren't very close to the choirs, so it made it difficult to get a good, clean sound without a lot of hard work. This first one was kind of a test for me, too, and might have had a lot to do with my future, now that I look back at it.

Milton, or Mr. Biggham at the time, had booked the session for 11 a.m. Of course, I was there at 10 a.m., which is a habit I got into when I first started to be accountable. I was always either early or at the very least on time, with a few minutes to spare. And I mentioned earlier about engineers always being the first ones there for a session and the last ones to leave. That never changes. It is carved in stone.

So, I got everything ready, and all I had to do was get the tape from Mr. Biggham and put it on the tape machine. I mixed it on a Neve console with automation, also the best of the best consoles. I used a computer to help me remember moves on the faders. Once I made a move, I didn't have to worry about it any longer, because the computer would make the move for me.

So I waited and waited, and it turned to 12 noon, then 1 p.m., then 2 p.m., then 3 p.m. Finally, at 4:30 p.m., Mr. Biggham pulled up in front of the studio. I walked out to his car and introduced myself to him, asked him where the tapes were, grabbed the tapes and proceeded to walk into the studio. All the time, he just stood there and stared at me. I went back out to the car to see if there was anything else to carry in, and he was still standing in the same position looking at me.

Finally he said, "Do you mean to tell me that you've been waiting here all this time for me to show up and didn't say a single thing about what time it was or the fact that I was extremely late or anything?" I said, "No Sir, we have a record to mix, don't we?" He laughed and laughed, and I didn't think he would ever stop laughing. He said, "You know, I've been in this business for many, many years, and integrity is not a word I'm accustomed to saying, but you, Mr. Masters, you are a man of integrity! I can't believe you have been waiting all this time on me." So, we proceeded to go inside; we had some fresh coffee, talked for a few minutes, came up with a game plan as to how many songs he had to mix, and how much time he had to get it done, and the schedule worked out well for the both of us.

Before we go any further, there's one thing I want you to know. Savoy or Malaco/Savoy was based out of Jackson, Mississippi, and was owned by three guys: Tommy Couch, Sr., Stewart Madison, business manager, and Wolf Stephenson, vice-president and chief engineer. They were all partners, plus, they had stock holders. They bought Savoy Records a couple of years earlier. Savoy was one of the oldest gospel record labels in the business and had been around since the 50's. So when I was working for Savoy, I was really working for Malaco, because Malaco had also bought Muscle Shoals Sound Studios in 1985, which was now down on the river in that huge building Jimmy Johnson showed me before I moved to Miami. And it was a class studio, to boot. It had two of the best-sounding rooms I have ever worked in in my life.

Wolf and Tommy used to come up to Sound during the 70s to try and find songs for their artists and to also see how in the world we were getting such fantastic sounds out of that funky little shotgun building we were in at 3614 Jackson Highway. They also wanted to do what we were doing, so they sort of looked up to us as a template for success in the record business at that time. And if you'll remember, I took Paul Simon and Phil Ramone down to Jackson and Malaco in '73 to put horns on "Mardi Gras," and also cut that track for Paul, "Learn How to Fall." That's when the illustrious and famous "stingy man of music," Tommy Couch, Sr., bought one of the top artists and top record producers in the country boxes of KFC for dinner along with a roll of paper towels.

So I dove in, and with a lot of hard work and a lot of help from Milton, we got the Clay Evans record mixed. It was a great experience for me, but I wasn't that crazy about mixing live music because of the bad sound you get on all the instruments, vocals, and even the choir itself. When you turned the lead vocal off, you could still hear it bleeding into all of the other mic's all over the stage, so the sound was less than ideal. But after talking with Milton about the reason for recording live, I understood why getting the world's best sound wasn't a priority in gospel music. The reason for recording live was to capture the Spirit of what was going on during the concert.

I later was told they weren't called concerts, but services. They were having "church." And you could tell. I began to appreciate what they were attempting to accomplish in the first place, and it started to make perfect sense in a spiritual way. It wasn't about the choir, or the singer, or even the sound they captured. It was about Him. It was about Jesus and the Holy Spirit working on people's hearts in these services when the choirs and vocalists were singing. They were recorded church services.

That's why my entire attitude toward the mixing process changed. I started using mics to capture the audience like they were another instrument—the way the congregation responded to certain songs and how they were being affected and ministered to. It was an entirely different world, and I loved it. The more records I mixed, the more I loved it. Milton came in next with the Dallas/Ft. Worth Mass Choir, followed by a couple of more mass choirs, and I was really starting to get into it.

I also promised myself that if I ever had the chance to record the services myself, I would make a concentrated effort to get more separation on the different signals and really try to get the best out of the sound and let the Lord take care of the music and the response. I also thought of ways to get more and better audience sound. But at the moment, I had to take what I had and make the best out of it, and I enjoyed it very much.

I took a break from mixing to go back out with Will several times during that period, but I couldn't get those choirs out of my head. But I also loved to play bass more than anything in the world, and I loved being with Will. Even though we both had idiosyncrasies, we knew God would work it out and show us how to overlook the small things in each other's personalities. I knew I was created to be a minstrel, and I appreciated the opportunity to go out and use the gift God gave me to draw men unto Him.

It wasn't we who saved men; it wasn't the music that saved men; it wasn't the things that Will said from the stage that saved men; it was the Holy Spirit that saved them. He would move on them just the way He moved on me that day up on the second floor of Fame studios. It was a supernatural act of God that saved me and filled me with His Spirit. It wasn't what I did or didn't do, either; it was what He did on the Cross that saved my soul. It was His grace and mercy that allowed me to make mistakes and make wrong choices, but I was still a new person inside, and I knew it. Curse words wouldn't come out of my mouth any longer. Talking about having sexual relations with women wouldn't come out of my mouth any longer, and dirty jokes wouldn't come out.

I did have problems with other people's personalities occasionally, and that was a big hang-up for me. That was before I got the revelation that "iron sharpens iron." I even started to get irritated with Will always being so opinionated about certain things, constantly running off at the mouth and controlling conversations. Just little things about other people's personalities irritated me after being around them night and day and riding with them mile after mile, hearing the same old things over and over again. You would think that after being on the road with other musicians for so many years that I would be accustomed to putting up with other diverse personalities, but I was a different person then and didn't have the same values that I had inside me now.

The straw that broke the camel's back was something we did every fall for about four years. The North Carolina State Fair was in Raleigh every late September or early October, and there was also a ministry there which was one of the most organized evangelical ministries I had ever seen. And talking about success, they would literally have hundreds of salvations as the fruit of their efforts each year. I found out that they prepared for it an entire year ahead just to make sure it did have the best results in bringing lost people into the Kingdom of God.

They always had this huge tent right inside one of the main gates of the fair. They booked it years in advance, looking ahead to the future to make sure that no one else booked that spot ahead of them. They would put a stage up inside the tent and about 200 chairs for people to sit and rest. If you've ever been to a fair, you should know that it's almost impossible to find a place to sit down and rest without buying something.

So they had a stage, and they had us set up our instruments and play for fifteen minutes every hour from 10:00 in the morning until 11:00 every night. On the weekends we would play until midnight. So that was anywhere from thirteen to fourteen hours a day and only playing for fifteen minutes every hour. When we would play, people would come in and sit down to listen and just rest after walking from their cars, which were mostly parked quite a ways away from the gates. If they were walking around the fair, they would hear us playing and see a place to sit down and rest. When we finished playing, the place would be totally full of people just taking the load off and resting for a few minutes; plus, we played very good music.

Then, after playing for just a few minutes, we would tell them we were going to take a short break, and the ministry had trained counselors (who had trained for an entire year just for this occasion) move among the people and be led by the Spirit to certain ones and ask them if they were sure if they were going to heaven when they died, or something to that effect. They would engage them in conversation in one way or the other, and would always end up praying for at least forty to fifty people an hour, or more. At the end of the ten days, they would usually have hundreds of either new converts or people who would recommit their lives to the Lord or who just needed prayer. Sometimes, believe it or not, people would get healed right there in the tent, and have their entire lives changed just because they sat down to rest and listen to the music for a few minutes.

They kept a trailer outside the tent for us to hang out and rest in, and they would continually bring us food of one kind or the other. We could always count on gaining at least ten or fifteen pounds each when we played at the NC State Fair each year. All we did was play and eat, eat and play—and a lot more eating than playing. We also talked a lot, and that was where we started getting on each other's nerves. Sometimes it would be so cold we could hardly play our instruments, but we were troopers. We got the job done, but we were totally exhausted after ten days of the same thing over and over. Thirteen to fourteen hours a day together, plus being together in the van when we were traveling, required a lot of grace for us just to stay together as long as we did.

Will's obsessive talking and preaching, and my listening to him say the same things I had been listening to him say for years really started working on me. After four years of it, I couldn't take anymore, so I took a temporary leave from the band, and I wasn't the only one. Ronny was having the same problems. We sort of took a sabbatical, officially, with no hard feelings, but with much prayer on behalf of what was a really great band, with very professional players who, more importantly, were committed to the cause of Christ from the very start.

Will McFarlane remains to this day one of the very best friends I've ever had in my life. My love for him goes much deeper than anything this worldly system can explain. I went out with him a couple of times after we broke up, and when I got into the van, Will started saying the same things that used to irritate me so. I was sitting there dumbfounded, so I said to the Lord, "I thought you were going to change him." And I got an answer back real, real fast straight from Heaven: "Who said I was going to change him?" God nailed me. My Heavenly Father nailed me to the cross just like they did the Lord Jesus at Calvary. And to top it off, nothing Will McFarlane has ever said from that moment on has ever bothered me again. And it remains that way until this very day. As a matter of fact, it caused me to love him even more than I had before. Will is a class act and sold out to the Lord. Besides that, he's the best father and husband a man could possibly be, and now he's the best grandfather a man could possibly be. He is truly a mighty Man of God.

Mixing for Malaco/Savoy was getting to be a regular thing. Every once in a while I would have to call down to Jackson to find out when my check would arrive, but sometimes it would be weeks before I would finally give up and call. Stewart Madison was the man with the checkbook, and at times the producers would forget to turn my invoice in for a particular session. If I didn't call, Stewart wouldn't even know that I had worked on a session for him. The director of gospel music at Malaco was a gentleman by the name of Frank Williams who turned out eventually to be one of my best friends in the world. But he also had a secret side that I would see occasionally, just as we all do. He had a tendency to be absent-minded when it came to turning in my bills, too.

In late November of 1988, I got a call from Frank, and he said he had an album he wanted me to mix. I asked him who it was, and he said it was the "Mississippi Mass Choir." I was thinking to myself, "Oh boy, that's all I need, another mass choir record," but I said, "Bring it on up." He mentioned that they had just recorded it, and it needed to be finished yesterday, which was the music business way of saying, "I need it in a hurry." When I put the tape on the machine and started running it down to get a feel for what was I up against sound wise and how well it was recorded, etc., I realized that there was something very special about this choir that I hadn't heard on the other mass choir records I had done over the last year and a half.

Frank was a very gentle person, and the only way I can describe what it was like being in the same room with him was it was sort of like sitting in the same room with Jesus. Frank had such a loving, soft spoken, gentle spirit, and I never to this day have heard a foul word come out of his mouth. The worst thing I ever saw him do was to make a certain female artist wait out in the lobby for him for over two hours once. I was unaware of her history, but I eventually understood completely why he made her wait for him.

He also brought along Tom Easley, the engineer from Malaco who helped Wolf. It was kind of strange. It appeared that Tom came up to help me out with mixing the Mississippi Mass album, but once we got all the tapes into the control room the first day, I hardly ever saw him again. He was hanging out with one of MSS's female engineers, Vicky. She had a private office upstairs, which was her living quarters, and they had a tendency to smoke some of those funny cigarettes up there occasionally, so that's where he spent the majority of his time. Besides, I didn't need him anyway.

The good thing about mixing live albums was, once you got all the instruments sounding the best you could and the choir sounding the best you could, then you could move pretty fast, because the only thing that changed with each song was the lead vocals. So we mixed the entire album in about four and a half days. And I must say it was, without a doubt, the best gospel album I have ever worked on in my entire life. And the sound, which was recorded live by a company called Omega Sound out of Dallas, Texas, with owner/engineer Paul

Christensen, was just absolutely superb—the best live sound I had heard since I had been an engineer.

After Frank left and went back to Jackson, I had to call Paul Christensen in Dallas and tell him what a fantastic engineer he was and how excellent the sound was on the Mississippi Mass album. Little was I to know that Paul was going to be a major part of my life for the next twenty-five years. We definitely hit it off when we first conversed, and I also found that my reputation had gone before me, so we had a mutual admiration friendship beginning.

Chapter

30

Edie and I had reached a point where we were outgrowing our little apartment at Quail Run, so we moved across the street to a two-story townhouse, and the rent wasn't that much more. The manager still had a soft spot in his heart for us because of the way I had handled the resident manager's job at Quail Run. Quail Run was just overrun with college kids who had no sense of time or noise, and having neighbors upstairs was always a crapshoot. Occasionally we would get someone that had soft feet and wasn't too noisy above us, but then again, at times we would have someone who must have had size 13 boots on 24/7, and it seemed like he had twenty-two roommates living with him. The parties down at the pool were also keeping us awake at night. It was just turning into a party complex for college kids that went to the University of North Alabama. I was young once, and I didn't want to deny them the fun part of their young lives.

As a matter of fact, I taught a course there at the University for a year on Recording Studio Engineering. I only had one class a week for an hour and a half, and it paid really well. The only major problem was when I first started, the professor and head of the music department told me I had to put a syllabus together for the class. I had no idea in the world what a syllabus was. At first I thought he meant "silly bus," and that really took me for a spin, so I asked around and was finally able to put one together just in the nick of time.

I had about thirty students. It was strange, too. They either got it or they didn't get it. I had to give a test at the end of each semester and at the end of the year. Fifty percent made "A's" and the other fifty percent made "F's." I think the funniest part of it was the staff meetings I had to attend. All of the teachers had degrees, of course, and were tenured, and I only had a high school education, so it was professor this and doctor that and Jerry. Needless to say, I was out of my element from start to finish.

Teaching only once a week and for only one semester, I received a check every couple of weeks for almost $500. What a godsend that was. And it just sort of came out of nowhere. Of course, I know who it came from, and that was another thing. I spent about two thirds of my time talking about technical things and the rest of the time explaining the Gospel to my students. By teaching that class, I really got a look at the average college-age young person and realized how truly miserable they were if they didn't have God in their lives. I tried to be encouraging and explain to them that there is a better way, and not only that; it has a perfect retirement program. There were a couple of students that got saved during that semester.

In June of 1989, I got the phone call I had been waiting on for seven years. I had just returned home from church, and Edie was at work. I was in the kitchen washing dishes, of all things. It was Wolf Stephenson from Malaco in Jackson, and he said that they were going to let Tom Easley go. Tom was the guy that was so much "help" during the mixing of the Mississippi Mass Choir. It seems he had worn his welcome out there after so many years of "helping" Wolf like he helped me. Wolf said that if I was interested I should come down there some time in the next week or so and talk to Tommy Couch about the possibility of taking Tom's place. I just laughed and said, "I'll see you in the morning, Wolf." He said, "There's no big hurry," and I said, "Wolf, I'll see you in the morning!"

I immediately went upstairs and started packing for at least a two-day trip. It was a five-hour drive to Jackson straight down the Natchez Trace Parkway, which is a federally managed two-lane parkway that runs from Natchez, Mississippi, to Nashville, Tennessee, with no commercial vehicles allowed, but the speed limit was only 50 mph. I left the Shoals at 5:00 the next morning, and by the time Tommy Couch got to work, I was sitting in the lobby waiting for him.

He buzzed the receptionist and told her that as soon as Wolf got there, we would get together. So I ran out and got some breakfast.

When I returned, Wolf had just arrived, so we both grabbed a cup of coffee and headed for Tommy's office. We just kind of talked about when they used to come up to the Shoals in the 70's, and we briefly talked about Paul Simon's trip down there. I didn't mention anything about the KFC, because I didn't want to bring up anything negative. We discussed the excellent string sounds I had gotten for Wolf all the times he had come to Miami to record with Mike Lewis. He mentioned they had never had strings sound so good since they had been in the business. Of course, they were using local string musicians, too, when they would do their own strings in Jackson, which made a world of difference. He asked me what I wanted to do. I told him I wanted to come down to Jackson and work for Malaco until I was too old to leave the house any longer.

The starting salary he offered was almost minimum wage. I looked at him and said, "Tommy, do you have any idea what kind of experience I'm bringing to this company?" He didn't say anything, so I raised the amount he offered me to where the original offer would be my net pay weekly, and he reluctantly agreed. He also gave me $1,000 as a signing bonus to clear up any debts I might need to pay before I left Florence, and he said he would allow me to use one of the company trucks to move my furniture. I told him Edie wouldn't be able to come down until the first week in July, but I could start on Monday of the following week.

So I drove back and forth on Mondays and Fridays and looked for a place for us to live in my spare time. We finally moved down on the fourth of July weekend, 1989. I have to be honest and say that I expected to be paid a lot more than I was offered until I finally learned that Tommy Couch always got everything as cheap as he possibly could, especially people. But all I needed was a chance to prove myself—at least that's what I thought it would be like.

One thing he did say during our negotiations was that he didn't think I was able to perform all the duties that were going to be expected of me, and I told him I could do those things blindfolded. I was determined to prove myself and make myself indispensable to Malaco, until I found out after twenty years that nobody at Malaco is indispensable. I was so grateful to the Lord. His way is much better than our way.

The first week I was there, I just kind of tried to establish a place to work from and feel things out to see what was what and where everything was. In addition, I had to find us a place to live. After searching around for a few days, after I got off from work, I finally settled on a one-bedroom, one-bath up in Ridgeland called Pear Orchard Apartments. It was a huge complex with tennis courts, swimming pool, the whole kit and caboodle. It was very small, but it had a fireplace. It was $475 a month, which I thought was pretty steep, but I wasn't going to live in a match-box that was for sure.

We signed a year's lease and agreed to move in the weekend of the 4th of July. As far as the studio, I found out real quick that everything was everywhere except where it was supposed to be. I had never seen such a disorganized place in all my life. It was a total disaster. I spent half my time putting tapes on the machine and listening to them, trying to figure out what they were, who they were, where they belonged, and if they were important or not. It was hard to determine whether or not they were important enough to keep, because once I started, Wolf just sort of disappeared and left the entire thing in my lap.

I finally dug myself a hole over in the corner of the production room next to the lounge. I made a space about four feet wide where the telephone would reach, put a clip-on lamp over that section, and tried to establish a beachhead of some sort that I could call my own. Then I sort of worked my way out of the hole I was in, and tried to put things that belonged together in one spot with other things of the same species, so to speak. I think you might say I was trying to organize and de-clutter the place.

Can you imagine walking into a junk yard and trying to organize it by putting everything of the same kind in one spot and remember what goes where? I spent my entire first year trying to make heads or tails out of one of the biggest messes I had ever walked into in my life. That was one thing I learned in the Army, organization and discipline. I asked Wolf what my hours were supposed to be, and he gave me a starting time and an ending time. I added an hour onto each one of those to show how serious I was about that job. I came an hour early and stayed not only an hour late, but spent hundreds of hours of overtime and weekends of my own time working for them, with no overtime pay of any kind.

Do you want to hear something that will blow your mind? From the first day I walked into Malaco (the first workday after the 4th of July weekend of 1989) until the middle of December 2008, not one single person ever said "good job," "way to go," ,"good album," "good mix," "attaboy," or "thank you." Nothing that would indicate that anyone in the organization ever appreciated one single solitary thing I did in the twenty years full time and five years part time that I worked for Malaco Records. Not one single positive word.

It appeared that I, by happenstance, started running into a lot of demos that were just lying around. We had two different major publishing companies at the time. We had Malaco Publishing and Muscle Shoals Sound Publishing, which we had purchased in 1985. So I not only had to put them all together on one format, but keep them separate by publishing company, too. I had recording sessions coming in quite often, too.

That was another thing I wanted you to know about our Director of gospel music, Frank Williams, or Franklin D. Williams, as he was officially known. He did have one major fault, as we all have faults. I would come in on a Monday morning and be sitting there trying to decide which disaster I was going to attack that day, when all of a sudden all of these musicians would start walking into the studio or into the lounge.

We had quite a few gospel quartets that did most of their recording in the studio, and Frank wouldn't tell me when he had booked them to come in and record. They would just show up— SURPRISE! The studio wouldn't be ready. I wouldn't be ready, mentally, at least. My plans for that day or that week would be shot all to hell. It would be a total surprise to everyone except Frank and the group themselves. So I would have to go out in the studio and start setting up for a recording session. Had I known they were coming, I could have been practically ready to record. But with no advance notice, they ended up sitting around for at least a couple or three hours as I sat up mics, music stands, headphones for each person, then got the control room ready to record, which takes an hour at least. It just takes a while to get ready to record an entire act, especially when you have absolutely NO HELP whatsoever.

That's another thing, when I first started to work at Malaco, for some reason Wolf had a license to disappear for one reason or the other. He always had something he had to do that was more important. I was under the impression that I was to be there to help Wolf in the studio. I wasn't aware that the entire load of the studio was all of a sudden on my shoulders. And that's the way it was for about the first eight to ten years I was there. I would see him walk into his office now and then, and he would stick his head in the control room occasionally, but it was always after I had everything set up and was ready to go. His timing was perfect. He always showed up when I didn't need help any longer. He came in every two weeks, got his check, and was gone. He had a lot of "personal" business. It was all in my lap for years and years.

Finally, after I had been there for about a year, I was driving home one afternoon, and I started to feel like I was having a heart attack. I had so much pressure on me that first year, because it was all in my lap from the start, plus, I was trying so hard to make myself indispensable. I sort of slipped and started smoking a little "whacky backy" occasionally, and I also started having a beer now and then, which led to two beers, which led to a glass of wine with dinner, which ended up eventually a couple of vodkas and grapefruit juices before bed, and eventually I was right back in the same pigpen God had drug me out of in 1982.

Once we moved to Jackson, I wasn't accountable to anyone any longer. I felt like the Lord had given me a break from ministry, too, so I stayed out of church for about a year. In essence, I was what you would call BACKSLIDDEN. I had crawled right back in the same old hole I was in when the Lord gave me new life. There was just one difference; I never lost my relationship with Him—even though I was doing all of that, I was still in touch with Him constantly by prayer and meditation. Grace and Mercy! I was just in a rebellious state of mind and was doing all the things He had set me free from.

So I smoked a joint on the way home, like I had gotten in the habit of doing, and all of a sudden it seemed like my heart was beating out of my chest. I came wheeling into the emergency room, which was on the way home for me, and I went scurrying into the ER and told the nurses I was having a heart attack. I looked like Fred Sanford in Sanford & Son when he would grab his heart and pretend like he was dying, but I felt like I was.

They hospitalized me that night, settled me down, and ran me through all kinds of tests the next few days to check my heart, but could find nothing wrong. I finally realized it was just stress. I was trying so hard to impress Tommy and Stewart, trying to show them how good I was, that I was taking it all home with me and living it, and it was becoming more pressure than I could handle by myself. I knew I had a strong heart, from swimming as much as I had when I was young, and I stayed athletic all the way up to my 60's, so I knew there was nothing wrong with my heart. I was just overloaded with trying to impress everyone, and no one really cared. Not one single bit. Never did. Never will. I learned during my long career at Malaco to do everything as unto the Lord. He was the One I had to answer to as far as my work. If I was pleasing Him, that was all I was concerned about, and after a period of time, I realized they really didn't care. When they would tell me to do something, I would just do it.

When Tommy first hired me and we were all discussing where Edie and I could live, someone mentioned that we could possibly live in one of Tommy's condos. He immediately said, "No, they couldn't afford that," which really surprised me. It sort of put me in my place socially and salary wise. That was the moment that I realized that he had no plans whatsoever of ever paying me more than the $300 a week he was then paying me. That was extremely encouraging to know that he had a real lucrative future in store for me. It actually made me livid.

So after we had been there for a year and were living in a small one-bedroom apartment all the way out in Ridgeland, in a complex that was more like a college campus than a residential area, I was determined to find us a place with more room, peace and quiet, and at an affordable rent. The rent for Tommy's condos at the time was $500 a month. So all of a sudden, much to my surprise, the best one, the roomiest and most open one with over 1350 square feet came up for rent. I told him that if he would make it affordable to us, I would also act as resident manager. He reluctantly agreed, and we moved in exactly a year after we had moved to Jackson. It was a great apartment, with everything I wanted: peace, quiet, no parties; but in a dangerous area of town, as far as crime. I depended on the Lord to protect us, and though He did it His way, He did what I had prayed for. I'll explain later.

You know, even though for many years this job was exactly what I had been praying and waiting for, it appears that all I've been doing is complaining about it. I just didn't expect to walk into such a disorganized organization. If you walked into Tommy's or Wolf's office and looked at their desks, you would understand why the entire place was disorganized.

I've always believed that a man's surroundings or office where he worked was usually a reflection of the way he lived, and they made that theory come to life. Their offices were so messy that the only hope for either one of them would be to walk in and toss a grenade in there and run out and hide before it went off. That would put it in more order than it had ever been in their entire lives, I'm sure. But please don't think that I wasn't grateful to have a check coming in every week after such a long, long time. I couldn't count on that at Criteria, but I did in Birmingham. (Remember God's word to me in Deuteronomy 24:5?)

Another thing we had to work on once we got settled in was finding Edie a job. I hated her having to go back to "slinging hash" or working in restaurants. She deserved better than that, and she was much more qualified. While living in Florence, she went to a business school and majored in secretarial law and graduated with a 4.0 GPA. She had more to offer someone other than bringing them food. She tried working at a Mexican food place not far from the apartment in Ridgeland, but she had to carry trays sometimes with as many as seven or eight entrees on them. They were just too heavy for a woman to be carrying for nickels, dimes and quarters again, no way.

Finally, one night she ran into another waiter and spilled a huge tray with seven entrees on it, and that was the proverbial straw that broke the camel's back. I told her to turn in her apron. I went to Tommy and asked him if he had any ideas. It was then that I discovered that Malaco had an opening in their telemarketing business. I knew Edie would be great on the phone with anyone, no matter what she was discussing. She has a perfect telephone voice and the personality to sell icemakers to Eskimos, if given the chance. They interviewed her and hired her right on the spot.

The business, Malaco Telemarketing, was headed up by Joe Speetjens, and the overall supervisor of the telemarketers was a lady named Fran Spencer. It turns out there was a huge personality clash between Fran and Edie, which later turned out to be a huge clash with Fran and everyone who worked there. Malaco had a huge catalog of LPs, cassettes, and eventually CDs and videos. They would go back and take some of the old Savoy artists, add in a few of their recent releases that didn't do so well, and come up with different packages to sell to people that had bought from Malaco's catalog in the past. They did R & B packages and gospel packages. It was a very lucrative business for them, and when it first started it looked like it was going to be a gold mine for the company. But like everything else, greed destroyed it. But we'll talk about the business side of Malaco later.

At the time I came to Malaco, just like the time I came to Fame, Muscle Shoals Sound, and when I went to work for Criteria, it was the beginning of the most successful run in their history. That's why I knew that God had His hand on me all my life. He would always have me at the right place at the right time all throughout my life. At first I thought that it was me that brought all of this success to these places, but that was not the case at all. So I'm not saying these companies all of a sudden hit their peaks because I was there. It was just the opposite. The glory belongs to Him.

So Edie was an overnight sensation at the telemarketing job, which was no surprise to me. Within two weeks, she was their #1 saleslady and stayed there most of the time. And she really enjoyed it, too. She's a talker and loves to chat with people. And she's very well-versed on just about everything. I was falling into my gig alright, but I sure could have used some help. The hospital couldn't find anything wrong with my heart, which wasn't a surprise to me, but I just had to slow down a bit, which no one noticed anyway, so it made no difference.

Chapter

31

After a while, I had to start making frequent trips back up to Muscle Shoals for mixing purposes. I had learned, with the help of Paul Christensen, how to transfer mixed audio to video, once we started shooting videos more often. The first video we had was the Mississippi Mass Choir's first album, which I had the pleasure of being a part of at the very end by mixing it with Frank in Muscle Shoals. I might also mention that the album which was predicted by the business manager, Stewart Madison, as "not going to sell ten albums," ended up being Billboard's #1 gospel record for forty-five straight weeks. That's FORTY FIVE—only seven weeks short of being #1 for an entire year.

In my entire career, I have never been a part of a record that was that successful, for that long, and that still sells today. To say they were an overnight sensation would be an understatement. They were the most popular choir in the world for years, and a lot of people think they always will be. Right after we moved to Jackson, I took Edie to one of their services, and she fell in love with them. After talking with Frank on a flight he and I took to Tampa, Florida, to record the Florida Mass Choir, I mentioned to him the idea of Edie joining the choir. He said not only yes, but heck, yes. He said that the choir was originally formed to give every kind of person in the state of Mississippi an opportunity to join. There was already one white girl in the choir, so

Edie called the music director, Jerry Smith, and asked if she could audition for the choir.

A few days later, she was invited to be a part of the choir, to which she remained until the trips on the road started to bother her physically in 2006, when she then resigned. She even got to make a trip to Spain with them for ten days. She was a very powerful soprano, and you could tell she was accepted by most all of the choir members, with a few exceptions which I won't go into, but she loved each and every one of them, and still does.

She recorded with them on album #2 all the way up to the present, so she definitely did her part and earned her wings, so to speak, as far as breaking the barrier so many people "think" exists in Mississippi. When she would go out on the road with them, and they would play in various cities throughout the United States, it was always the older people in the crowd that would grab her and hug her and tell her how much they enjoyed seeing her up there in the midst of what was considered a "black" choir.

It's very strange that so many people considered it a "black" choir, yet there was nothing in the rules and regulations that said it was for blacks only. It was only in people's minds that they considered it that way. But that was "their problem," not hers or anyone else's in the choir. The only segregation in that choir was in people's minds and their wicked hearts.

Back to their first album and video, the audio on the video was straight from the track the night of the service, even though we weren't able to go in and sweeten anything (add strings or horns), fix any mistakes, or even mix it. What came straight out of the console was so anointed it really didn't have any major noticeable mistakes to fix. It was a superb mixing job on the part of Paul Christensen and Omega Productions. But once I saw the potential of having a system to lock up the audio with the video, using time code for mixing, editing, and fixing mistakes, and sweetening became quite obvious. I got Wolf involved in the process to where he could at least order the system, and I pretty much took it from there for the first few years.

About two or three times a year, I went up to the Shoals to mix. Wolf would come in and do an R & B album on one of our blues artists, Bobby Bland, Johnnie Taylor, or Little Milton. It would take Wolf literally months to finish an album on one of his blues artists, yet I would be required to record, overdub, and mix an album sometimes within ten days to two weeks, and that was it. They wouldn't even let me touch a blues record for quite some time when I first started. I guess they didn't think I had enough "experience" (smile). I had cut more hit records on the first day I came to Malaco than every single engineer in the state of Mississippi put together, but I couldn't work on their blues artists. Go figure.

It wasn't a whole lot of fun driving back and forth to the Shoals. There were so many memories stirred up every time I would pull into the city limits, but I just grinned, put it all behind me, went ahead and did what I had to do, and then headed back to Jackson. I always stayed at the Holiday Inn, which was the only decent motel in town at that time, and Malaco picked up the tab for my gas, room, and food, so I could handle it. The only problem is that at one point, after having my car stolen from in front of my house, I ended up with a new Toyota, which I leased, and which also had a mileage limit on it of 12,500 miles a year. At the end of the year, I would always be in the hole, mileage wise, but they would just tack those miles onto my next lease and make my payments go up about $50 to $100 a month. But I'm tired of complaining about my "dream" job, so let's just move on.

There was a young engineer named Kent Bruce working at Sound when I started going up to mix. He was a brilliant young man and very talented and gifted technically, but I later found out what kind of a person he was, and that will be the last I'll talk about him. But he was a great help to me when I was going up there, and I want to thank him for all the help at the first of our doomed relationship. Once they closed the studio in Muscle Shoals in the early 2000's he moved to Jackson and joined forces with Wolf. It was then that I eventually found out what it was like to work in hell. If just one of them had had the guts to tell me what it was that I was or wasn't doing to turn them against me, I could have dealt with it, but neither of them had the intestinal fortitude to do that one simple thing—simply tell me the truth.

I mentioned earlier that we had quite a few gospel quartets signed to Malaco. Some had been signed for many years, but once the Jackson Southernaires broke the ice with their Malaco LP, Malaco's first gospel project, people started expecting more gospel music from Malaco, so they started signing groups left and right. Besides the Southernaires, they had the Sensational Nightingales (my favorites, personally), Willie Neal Johnson and the Gospel Keynotes, the Pilgrim Jubilees, Margaret Allison and the Angelics, just to name a few.

The Sensational Nightingales were without a doubt my very favorite group to work with. Their illustrious leader, Joseph "Jo Jo" Wallace, was one of the godliest and most sanctified gospel singers I have ever met in my life. Please don't take me wrong here. I loved all of these groups and befriended each and every one of them all the way down to their musicians and roadies. They were all the most wonderful people I have ever met since I've been in the music business. It's just that some of them were in it because it was all they'd ever known in their lives. They grew up doing it and just followed in someone else's footsteps. Some, however, were called by the Lord to do it, because being on the road as much as they all were; they had more mileage on them than a room full of truck drivers.

We did a concert in Birmingham, Alabama, on just three of the groups, and among the three groups, they had a combined 150 years of gospel music under their belts. And that's what we ended up calling the combined DVD and video: "150 Years of Gospel Music." We recorded it in one of the most beautiful auditoriums I've ever been in. Situated right in the middle of downtown Birmingham, Alabama, it was called The Alabama Theatre. The interior looks like it was a hand-carved masterpiece from the stage and walls all the way up to the ceiling where there was a huge glass centerpiece that looked like the Sistine Chapel in Vatican City.

The three groups we recorded were the Nightingales, which we called the "Gales," The Pilgrim Jubilees, which we called the "Jubes," and the lovely Margaret Allison and the Angelics. We shot a video plus the audio, and our original intentions were to make one long concert with the three of them, but we ended up making individual DVDs and CDs on each group. We ended it with a grand finale, which had all three groups on stage at the same time, which we put at the conclusion of each DVD and CD.

The Nightingales came to Malaco every year in October, just like clockwork, and did an album. Frank Williams was the original producer, but eventually he handed the reins of producing them over to me. I also did some of the bass playing on a few of their albums. "Sug," or Horace Williams, the bass player with the group, didn't quite have the studio touch when it came to recording, and we could never get a good bass sound from him. So when I stopped playing bass, we started using another bass player. The other two gentlemen in the group, who have passed, were Bill Woodruff and Calvert "Mac" McNair.

Mac was only in his middle 40's when he died of brain cancer. He knew he was going to die, so he went up to Muscle Shoals when they weren't busy and did a solo album as sort of a remembrance LP for after he was gone. But Jo Jo and I were joined at the hip, spiritually, as was Bill, who also passed away in the mid 90's.

That was the problem with most of these groups. I don't want to be critical in any way, and I loved all these people from the very bottom of my heart, but their motivation for being out there playing all over the country night after night was not very heavenly inspired. It was just an economic and carnal way of having fun with music using gospel music as a tool. It was a culture. Their parents did it, so they did it. They knew all the right things to say and sing about when they were on stage, but when they came off stage, it was wine, women, and talking about the next song. Some of them were very promiscuous as a rule, except those like Jo Jo and Bill with the "Gales."

As a matter of fact, as I was sitting in the studio one night mixing. I was alone with the Lord, just trying to make a "silk purse out of a sow's ear" as they say sometimes when they have a bad-sounding record that they are trying to make sound as good as possible. As I was mixing, I stopped to rest for a few minutes, and I didn't want to get up from where I was sitting, so I just put my head down on the console and closed my eyes. I started thinking about how it had been since that first session with Milton Biggham at MSS in 1985. As I always do when I'm alone, I was talking to the Lord out loud, and I just happened to say to Him, "Lord, why have you got me here? Why have you stuck Edie and me right smack dab in the middle of the black culture and black music business in a state I NEVER thought I would end up in? What do you want from me? Why this, Lord?"

I wasn't complaining, either. I was having a ball doing the music and enjoying the majority of the people. I was treated worse by the white people I worked with than any of the scores of black people I worked with. They showed me respect. They called me "the Doctor," and when it came to the studio, I was known to all the blacks as "the Man." A lot of them also asked me if I was a preacher. I would get wound up sometimes and start preaching the Gospel with power, quoting scriptures to back me up, and many times they would just sit there in awe of the things that were coming out of my mouth. I even said things at times that I didn't even know I knew. As far as the people I worked with, though, it was a whole different story. Not a single white person ever said anything nice to me, except my friend Jane Galloway over in the accounting department.

So, as I was sitting there meditating, I said, "Lord, why me, why this?" He said just as plain as if He were sitting right there in person, "Son, I've sent you into the gospel music business as a missionary." Then the light came on. By then Edie and I were attending a predominantly black church, the Jackson Revival Center. It was 90% black with a white pastor and a white associate pastor, but the choir was all black except for Edie and the pastor's daughter. I played in the worship band, but I was the only white guy in it. But I never noticed color. I had put all of that behind me so very, very long ago.

Someone once called me wanting a reference on a guitar player he was thinking about hiring. He asked me at one point if he was black or white, and I stopped for a second. After a long quiet period, I simply said, "You know, I never noticed." It got very quiet on the other end. He then hung up after quickly saying thanks.

But the point I'm trying to make here is that many black people grow up in the church. It's simply a part of their life from the moment they are born. They are often raised by either their mother or their grandmother. Many black men don't seem to stick around very much when the kids start coming along. They split for new territory where they can sow their seed elsewhere. So black people know exactly how to act in church, what to say, what to sing, how to dress and talk the talk, but in general, once they leave the buildings, many of them don't seem to walk the walk. So the Lord put me in this position to try and show them, whenever I had the chance or the opportunity arose, exactly who the Real Living God is.

I think the highlight and biggest reward of working at Malaco and in black gospel music was my involvement with the Mississippi Mass Choir. I had the pleasure of overseeing and mixing the recording of every album they did since I mixed the very first album in the Shoals in 1988, and it was nothing but smooth sailing the rest of the way. My mixing of that humongous-selling first album (which set record sales and chart positions that will probably never be equaled) was pretty much the catalyst for my going to work at Malaco full time in 1989. My relationship with Frank Williams, the executive director, who actually formed the choir himself from the start, had a lot to do with my accepting the opportunity.

The first people he got to help him put the choir together were Jerry Smith, Roy Wooten, and David Curry, Jr. The spiritual leader of the choir was Rev. Benjamin Cone, Jr., who eventually became one of my closest and dearest friends ever. Frank's original intention, as I told you earlier, was to get people from all over the state of Mississippi of every shape, size, color, denomination, and age that wanted to lift up the name of Jesus in song. What he ended up with was approximately 150 to 170 of the most talented people in the state. We had people that lived as far away as Memphis and Tupelo that would drive down daily for a simple meeting or rehearsal.

The song-writing that was accomplished in the process was above my wildest expectations, with Frank being the most prolific of all the composers, and Jerry Smith putting the music along with it. They produced some of the most historic gospel music in the decade of the late 80's and 90's. The biggest individual song for the choir, which was written by Frank himself, was called "Your Grace and Mercy," and it has never been equaled to this day that I know of in gospel music.

Edie joined the choir shortly after we moved to Jackson and was able to be part of the second album. We recorded it at the Memorial Coliseum, which seats about 8,000, and I can tell you right now, it was SRO (Standing Room Only). By that time, the MMC was the biggest, most popular choir in the country. People came from all over the United States, literally, just to hear their second album. It was one of the most anticipated concert/services in the history of gospel music.

Those people practiced and rehearsed for weeks and weeks to get prepared for it, and believe me, they paid their dues as far as holding up their end of the bargain. They made sacrifices in their homes, their jobs, with their children, with their free time, etc. By the time the concert was done and over with, Edie had a smile on her face that took at least a week to wipe off. The concert was just fantastic.

But the album that sticks out in my mind more than any was the third album, "It Remains To Be Seen." It has so much history behind it that it will always be in my heart. First of all, they were invited to come to Washington, DC, to be in the Inaugural Parade to welcome the new president of the United States, Bill Clinton. They were to be the last float in the parade and then stop in front of the new president and sing a song from their first album, "He Was There All The Time."

The inauguration parade was on a Thursday night, and the choir was due back in Jackson two days later to record on Saturday night. It appeared that *all* the choir members wanted to be part of the inauguration, so they used any mode of transportation they could to get there. Some flew on commercial flights (which was almost a disaster); some drove in their personal cars; plus, they took two buses-full. They had over 150 members there to get on the float, plus the band, leadership, and the elders.

As they all prepared to leave for Washington, the weather was atrocious. The plane that most of them went on, including Edie, was a twin-engine, turbo-prop commuter flight to Houston, then a regular flight from Houston International to Washington. When the plane took off from Jackson, I walked outside the studio and looked to the southwest, which was the direction the plane was headed, and it was solid black. There was nothing but intense, dangerous thunderstorms solid—all the way from Jackson to Houston, some as high as 60,000 feet. On the radar, it was solid red from here to there. I thought to myself, surely they would never allow a plane to take off in that kind of weather, especially since it was the same all the way from Jackson to Houston. At least they would delay it or fly around it. But was I wrong.

Edie has flown all over the world in every type situation, in every aircraft and weather condition you could imagine, and she's never had fear in her entire life while flying. But she told me after she got there that she was absolutely scared to death on that one-hour and fifty minute flight. She said it was solid, intense turbulence and lightning all the way, not one second of anywhere near smooth flying. They had no idea what was keeping that aircraft in the air. I've been on flights like that in the East China Sea when I was in the Army, but she said they were the worst flying conditions she had ever flown in her entire life. I was praying for them all the way until I knew they were safely on the ground.

One of the ladies had an epileptic seizure during the flight, and almost everyone was throwing up in the barf bags. They practically ran out of bags. They all referred to it afterwards as the "flight from hell." But that was just the beginning of this episode.

Originally, Frank had wanted to do two concerts at the University of Mississippi and record them both. When he told me that, I mentioned to him that if we did it that way, the second service would be the best, because they would all be so tired and "out of themselves" after the first one, and God would be able to use them more spiritually for the second one. Let me explain quickly without going into a sermon.

We get so wound up at times when we're performing that we're not sensitive enough to the Spirit that's leading us. But when we're exhausted and more or less "run out of ourselves," it's easier for God to use us because we're more relaxed and open to His leading. It's an ideal situation for Him, because we just have nothing left of "ourselves" to take over, so He takes over. That's why fasting is so beneficial. Because of the lack of fuel and nourishment, the body or "flesh" becomes so weak that the Spirit takes over.

There were so many people on the float (and a lot of them were very heavy) that the wagon that the float was on couldn't move. Because of the security of the Secret Service, each participant float was in their own special "pen," which was fenced in and guarded by armed guards to make sure that no one who was not authorized could be involved or get close to the president and first lady without them knowing EXACTLY who they were, where they came from, and their reason for being there.

So, once it was determined that the float was not able to move, they had to cancel the float, and they locked the gates where they all were parked. They wouldn't allow anyone to leave the compound until the area was completely secured and the president and first lady were safely out of that area of town. By watching the parade on TV, you could tell that everyone was anticipating the arrival of the last float with the choir stopping in front of the reviewing stand and singing to the president, but they never arrived. They never got to rolling. Even President Clinton and the staff kept looking down the street, anticipating their arrival, because they were genuinely excited about hearing the Mississippi Mass Choir put the final touches on such an important event. Everyone there kept looking down the street for the float with the choir on it, but they never showed.

I think it went about ten feet and then wasn't able to go another foot. There was simply too much weight. I won't elaborate on that, but there were a lot of very heavy people on that float. This was such an important occasion for them as a group that they all wanted to participate, and that's very understandable. But, other than the fact that they were trapped in the compound, unable to go anywhere, had nothing to eat or drink for hours, there was just one more minor problem. It was about 16 degrees outside and breezy. It was freezing cold, and there was no place for them to go to stay warm except for a few cars, the buses, or bundling up with something. Edie said it was so cold that it just cut right through you. And Frank was a very sick man at the time, having major problems with his lungs. We all knew he had been sick for quite some time, but he wouldn't talk about it or discuss it with anyone except his wife, Katrina, who also was pretty close-mouthed—at least about that.

It appears that the entire trip was very timely for God, yet very traumatic for everyone else, and what's even better, EXHAUSTING. Now, I know you think I'm cruel and insane for saying that, but I have a reason. There is a scripture that says, "All things work together for good for those that love God." All of this happened for a specific reason. I truly believe that God wanted this to be the best album they had ever done, so he had to take them all, each and every one, and cut them down a notch or two so He could use them for His glory only. Their egos had been shattered. They were so tired they had to depend on God for their strength and stamina.

Some of the choir didn't make it back until the afternoon, just a few hours before the service. In other words, about all they could do was stand there and sing, no over-singing or trying to do anything extra, but just sing to His glory. God took it and made it the best album Mississippi Mass Choir ever did or ever would do. And I truly believe that for another reason, too.

After the concert was over, which was January 22nd, we let the dust settle and every one rest up for a few weeks. Then around the end of February, we started going through the tapes and determining what needed to be done. We started fixing small mistakes, taking our time, not completely redoing any instruments, but just punching in where they made simple mistakes and then leaving the rest alone. We spent a couple of weeks doing strings and horns, then about the second or third week of March, we started repairing vocals, just punching in one or two words here and there, and basically making all the performances as tight as possible without major surgery.

On March 18th, a Thursday afternoon, Frank called and said he was leaving town and wanted to come fix a couple of vocal parts before he left. I told him to come on and we'd get it done. When he arrived, before we got started, he said "Come outside to my car, I have something for you." So we walked out to his Benz, and he opened the trunk. There were about six suits, a couple of sport coats and a tuxedo with cummerbund, bow tie and all the extras. I asked him what those were for, and he said they didn't fit him any longer, because he had lost so much weight in the last few months, and he thought they would fit me perfectly. I said jokingly, "Where's the shoes, man?" He said, "You'll have to take care of that yourself," and then he looked down at his size elevens (I wear a nine), and we both laughed hysterically. I thanked him, hugged him, and we went back in. It took less than an hour to fix his vocal parts, then he got in his car, gave me another exceptionally big hug, told me he loved me, which he hadn't done in a long time, and got in his car, headed for the airport to go to Savannah, Georgia for a week-end service by himself. I never saw Frank alive again.

I felt something was not right, but I didn't say anything. He was going to be the guest soloist and preach a little, too. On Monday morning, the 22nd of March, he got up, went to the airport to get his flight home, and half-way to the gate he fell in the terminal and was dead of heart failure before he hit the floor. He was 45 years old. It happened about 8:30 or 9:00 in the morning. When I got to the studio at 9:30, I knew something was wrong because Roy Wooten met me at my car. He walked up, and I could tell he'd been crying. He said, "Jerry, Frank's gone. He passed this morning at the airport in Savannah; he's finally at home now."

About all I can say is that I cried for three days. I had never had anyone's death affect me like that since my baby brother Jimbo's death. Every time I would pull up in front of Malaco for about a week, I couldn't come in the door until I quit crying. I'd never missed anyone so much in a long, long time. The funeral was the following Monday at the largest church in Jackson. It held over 5,000 people, but there wasn't a place to sit, and people were standing on the outside of the church by the hundreds. People came from all over the world to his funeral. The choir actually got up and tried to sing, but only got half-way through the song and had to stop. I still miss him. He was a dear, dear man.

For some reason, without even searching for someone or thinking as to whether or not he was qualified to do the job, they automatically appointed Jerry Mannery as the new Director of Gospel Music. I think they were just too lazy to launch a search for the best possible person to fill those important size eleven shoes. Even though Jerry was very efficient and knowledgeable about the ins and outs of what Frank was doing, and was very good at administration, he wasn't musically-inclined to do that job, even though he did write a couple of really good songs while there at Malaco.

Jerry was a captain with the Jackson Fire Department and had worked for them for many years. He was highly respected as a Christian and man of integrity. The only problem was that he wasn't effective in the studio because he really didn't understand the recording process at that time. He had a tendency to pick songs based on who wrote them, as opposed to whether or not they were good commercial songs or not.

We became dear friends, and my hope was that he would slowly adapt to exactly how records were put together and would become more knowledgeable of the recording process. Almost all the artists that came in after Frank died were artists that Frank more or less had produced and guided through their albums. So now when they would come in to record, they would be like deer caught in the headlights—not exactly sure what to do or what to record. Even worse, they wouldn't be prepared when they came to record. Instead of preparing ahead of time, they would use the studio to learn their songs and the arrangements, which meant that I spent hours just sitting there waiting and watching them, totally helpless and not sure what to do next.

I tried to use my knowledge as a producer and engineer, but they just wouldn't receive from me, so it started to become a major problem. I would get tired of sitting around, and when I would try and take control of the recording process, they would be offended that I was trying to do Frank's job. That, they would not even consider.

Jerry wasn't a lot of help at that particular time in the studio. They all knew it, yet they were afraid to tell him to just stay out, so they would try to work around him. I would tolerate them, but pretty soon my toleration became quite short and started turning into hostility and words of anger. Frank really left a void that no one else could fill, and it was quite frustrating for all of us. Practically all of the artists would say to me, "I wish Jerry would just stay in the office and promote our records and leave us alone to record." But not a one of them had the courage to say it to his face. And I wasn't going to do it, either.

After a while, all of the artists started complaining that I was rushing them and being short with them. Tommy Couch knew why they were saying that and why I was doing what I was doing, but I was still disappointed that the artists didn't understand that things had changed and they were going to have to come into their future sessions more prepared and not use the studio (and my time) to write and arrange their songs.

Jerry was working part time at the Fire Station and part time at Malaco, but after about a year, he retired from the fire department and started working full time at Malaco. He was a fantastic administrative and detail person who not only had to try and keep control of all the artists and their recording schedules, but he had to fill Frank's shoes as far as having total control of the Mississippi Mass Choir. He was doing the work of about four people at once, in addition to trying to be a good father and husband. Once again, if he had stuck to the administrative duties of the choir and had found a good record producer for the choir, they could have remained on top of the recording world. But such was not the case.

Each album they did after "It Remains To Be Seen" was just a bit weaker as far as songs, selections of lead singers, arranging, etc. They continued to go down artistically with each album, because they just wouldn't listen to anyone else. There were a lot of good lead singers in that choir who never got a chance to sing lead parts simply because of politics and nepotism. One of the song writers and choir directors, along with his sister, Dorcus Thigpen, who was also a sensational choir director, was David Curry, Jr., who wrote quite a few of the great songs on the first three albums. It seemed like every song selected and every soloist came from that particular family, regardless of what anyone said. It was so frustrating to see such a wonderful group of singers with such a great anointing from God controlled by a small clique in leadership that eventually destroyed the entire thing that Frank had started. What a shame.

Even though I was blessed to be the overseer of the recording of every album they did, and was the mixer of all their albums, when I made any suggestions, it was like the words that came out of my mouth never got any further than the tip of my nose. No one listened to me as far as anything concerning the choir, and I'm sure, had Frank lived, that would not have been the case at all. What a loss—simply because of greed and wanting to be "stars."

I must admit that there was one person who was the glue that kept everything half-way together, and that was the "Professor," Jerry Smith, choir director, fantastic piano player, song writer, and probably the most talented person in the choir. He eventually put his own group together, "The Children of Israel," and they did their own thing and were beginning to spend quite a bit of time in Europe touring, singing, and spreading the Gospel. They are a terrific group of singers and players, and if you ever get a chance to see them, do it. You won't regret it.

Chapter

32

After our unfortunate retreat from the Jackson Revival Center, Edie started going out again and scouting various churches. She visited one church in particular called the Vineyard, which was a church that was one of 900 churches worldwide. It was started by a musician named John Wimber out in California several years before. John was the keyboard player and musical director for the Righteous Brothers, Bobby Hatfield and Bill Medley, two artists I had worked for in Muscle Shoals. As the Righteous Brothers, they had the big hit "You've Lost That Loving Feeling." Edie loved the church, even though it was quite small at the time—about 100 members total, of which usually about sixty-five or seventy would show up on a regular basis. The Pastor's name was Bruce Wimberley, and his lifelong love, Elaine, his wife, helped immensely in the everyday activities of the church.

Edie brought me home a couple of tapes of Bruce's teaching, and I was very impressed with his style and spirit as he taught from the Word. You could tell he was very Christ-centered and anointed as a pastor and teacher. After a couple of weeks of listening to his tapes and Edie's insistence that the Vineyard was where we belonged, I decided to give it a shot. It was, without a doubt, the place we were supposed to be at that season of our lives. It wasn't long before we both ended up playing in the worship band.

The building was small, but just big enough at that time for our needs. Soon after, we started growing, and we knew the time was coming for us to move to a larger place. As people started getting to know us and hearing about our lives, the better the fit. One Sunday night Bruce asked me to get up and give my testimony, and people started realizing that we had "been there and done that" as far as Kingdom Life was concerned, so we were a good fit, and we started feeling more and more at home.

One of the first couples to befriend us was Dave and Kathy Dixon. They invited us to dinner at their home after church one Sunday, and they really set the stage for what the Vineyard was all about. It was about love—unconditional, agape love, the kind that God loves us all with. We've been at the Vineyard ever since. Even though we now have a real church building, with a steeple and all, it still has that Vineyard feel that I first felt. After being appointed an elder a few years after we started going there, it set my heart in stone as to where God wanted us.

Our particular Vineyard has planted five churches in Columbia, South America, and the fruit has been phenomenal. Even though the drug cartels have murdered several pastors in Columbia, we have had favor with God the entire time. We have now grown to over 500 members in Jackson, MS, and I expect us to continue to grow as time goes on—or until the Groom comes to get his Bride. MARANATHA...Come Lord Jesus.

After a while at Malaco, I started getting the opportunity to work on some of the R&B producers and artists, which I found a pleasant change as far as genres' of music. My first really fun mix was an album on artist Mel Waiters. He had a song called "Hole In the Wall" about a club where it was literally just a hole in a wall somewhere, and they turned it into a late-night hangout for after-hours night people. It became an instant giant hit all over the country. It was such a simple and straightforward song that anyone could have mixed it, but it was an instant smash record. People were even starting nightclubs by that name or changing the name of their club to "Hole In the Wall." Anything to capitalize on the popularity of the song.

So they had me mix the album, which was fun. Mel Waiters was a classy guy and good friend and very easy to work with. He did most all of the music recording at his home, and when he came into the studio all he had to do was his vocals, which did take a while. But the final product was always outstanding, and it allowed me to get my foot in the door to work on more R&B records.

But talking about easy to work with, there was no one in the world easier and more fun than a producer and songwriter from Los Angeles by the name of Charles Richard Cason, born May 5, 1945. Charles "Rich" Cason turned out to be one of the very best, dearest, and loving friends I have ever had in my life. (Rich hated to be called Charles because he was harassed by a bunch of jerks in high school while living in Arizona.) He had talent just dripping off him, and he was the best at writing, playing, and producing. I love to work with producers that KNOW what they want to do when they come into the studio, and Rich Cason was the best of the best. He was originally from Arizona and then in 1970 moved to Los Angeles where he hooked up with his soul mate forever: Zuri, officially known as Veronica Dixon. Zuri was a very beautiful, talented, articulate, intelligent, classy lady and had enough love in her for the entire world. Rich was a blessed man, and he knew it.

Just to give you an idea of how well we worked together, Rich and I, along with an artist named Johnnie Taylor, had the privilege of recording and mixing the biggest Malaco record of all time. And all of it was done by just the three of us. Rich played all the instruments, sang all the background parts, Johnnie sang the lead vocals, and I mixed it. That record sold more records for Malaco on the Malaco label than any in their history up to this day. Johnnie didn't like the song, and it was like pulling teeth to get him to sing it, but Rich had a way with artists, and he eventually got Johnnie to throw in some of his famous Sam Cooke runs, and all of a sudden, the song came to life. It was simply called "Good Love."

Now don't get me wrong, Malaco had records that almost sold more than Good Love, but they were on other labels that Malaco had leased the records to, like Dorothy Moore's "Misty Blue," Z. Z. Hill, and Mississippi Fred McDowell, along with King Floyd's "Groove Me," Jean Knight's "Mr. Big Stuff," and Anita Ward's "Ring My Bell." But Johnnie Taylor's "Good Love" turned out to be the biggest all-time seller for Malaco Records, and Rich and I, together, practically did the entire thing without any help from anyone else except for Johnnie's vocals. What a producer he was.

Rich also got a Grammy nomination for production on Johnnie's record "Soul Heaven," which Johnnie didn't want to do either. He said, "I don't want to sing about a bunch of dead people." But he did eventually sing it, and it wasn't long after that that Johnnie joined them in soul heaven as well. His heart just couldn't handle that lifestyle any longer. He went to Soul Heaven himself on May 31st, 2000.

As Rich and I were talking one day in the studio, I mentioned some prostrate problems I had had recently. I had gone to the urologist to have my prostate examined, and had ended up needing surgery because my prostrate was starting to grow over my bladder. It was causing me to have a very rare infection, especially for men, called intercystial cystitis, which is an irritation of the lining of the bladder. It causes extreme pain, especially (I found out later) when you drink any kind of citrus drinks, like orange juice.

I found that out when I took my granddaughter, Cori, back to Memphis, where she lived with her mom, Mandy. When we left Jackson, we made a quick stop at McDonalds for an Egg McMuffin and a small orange juice. By the time I was half-way to Memphis, my bladder was hurting so badly I couldn't drive any longer and couldn't even stand up straight. Mandy's fiancé, Jeff Sappington, took me to the emergency room in Germantown, Tennessee, just a few miles away. I waited in the waiting room in incredible pain for an hour and a half to get in, only to have an intern, who had never even performed the procedure before in his life, catheterize me (it was the 7th time I had been assaulted like that), which was almost as painful as the bladder infection itself.

After scores of tests and about $1500 worth of nonsense, I was diagnosed with an "I have no idea what's wrong with you." It was the story of my life. Now I know why they call what doctor's do "practicing." Finally, my urologist, who is also a good friend and good drummer, Dr. Charles "Chuck" Secrest, diagnosed me correctly and put me on a drug called Elmiron, and after two years of pain, the infection was completely gone.

So, I mentioned my prostate problems to Rich, and reminded him that black men had a tendency to get prostate cancer more often than other races, and at his age, he should go get a PSA test as soon as he got back home, which he did. He called me about a week later and told me the results of his PSA test. Anything over a four is considered time to keep an eye on things. He said his PSA was 750, and he had full-blown prostate cancer. The doctors wanted him to go on chemo immediately. At that time, they gave him six months to live.

Rich and I did several albums together long before his prostate problems. We were a team and always knew exactly what each one of us had to do and when to do it. When it was mix time, Rich would put all the instruments where he wanted them to go in the track. I would then fine-tune the sounds of each instrument and then add the vocals, use echo where needed, in very small amounts, and do the final mixes.

Certain people there in the studio were constantly criticizing him for his lack of perfection in the vocal sounds, like maybe a lip smack here or a breath here and there, just anything to try and keep him off balance for some reason. I won't mention any names but the initials of the person that gave him the most grief were Wolf Stephenson. Why, I have no idea unless it was just plain, old fashioned jealousy. Rich didn't pay any attention to that nonsense, and I'm so glad he tolerated the criticism to where it didn't affect his creativity one bit. I was used to it. There were a couple of people in the engineering department that had such a critical spirit that they were always looking to find fault with other people's work. It just became a nuisance and made Rich feel unwelcome there at Malaco. Jealousy, the old "green monster," raised its ugly head again.

Rich respected me as a person, which, again, was a rarity around there. He respected my time, and would under no circumstances let me work any longer than eight hours a day, regardless of his or other people's schedule. He treated me with more respect than any person I ever worked with the entire time I was at Malaco—bar none. He went to church with me a few times, and we even played racquetball occasionally, but I couldn't even begin to keep up with him. He skunked me every time we played. He was very athletic, in real good shape, and a lot of it had to do with Zuri always making him eat right and take the proper vitamins and supplements. She was a godsend for Rich, and their relationship showed all over him. His beautiful personality and sweet spirit made him one of the most loved and respected producers in Malaco's history, as far as I'm concerned.

I lost my dear friend to prostate cancer on March 20, 2007. I still miss him very much. There will never ever be another Charles Richard Cason. Malaco lost its best record producer since its inception, and I lost my best friend. This world lost a beautiful creation.

I just want you all to know one important thing. As you've noticed, I have consistently referred to a lot of various people in this book as "my good friend" or "dear friend" or something in that regard.

I use those adjectives to describe them that way because that's exactly the way I perceived them in my life. Each and every person I referred to in that manner truly was good, or dear, or really special to me all throughout my life. And that separated them from hundreds of other people that I just simply knew, worked with or was merely acquainted with. I just wanted everyone to know that those endearments were true and real to me, and had a lot to do with the way my life ended up or is at this time. Without them, I would have never made it this far. I just wanted the world to know about how I felt about them. For real!

During my career at Malaco, I pretty much single-handedly recorded 122 albums, including videos in which I not only did the cassette and CD or LP, but also mixed the audio for the video. I also posted the video along with an extremely talented video producer named Perry Trest at Imageworks, Inc. Imageworks was a video post-production company that specialized in putting videos together with special effects, adding the mixed audio to the video, adding the credits and titles, and fading the ends of songs and starting the songs in the correct places. That was the most fun of all the things I did until that was taken away from me by people that thought they could do a better job. I'll leave that one alone, I've criticized enough people as it is.

It was strange that the person that took my job of posting videos, and who also had a lot to do with everyone's lack of confidence in my mixing abilities, learned how to post videos by sitting in the room with Perry and me hour after hour. Once he got the handle of how to get the job done, I was no longer qualified to do it. It was the beginning of an agenda by the "enemy" to eventually have me removed from any responsibilities on the creative side of Malaco, and it didn't take long to figure out who was behind it.

Perry Trest was one of the best creative posting engineers I have ever seen. He wasn't afraid to try anything. And he didn't mind spending time to experiment, regardless of how much time it took. He was the best. And another thing that was ironic was that Perry had been one of my students at Full Sail back in 1983, and he remembered me well from the first time I walked into the studio. I asked him what his opinion of me was when I was teaching down there, just out of curiosity, and he said only that I was "strange, but very knowledgeable." He said "strange" because I always tried to slip little nuggets about the Lord into my teaching. Because the students at Full Sail were from all parts of the world and represented all different languages, religions, and beliefs, I was really sticking my neck out when I did that, but I just couldn't help it at that time in my life. It was just my nature. One thing I never did, though, was apologize for it. And I never will.

There were many people that I enjoyed and befriended while I was at Malaco, and I'll carry them around in my heart for the rest of my life. The Nightingales were one group, Jo Jo Wallace, like I said earlier, was one of the most dedicated and sanctified men of God I've ever known, and he wasn't afraid to talk about it either. Sug was as bald-headed as I was, and he used to call the top of his bald head "a solar panel for a love machine." I thought that was quite humorous and also was a good example of the difference in the lifestyles of these men from one group to the other.

Margaret Allison was one of the dearest Ladies of Gospel Music I've ever known, and she could flat play that piano and sing. She carried a young lady and a gentleman bass player with her on the road and on recordings. Another Gentleman of Gospel was a man named Willie Neal Johnson from Tyler, Texas. What a dear man he was. And when he was on stage, he was almost like a clown the way he would cut up and tease the members of his band. He loved the Lord, and it really showed when he was up there singing gospel music. I must have done at least six albums and videos on Willie until he passed just a few years back.

One thing I noticed when I first came to work at Malaco was the age of most of our artists. I went to Tommy Couch's office one day and made mention of the fact that most of our artists were getting on up there in age, and Tommy came back and said, "Well, so are we." The point I was trying to make was that we needed to bring in some younger and fresh new talent, and start developing them for future recording. But it just wasn't in the cards for Malaco to go any longer than the people that ran it and worked for it, including me. Little did I know what was in store for me.

Another group that I grew to know quite well and love were the Pilgrim Jubilees or the "Jubes" as we called them. Clay Graham, his brother Cleve, Major Roberson, Ben Chandler, all the singers; Bobby McDougal, their fantastic guitar player who could play rhythms unlike any other gospel guitar player on the circuit, Eddie Graham on guitar, and last but not least, Mike Atkins, the bass player and band leader, who had one of the funkiest bass lines in gospel music today. They were an unusual but very tight and exciting group to watch. I loved them all, and I especially loved some of Mike's fantastic bass lines.

Another gospel artist who really touched my heart was a gentleman named Willie Banks. Willie was a giant of a man physically, and had that deep, deep, Southern black voice that only he could put out. He was known by his musicians as a disciplinarian, but I think he was just trying to teach them obedience. Willie, after smoking all his life, finally came down with lung cancer. We had to try and get a last album on him before he went to be with his Master. When he did his vocals while recording that last album, he would have to cough and clear his throat between every line he sang. When we played the song back for him to listen to in order to check for mistakes and such, it would be so painful for him to listen to his coughing and hacking all through the song.

Each day before we would get started again, he would listen to what they had done the day before, so I made it a point to come in extra early each morning, go through each song, and hand erase all the coughing and throat noises he had to make in order to sing the next line. When he would listen back the next day, the vocals would be just as clean as they could be. All he heard was his clear, pure vocal. He never said anything to me for doing that, but when he would hear each one, he would realize what I had done, and he would look at me and smile and wink. He didn't smile much, so I knew it meant a lot when he smiled at me, and that was his way of saying thank you without blowing his cool in front of his band. Those smiles were worth a million dollars to me.

Another artist that I loved very much was probably the very best gospel singer that I ever put my ears to. His name was James Moore. I had never heard anyone come anywhere close to him and his style of singing. It was powerful, anointed, and just as clear as a bell. But like so many gospel artists, he didn't take care of himself physically. He would overeat and eat entirely too much sugar and sweets, which caused him to be at least 200 pounds overweight. After a while he developed diabetes and had to take dialysis three times a week.

He went to the doctor originally with nosebleeds, only to find out at age thirty-eight that both kidneys had shut down on him. The toxins in his bloodstream eventually caused him to lose his eyesight. He went on ministering, and in '97 he starred in the cast of the New York play "Why Good Girls Like Bad Boyz," and he even toured with them for a while. He then developed colon cancer, and after doing his last album in his hometown of Detroit, he went to be with the Lord in the year 2000 at the ripe old age of 44.

I miss all of these wonderful men and women that devoted their lives to spreading the Gospel through music and song. They really paid the price with traveling and sleeping in a different bed every night and having hardly any time at home with their loved ones. They were called of the Lord to do that, and that's why it was their nature to do it their entire lives.

Speaking of people who have been called to minister to others, I have recently been volunteering at a local hospice in Ridgeland, Mississippi (which is just a suburb of Jackson), and I have begun to know a lot of the nurses there that work with the patients that literally come there to die. When I first met several of them, I didn't feel they had a lot of compassion, the kind it takes to take care of dying patients. But as I worked there, I watched families walk in after their close relative had died just minutes before, and the nurses would walk out and not only talk with them, but actually embrace them and weep with them in their sadness and loss.

I asked them, "How do you do that without getting personally involved with the patients?" They replied, "You must be called to do this job. It takes a certain amount of mercy and grace to get attached, yet not fear letting them go, knowing they are going to a better place!" It was then that I understood the work of ministers of any kind, whether it was in music, nursing, taking food to foreign lands, or simply being a shepherd to a flock of sheep. We were all created to make a difference one way or the other.

I also want to mention a few other artists I loved and spent so much time with. Even though they weren't singing the Gospel, it doesn't mean they weren't doing what they were supposed to do. They include my dear sweet lady of song, Shirley Brown, who I think is the closest thing, vocal wise, to Aretha Franklin that ever lived. She is a darling of a friend. Also Stan Mosley, my Chicago pal, along with another gentleman of song who didn't quite make it all the way, "Little Milton" Campbell, one of the best blues singers and guitarists in blues music.

And last but not least, my miracle champion, worldwide-known songwriter, George Jackson. I've known George from the time I started at Fame in 1969 when he used to ride a Trailways bus down from Memphis to Muscle Shoals to do his demos. He would always get a six-pack when he got on the bus in Memphis, and by the time he got to the Shoals two and a half hours later, he would be three sheets to the wind. But he doesn't have that problem any longer since Stewart Madison got hold of his life and had him go through detox. He dried out and got a brand new start. He's now been sober for almost fifteen years, and his song-writing is extra special. He wrote "Old Time Rock and Roll," which was a monster hit by Bob Seger; he wrote "One Bad Apple," which was a huge record for the Osmonds back in 1970; he wrote "Down Home Blues" for ZZ Hill; and many, many more over the years. He's a classic song-writer, and he's not through yet.

And just one more classic George Jackson story. George had never owned or driven a car when he moved down to Jackson, Mississippi. It wasn't because he couldn't afford it; George made a lot of money. But he was so smashed all the time, he never learned to drive. Finally, Stewart told George that if he would take driving lessons, he would buy him a car. So George took driving lessons, and it took him a full year to learn how to drive.

After a year's worth of lessons, he finally decided he was ready to go take his driver's test. He was so prepared; I just knew he would pass it. When he finally came back and walked in the door, I asked him if he had passed, and he said no, he'd failed. I said why? He said that during all that time, the driving instructor had never taught him how to parallel park. So he had to do his lessons all over again, except this time he had to learn how to parallel park. That took him another six months, but finally, after a year and a half of lessons, he passed his test. George had his driver's license. Stewart took him out and bought him, with George's money of course, a new Toyota Camry. Man, this guy was in heaven now. You should have seen him driving down the road by himself. It must have taken him three weeks to wipe the smile off his face.

Early one morning, a couple of months later, he came driving into the Malaco parking lot. He jumped out of the car, came running into my office, and cried, "Jerry, Jerry, you've got to come help me. There's electrical wires sticking up out from under my hood, and I'm afraid it's going to catch fire." So I calmly walked out to George's car, looked at the hood, and reached over and pulled out some pine needles that were sticking up between the hood and the fender. He always parked under a pine tree. What a character. I love him to death. He's a class character, very sweet, and a terrific song-writer, to boot.

Chapter

33

One day after the turn of the century when everyone realized that the world wasn't going to come to an immediate stop, everyone at Malaco was sitting out in the lobby taking an afternoon break just having conversation. I happened to mention that when I reached the age of sixty-five, I would love to be able to retire. That was my desire and hope, but of course, it all depended on my income building and my profit sharing continuing to grow, which at the time had a nice chump of change in it.

Wolf was sitting out there with us at the time, and when I mentioned about my "wanting" to retire, it must have imprinted on his mind very indelibly. I was having a lot of problems with my lower back at the time, and I eventually was put under the care of a pain specialist, Dr. Carol McLeod, who turned out to be not only a great and passionate doctor, but a good friend as well. It seems that I had two lower vertebrae that had no cartilage between the L-3 and L-4, and the pain started to be a real chronic problem to the point where it was hard to make it without taking some kind of pain medication. I tried Aleve, Motrin, Tylenol, and such until it was starting to make me sick to my stomach.

So I went to Dr. McLeod with my problem, and at first he tried what they called a "spinal block." They put you to sleep for just a minute, and inject Fentanyl mixed with steroids directly into the area that's causing the problem. I must say that after four months of those, one about every two weeks, they offered no relief whatsoever. They might as well have injected me with chocolate.

Then they tried Fentanyl Duragesic patches, but they didn't work either. The thing that activated the patches was the warm blood flow in the skin. In other words, when you're asleep and your body is still, there's little blood flow, but when you wake up and start moving around, the blood flow to the various parts of your body increases, and it activates the patches. So, the patches would hardly work until I got up in the morning. Then I would grab a cup of coffee and start moving around, and the Fentanyl Duragesic patches would kick in, and I would fall asleep sitting on the couch drinking my coffee.

Then they tried all kinds of oral meds, including Hydrocodone and Oxycontin. I got to the point where I couldn't even tell when I had taken any because my body had built up such a resistance to painkillers that nothing seemed to do the trick. Then Dr. McLeod came up with the answer that actually changed my life. It was a Medtronic Pain Pump. The pump itself was about the size of a bar of soap and had to be surgically implanted in my abdomen, just below my rib cage and to the left a little.

It has a small input hole in it that is used for refilling the tank with morphine, which sends medication in very small amounts through two tubes that are implanted along with the pump. They run from the pump into a catheter at the point of my spine where the pain originates. The pump feeds very small amounts of morphine into my spinal column on a regular basis, but into my spinal fluid only. That way the morphine doesn't affect any other parts of my body or make me drowsy or stupid or anything like the oral meds and the patches did. It is the perfect answer.

When I told Wolf and Kent that I was going to have to go into the hospital for a week and have surgery, it was the happiest I have ever seen them since I've known them. I mean, they were elated. I think they thought it was the beginning of the end for me at Malaco. And now I realize, as far as they were concerned, it was the beginning of the end. It just took a while.

I had the pump inserted in February of 2003, and they say that after six or seven years, you occasionally have to have them replaced because of the battery inside that is the power source. It is also controllable on the outside with a wand that they place over the pump.

It controls the amount of output, tells you how much serum is left, and when your alarm date is, so you can have everything you need when it's time for a refill. It's important to be able to turn the pump up or down to control the amount of pain you are going through.

At the beginning, it caused some minor problems, but they were major problems to me. Dr. McLeod had hired a practical nurse to make sure that my pump was always full and never got to the point where I would be without. The only problem is that she didn't do her job correctly at all, and I ended up in morphine withdrawal three times before we figured out what was wrong with me.

Each time, I was so sick for ten days that I literally asked God to kill me and take me home. I couldn't move without throwing up, and I had nothing in my stomach to throw up. I couldn't put any kind of anything, not even water, in my body without getting sick. I was freezing to death, yet I was burning up with fever. I couldn't sleep I was hurting so badly. I literally thought I was in hell. It took ten days, and then the nurse would show up and fill my pump, and all of a sudden, I would start to get better.

I was gone from work for ten days each time it happened, yet not one single person from Malaco called to see, first of all, if I was alive or dead, and if so, what was the problem? Nothing, nada, no kind of communication at all. But that was what I expected, because that's just the way it was there. I must say that my only real friend there, Jane Galloway Hart, did keep in touch with Edie to make sure I was still alive. But I received no phone calls from anyone.

This happened three times before they finally figured out that the nurse was causing this. I was in hell each time it happened, and I truly wanted to die. But we've got a handle on the pump now, and it's only happened one time since then. That was because we got my refill date mixed up, and I came in a few days too late. The pump had gotten so low that I wasn't getting any meds, and that wasn't anyone's fault, so it was just one of those things. But Dr. McLeod got a chance to see what would happen to me when I would start to go into withdrawal, and it really opened his eyes to how it affected me. So it was very educational for him and the nurses.

As I get ready to start talking about my last few years at Malaco, which were not very pleasant, I just want you all to know that I loved coming to work. I still, in spite of how I was being treated, couldn't wait to get to work, because that was where God had put me. I still had the joy of the Lord all over me, and I hold no ill feelings toward anyone involved in my last days. I've forgiven anyone I might have thought was trying to hurt me, and I count all as forgotten. I loved working at Malaco. I loved the people, all of them, unconditionally, and I still do. I hold NO HARD FEELINGS toward anyone that is mentioned in this book. Please understand that as you read this conclusion. I just had to tell the truth of how things were and still are there.

When the economy and the record business started really changing after 2000, Wolf finally realized that it was his company, too, and he got his personal life together and started coming in more and getting more involved with what was going on in the studio. He and Kent became like Siamese. They spent most of their time together, and if I happened to walk into a room where they were talking, they would immediately stop whatever they were doing or saying to each other, and look at me like, "What are you doing in here?" They would ask me if I needed anything, and if I didn't, they would just sit there in silence until I left. Then they would continue their conversation.

You've heard the old saying, "two's company, three's a crowd"? That was the case with Wolf, Kent, and me. They simply didn't need me or want me around any longer. I would constantly try to get involved and ask if they needed any help, but they would never let me in on what they were doing. They wouldn't even let me plug an electrical cord in the wall for them. They got all they could out of me for twenty-four years, and they simply wanted to throw me away. But what bothered me the most was the fact that neither one of them had the guts to level with me. They wouldn't even engage in conversation with me any longer. And it all started after my 65th birthday. What a coincidence.

Another thing I couldn't understand was, when I had something to do, neither one of them would ever lift a finger to help me. Whenever Wolf had a session, I would be out in the studio setting up for him, and he wouldn't even have to leave the control room. But when I did a session, before I was totally ostracized from the control room, not one of them would even help me plug in a set of headphones unless I actually went up and asked them. Then Kent would help, but he would be complaining the entire time, because "he had other things to do," according to him. Then he would go back into his office, pick up the magazine he was reading, and continue reading.

As I told you before, Kent was a brilliant young man when it came to sound equipment, and Wolf had become so dependent on Kent that I'll swear he couldn't do anything without asking Kent if it was okay or "is this how you do it?" If Kent couldn't be found, he would call him on his cell phone. Wolf was lost without Kent. I told Wolf once that I would love to have a nickel for every time he called Kent for technical assistance. I could then retire, like he wanted me to, and become a multi-millionaire, to boot.

In addition to being eased out of the control room as far as doing sessions, we found out that the company had lost at least 35% of the profits from our profit sharing accounts in the stock market. So they decided to eliminate profit sharing for the employees, which we were all depending on for our retirement. They gave us choices as to which financial broker to give our profit sharing to, and they turned our money over to the brokers of our choice as IRA rollovers. Like I said earlier, at one point my profit sharing account had quite a bit of money in it, but by the time they had dispersed the money, I barely had half of the original amount to last me the rest of my life when I retired.

It finally got to the point to where I was hardly ever allowed to work in the studio unless it was an emergency. They kept complaining that I didn't know how to use the new equipment, yet you can't learn how to use something unless you can sit at it and work on it. Wolf even had the same kind of equipment in his own home, so you might say he had quite an advantage over me. He once suggested that I spend more time sitting in the back of the control room watching him and learning that way. After forty years of setting the standard for recording hit records, and being accustomed to having some of the top recording engineers in the country sitting there watching *me*, I guess my pride just wouldn't let me go back to that level, especially at my age.

I would occasionally get a chance to work with some of my friends, like George Jackson, whenever he needed to do some demos or something like that, so I was learning the new equipment slowly but surely. About the time I would get to a certain level of knowledge, they would update the system to where it was totally different than before. I was getting the picture finally. My time was about up.

I loved my job. I loved getting up every morning and going to work, even when my "cohorts" wouldn't even talk to me. The last time I counted, Kent went about six or seven years without ever saying a single word to me unless I happened to ask him a question. He would then give me the shortest answer possible, with a little sarcastic remark to follow. But that was it as far as Kent and me having any kind of relationship. With my superior, Wolf, I spent most of the time talking to his back. When I did try and talk to him, he wouldn't even look at me. He would continue doing what he was doing and just sort of grunt answers at me or mumble some kind of response. Those were the conditions under which I worked for the last six or seven years I was at Malaco.

I think the straw that broke the proverbial camel's back was the last two albums I mixed. I wouldn't even have had a chance to do that if it hadn't had been for Tommy Couch. He had known Wolf for most of his life, and he knew, sort of, what I was going through back there, but he didn't know what to tell me to do about it. The mixes I was given, thanks to Tommy, were the Nightingales and Margaret Allison with the Angelics.

When we normally mix, we take at least one complete day per song. We'll mix on it all day, then come back the next morning and fine tune it, then move on to the next song. So we would end up spending about three days on two songs. All of a sudden, I was given three and a half days to mix twelve songs. That's almost four songs a day. I'm a pretty fast mixer, but we had all new equipment and a new workstation. As opposed to mixing from two-inch tape analog, we were mixing strictly digital from a great, but very complicated format called Nuendo. It was an audio and post-production system that allowed you to not only record, but to do just about anything to a signal that you wanted to. It was state of the art from the word go.

So I did what I was asked, as far as mixing the first album on the Nightingales. I thought it sounded pretty good; however, I would have loved to have had a little more time to spend on each song. Another thing that was missing from the mixing was the actual producer of the record, Darrell Luster. If he had been there with an extra set of ears, it would have made all the difference in the world in how the mixes turned out. But he wasn't "allowed" to come down and help out, because it cost too much for him to come down, according to the money man, whoever it was that day.

I couldn't really fine-tune each mix like we were accustomed to, because I had to literally fly through the mixes. There were several different things I would have gone back and changed, but because of the time element, I had to move on to the next song. I couldn't work twelve to sixteen hours a day like I used to, so I spent about ten hours a day and just barely got the twelve songs mixed in the time allotted.

A couple of days after I finished the mixes, Wolf came in and sat down and listened to each song over and over. He literally picked them to pieces. Every little thing about the mix he picked out and really made me feel like I was a first-year mixing engineer, as opposed to the forty-year veteran engineer and former good friend that I was. The way he described the mixes made me feel so bad that I literally asked him if I was going to be fired because of it. He said, "No, you're not fired, but I want you to go back and re-mix the entire twelve songs again and make these changes I wrote down." It was a long legal pad, and it was full of changes he wanted me to make. I was humiliated. In all my years as an engineer, I had never felt so incompetent and useless. So I did as he asked and then submitted the re-mixes to him. I guess they were acceptable, because he never said another word about it. I could see the writing on the wall.

A few weeks later, he did the same thing with the Margaret Allison LP. This time I had thirteen songs to do, but I had an extra half-day, which meant I had four days to mix thirteen songs. It turned out to be a repeat of the Nightingales' mixes, but this time, I only had to go back and re-mix half of her songs. Wow, half a success. I could feel it coming.

If you remember, I mentioned earlier about the time we were all out in the lobby just shooting the bull, and I mentioned about how I would "love to be able to retire when I was sixty-five"? I tried and tried to get Wolf and Kent to tell me what it was about me that caused them to treat me the way they did, but Wolf always came up with some kind of lame excuse like, "I'm just having financial problems," or "I've just got a lot on my mind." But when I asked Kent, he wanted to fight. He literally got in my face and accused me of accusing him of mistreating me. It was so ridiculous that I just finally stayed back in my office most of the time. If Tommy or Stewart asked me to do something, I would jump right on it. Otherwise, I spent about the last three or four years just hanging out in my office, trying to help various new followers of Christ to grow or helping them with their problems.

I read a lot of Christian web sites and studied the Bible. I did try to keep the tape vault in half-way decent order so that when someone went to look for a particular tape, if they asked me where it might be, I pretty much knew its location. There were hundreds of tapes back in that vault, and they went all the way back to the 50's and 60's. Plus, it was the dumping ground for anything that anyone didn't want in their office any longer. So it was actually a replica of the desks I mentioned earlier. It was the same mentality, except it was in a much larger room.

All of Savoy's master tapes and all of Muscle Shoals Sound's master tapes were kept there, plus all the demos from all three publishing companies: Savoy, Malaco, and Muscle Shoals Sound. I had the artists' names, dates, formats, and any other info available on each individual tape logged on an Excel data input log. I actually had the entire vault on paper, but only about two-thirds of it in the computer by the time I left. You could locate any tape you wanted by the artist's name, the date it was recorded, or the format (kind and size of tape), so hopefully it has made tapes easier to find for those who have come along behind me.

You know, the time I spent at Malaco appears to be really on the negative side, but it was where God put me for all of those years, and He put me there for a reason. I tried to simply be who I was without offending any of my fellow workers or trying to "act" like a Christian. But what happened the last few years is just a good example of the fact that we live in a spiritual world. Things are either black or they're white, not in racial terms, but comparative terms. There is no in between, no gray area, as a lot of folks think. And there is a constant battle going on in the heavenlies between the two. You either are FOR Him or you're AGAINST Him.

Many times you might wonder why people don't like you and treat you ugly or rudely, but it's not the real you they are against; it's Who lives in you. It's spiritual warfare. There's been a war going on between the two sides since Adam and Eve ate from the wrong tree in the Garden of Eden. I suspect that had a lot to do with how I was treated, too, so that makes it much easier to understand and handle. I loved what I was doing there, and I'll always love all the people I met, recorded, worked with, worked for, and befriended. In some cases I never even got their names, but still they were part of my life for a season, and I won't forget them ever. I'm constantly running into people who, when they meet me and hear my name, the first thing they say is, "Oh yes, I saw your name on the back of my tape, or CD, or LP, or video."

In the middle of August 2008, Tommy called me into his office and said, "I'm going to have to let you go." When I asked why, he said, "You're just not making me money anymore." Of all the reasons he could have given me, I thought that was the most absurd, but I had a feeling it was coming anyway. I'll tell you right now, I have never lost for one second the peace or joy that I received on April 29, 1982, on the 2nd floor of Fame Recording Studios. Do I understand why I was the only full-time employee in the organization that was fired? No, I don't. Do I believe that it was God's timing for me to leave Malaco? Yes I do.

I was curious as to what kind of financial arrangements they were going to offer me after twenty-four years of faithful service, not to mention hour after hour after hour of overtime and week-ends, and mileage put on my leased car driving back and forth from Jackson to Muscle Shoals at $.25 a mile. (I must have made at least twenty-five trips of 500 miles round trip each time.) They gave me full pay for August, September and October and half-pay for November and December. That was it. I told you way back there that Tommy Couch always got everything as cheaply as he possibly could, and that included my dismissal and possible end to my career as a recording engineer. I figured that as long as they were paying me anything, I would continue coming into work every day just like normal, just in case they needed me. But about the middle of December, I finally had had enough of Wolf and Kent, and I packed my stuff and got the hell out of there.

I had accumulated a lot of things over twenty years of working there full-time, so it took me two days to get everything off the walls and all my drawers cleaned out, plus a lot of "stuff" put back in the vault I had saved. Once out of there, I simply went over to the warehouse and hugged Mary Holmes, Annie, and Robert, three people I had gathered with every Tuesday morning for devotions and prayer; and of course Jane Galloway Hart, my friend whom I love dearly. Then I got in my car and drove home.

I don't regret one single day I worked for Malaco, and I learned a lot of things about myself, human nature, and what drives people. We were like a big family at one time, but little by little, things started changing. What I thought was my dream job came at the perfect time in my life. I told Tommy when he first hired me that I wanted to finish my career there, and it appears at this time that that's exactly what happened.

I was hoping that they would let me work back in the vault or something and keep me there as long as they possibly could, just out of loyalty, but for some reason, they didn't want me there any longer. Loyalty and integrity are not words associated with Malaco. And like I've said before, "Things usually happen the way they're supposed to." Technology changes every day, and if you don't keep up, you'll never be able to hang on in this business, or any other, for that matter. The truth is, the record business, as I knew it most of my life, is gone, never to return.

I knew when I was in my grandparents' house that night listening to my mother playing the old-fashioned-style melody of "Goofus" on the piano, and the rhythm guitar smoothing out the feel of the song, that music would always be my life. It still is and always will be until I make the transition, and who knows what's in store for me when I go to be with the Lord for eternity. But one thing I know for sure. It all began when I was five years old, lying on my cot up against that wall at 2016 S. Cedar St. in Little Rock, Arkansas, my hometown.

Breinigsville, PA USA
25 January 2010
231304BV00001B/7/P